GOOD
MOOD

BOOKS BY JULIAN L. SIMON

Patterns of Use of Books in Large Research Libraries (with Herman H. Fussler, 1969)

Basic Research Methods in Social Science (1969; third edition with Paul Burstein, 1985)

Issues in the Economics of Advertising (1970)

The Management of Advertising (1971)

The Effects of Income on Fertility (1974)

Applied Managerial Economics (1975)

The Economics of Population Growth (1977)

The Ultimate Resource (1981)

Theory of Population and Economic Growth (1986)

How to Start and Operate a Mail-Order Business (1965; fourth edition, 1987)

Effort, Opportunity, and Wealth (1987)

The Economic Consequences of Immigration (1989)

Population Matters: People, Resources, Environment, and Immigration (1990)

Population and Development in Poor Countries: Selected Essays (1992)

EDITED BOOKS

Research in Population Economics: Vol. I (1978); Vol. II (1980) (with Julie da Vanzo); Vols. III (1981) and IV (1982) (with Peter Lindert)

The Resourceful Earth (with Herman Kahn, 1984)

GOOD MOOD

The New Psychology of Overcoming Depression

Julian L. Simon

FOREWORD BY ALBERT ELLIS

OPEN COURT

La Salle, Illinois

OPEN COURT and the above logo are registered in the
U.S. Patent and Trademark Office.

© 1993 by Open Court Publishing Company

First printing 1993
Second printing 1993

Printed and bound in the United States of America.

Library of Congress Cataloging-in-Publication Data

Simon, Julian Lincoln, 1932–
    Good mood : the new psychology of overcoming depression / Julian
L. Simon.
        p.   cm.
    Includes bibliographical references and index.
    ISBN 0-8126-9097-4 (cloth). — ISBN 0-8126-9098-2 (pbk.)
    1. Depression, Mental—Popular works. 2. Cognitive therapy.
3. Self-esteem. 4. Self-help techniques. I. Title.
RC537.S54 1993
616.85′27—dc20   93-14946
                                                              CIP

"Life is hard," someone said to Voltaire.
"Compared to what?" Voltaire answered.

FREE COMPUTER-MEDIATED THERAPY OFFER

Purchasers of Julian Simon's book *Good Mood* can obtain an innovative, interactive program, OVERCOMING DEPRESSION, on disk. Designed as counterparts, both book and program were created to aid you in achieving peace of mind and greater happiness in your life.

OVERCOMING DEPRESSION is a unique, first-ever, cognitive-educational program for the treatment of mild to moderate depression. The program is not a computer simulation or imitation of a human therapist. It is a therapeutic method in its own right. With simplicity of use this computerized cognitive-educational program for understanding and dealing with your problems utilizes a unique dialogue mode. This 'breakthrough' technology allows you to express yourself freely in your own words and responds in meaningful everyday conversational language.

The program was created by Kenneth Mark Colby, M.D., Professor of Psychiatry and Biobehavioral Sciences Emeritus at the University of California School of Medicine at Los Angeles and former Professor of Computer Sciences specializing in artificial intelligence at Stanford University. Dr. Colby has published ten books and over 100 papers in the fields of psychiatry, psychology, cognitive therapy, and artificial intelligence.

OVERCOMING DEPRESSION, a $200.00 retail value, is available free ($10.00 for processing and postage) as a special offer to purchasers of *Good Mood* by writing to:

> Malibu Artifactual Intelligence Works
> 25307 Malibu Road
> Malibu, California 90265

Please enclose proof of purchase of *Good Mood* and $10.00 for postage and handling. PLEASE STATE CLEARLY whether you want a 3.5″ or 5.25″ disk. OVERCOMING DEPRESSION will run on an IBM-compatible machine with a hard disk and 640K RAM, or an Apple MAC using the program Soft PC.

This offer runs for a limited time, and the terms of the offer may be changed without notice.

CONTENTS

FOREWORD BY ALBERT ELLIS

Julian L. Simon's book on depression is a valuable addition to the literature and one that can be quite helpful to a large number of readers. Though Dr. Simon ended his formal study of psychology after the bachelor's degree and a couple of graduate courses—he then became an outstanding scholar in economics—he has devoted so many years and so much thought to the subject of depression that he has come up with one of the best books on this subject that I have ever read.

Good Mood is written from the heart and the gut—for the author has really suffered from mild and extreme melancholia over the years and is in many ways more in touch with depressed feelings than are most nonsufferers. He also aptly cites many other intelligent and talented depressives whose insights into their experiences are vivid and important.

Rather than come up with only one 'solution' to the problem of dysfunctional moodiness, Dr. Simon presents several very practical methods, all of which have their distinct virtues. His main technique, Values Therapy, has been hinted at by various other writers, including myself, but he operationalizes it and makes an original contribution that others have missed or have only vaguely outlined. For many depressives, it is a method well worth trying.

I differ with Dr. Simon on some issues, and in Appendix E below I argue with him about the proper way to think about my work and his, an argument which is itself a sign of respect. For now, I'll end by simply saying that Dr. Simon has written a fine book on depression. Enjoy and benefit from it!

Albert Ellis, Executive Director
Institute for Rational-Emotive Therapy
45 East 65th Street
New York, NY 10021

FOREWORD BY KENNETH MARK COLBY, M.D.

The approach of Simon's *Good Mood* to the problems of depression appealed to me for two reasons, theoretical and pragmatic.

The proposed theory represents an improvement over current theories of depression in that it accounts for, and unifies, more of the manifest phenomena, such as the making of negative self-comparisons. Besides providing more comprehensive explanation, a viable theory can also be pragmatically fruitful in generating new efficacious interventions in the natural order. The explanatory and remedial information contained in *Good Mood* is so clear that it seemed to me an interactive computer program based on it might be constructed as an interventional aid in relieving the widespread affliction of depression.

Such an interactive program would have several advantages. Since millions of people now have, and millions more are rapidly acquiring, personal computers, a computer program could reach large numbers of sufferers, 90% of whom never see mental health professionals for reasons of high costs, unavailability, or the unfortunate social stigma involved in having mental health problems. An interactive cognitive-educational program that one can run in private on one's own personal computer would provide a means of self-counseling and self-reprogramming at a low cost while circumventing the stigma problem.

In addition to providing explanatory and remedial information about depression, it would be desirable to have a computer program that would be more than a page-turner. It should be able to participate in conversations with the user about his particular depressive condition in unrestricted everyday language. An interactive program with dialogue capabilities arouses interest and emotion, conditions which facilitate learning. The dialogue mode of interaction also encourages free expression of thoughts and feelings, perhaps more freely than one might express to another human. A program that weaves together informational text and personalized dialogue capacities provides an optimal combination for therapeutic learning.

With the help of expert programmer Peter M. Colby and Julian L. Simon, I designed and implemented the computer program available to readers of *Good Mood*. It is the first ever cognitive-therapeutic program that combines instructional and dialogue modes of interaction in everyday natural language.

Kenneth Mark Colby, M.D.
Professor of Psychiatry, Emeritus
University of California School of
Medicine at Los Angeles

ACKNOWLEDGMENTS

Over the many years this book has been in the works, many people have given me the most valuable of gifts—their time, their thoughts, their good wishes, and some laughter. Most important have been Kenneth Colby and Albert Ellis, whose creative minds jumped out of their accustomed sets of ideas and quickly understood the explanatory and therapeutic power of the concept of negative self-comparisons; both of them gave me voluminous written comments which greatly benefited the book, and generous praise which kept me going in this work.

David Holmes, Arnold Miller, and Dori Seider read the book as professionals in the field, and gave valuable comments.

Howard Altstein, Nancy Bogen, Susan Krieger, and Sandra Philips provided helpful editorial suggestions. Several other people whose identities I have forgotten (please forgive me) also did so.

Z. and B. told me that reading the manuscript saved their lives by saving them from suicide. Knowing that I helped them helped me.

We are all indebted to those writers quoted in the book—from the composer(s) of some Psalms, to Shakespeare and Tolstoy, to (most recently) William Styron—who have set down their personal stories so that other depressed people can read and find help in them.

Thank you one and all.

Julian L. Simon

PART ONE

Introduction to Depression

INTRODUCTION

Are you sad? Do you have a low opinion of yourself? Does a sense of helplessness and hopelessness weigh you down? Do you feel this way for days or weeks at a time? Those are the elements of depression.

Depression comes in many forms. Psychiatrists consider that is is a heterogeneous set of diseases. But these are the rockbottom characteristics that are always present.

Depression is entirely different from the garden variety of the blues that come and go in a day or a week. You won't be likely to know how real depression feels unless you have been seriously depressed. As William Styron says, "depression remains nearly incomprehensible to those who have not experienced it" (1990, 7). If you have been depressed, though, you will fully understand how different that state is from the occasional gloom and bad mood, which only give a hint of what depression can be.

If this is how you are feeling, you surely want to regain a pleasant outlook on life. You also need to prevent depression returning later. Happily, there are now aids to attain those goals. But fighting depression takes effort. And there are certain benefits of being depressed which you may be reluctant to give up.

Nowadays, a depression sufferer can usually get relief with active cognitive psychotherapy, or with tested antidepressant medications, or with both. The U.S. Public Health Service summarizes as follows: "Eighty percent of people with serious depression can be treated successfully. Medication or psychological therapies, or combinations of both usually relieve symptoms in weeks."[1] Both kinds of treatment have been shown in controlled experimental research to benefit a large proportion of depression sufferers, within a few months or even weeks. Drugs, however, control the depression, whereas psychological therapy can cure it. (For information about the scientific results, see Appendix B and the books cited in the reference list.) All this is good news indeed for depression sufferers.

Only a quarter-century ago, medical and psychological science had little to offer depressed people. Traditional Freudian-based therapy put you on a couch or in an easy chair, and started you talking at random. You and your therapist hoped that in the course of two to five expensive hour-long sessions per week, continuing for many months or years, you would come across sensitive incidents in your past. You hoped that those 'insights' would relieve you of your pain. But the success rate was not high, nor was psychoanalysis proven effective by scientific tests.

Traditional therapy was founded upon the crucial assumption that people are irresistibly disturbed by their *past experiences,* and cannot change their emotional life by changing their current patterns of thinking. Recent scientific research has shown, however, that this assumption is false. People can indeed overcome depression by changing their *current* thought patterns. That is, though you may have *been disturbed* by events in your past, you now (in Albert Ellis's phrase) *disturb yourself* by your current mental habits.

Modern cognitive therapy—which fully coincides with the wisdom of the ages on this point—begins with the assumption that we have considerable control over our own thinking. We can choose what we will think about, even though following through on the choice requires effort and is not always fully successful. We can select our goals, even though the goals are not infinitely flexible. We can decide how much we will agonize over particular events, though our minds are not as obedient as we would like them to be. We can learn better ways to understand the data of our objective situations, just as students learn to gather and analyze data scientifically, rather than being forced to accept the biased assessments we have tended to make until now.

This book teaches you a newly-sharpened version of cognitive psychotherapy that has a more comprehensive theoretical base and wider curative outlook than earlier versions. You may use it by yourself to overcome depression, or you may use it in conjunction with a therapist. Most sufferers can benefit from the assistance of a wise counselor, though finding such a helpful person is not easy.

There is still more good news: Psychiatrist Kenneth Colby, famous for his artificial-intelligence computer simulation of paranoia, has developed a computer-based system of psychotherapy for depression based on the key ideas of this book. You 'speak' to the computer, and the computer speaks back on the screen, which helps you help yourself. A disk to run the program on an IBM-PC computer is available by request to purchasers of this book. It can be a help and a comfort to many readers.

MY PERSONAL STORY AND NEGATIVE SELF-COMPARISONS

This book emerges not only from the body of new scientific discoveries, others' and my own, but also from my personal experience of deep and prolonged melancholy. Here is my story.

I was depressed—badly depressed—for 13 long years from early 1962 to early 1975. When I say that I was depressed I mean that, except for some of the hours when I was working or playing sports or making love, I was almost continuously conscious of being miserable, and I almost continuously reflected on my worthlessness. I wished for death, and I refrained from killing myself only because I believed that my children needed me, just as all children need their father. Endless hours every day I reviewed my faults and failures, which made me writhe in pain. I refused to let myself do the pleasurable things that my wife wisely suggested I do, because I thought that I ought to suffer.

As I look back now, in comparison to reliving the *better* of the days when I felt as I did then, I'd rather have a tooth pulled and have the operation bungled, or have the worst possible case of flu. And in comparison to reliving the *worst* of those days in the first year or two, I'd rather have a major operation or be in a hellish prison.

Over the years I consulted psychiatrists and psychologists from several traditional schools of thought. A couple of them left me with the impression that they didn't have a clue about what I was saying and had simply somehow passed the necessary exams to get into a well-paying business. A couple of them were human, understanding, and interesting to talk to, but could not help me. And toward the end of that time, the psychiatrists and psychologists did not even offer me hope, and certainly no hope of a quick cure. My own training in psychology was no help, either.

Then I read about what was, at that time, a new and different approach to psychological problems—Aaron Beck's Cognitive Therapy, which in Albert Ellis's somewhat different form is called Rational-Emotive Therapy. (I shall consider them together under the label 'cognitive-behavioral therapy' or just 'cognitive therapy', along with Frankl's Logotherapy, recent variants such as Interpersonal Therapy, and also behavioral therapy.)

The core of cognitive-behavioral therapy is a thoughtful problem-solving procedure that can quickly get to the root of the depression, and directly yank out that root. Within that vision of the individual as *able to change his or her depressed thinking,* I then developed an analysis of the cause of depression centering on the depressed person's negative self-comparisons. And I worked out the logic of what I call 'Values Treatment', which can provide a powerful force for people to use the resources of cognitive therapy and thereby cure themselves of depression; that is what Values Treatment did for me.

Within two miraculous weeks I banished my depression, and I have since then been able to keep depression at bay. (Such a quick cure is not usual, but it is not wildly exceptional, either.) Starting April 1975, I have almost always been glad to be alive, and I have taken pleasure in my days. I have occasionally even been ecstatic, skipping and leaping from joy. And I am joyful more often than most people, I would judge. Though I must still fight against depression from time to time, I have not lost more than a minor skirmish since then, and I believe that—if my family and community stay safe from catastrophe—I have beaten depression for life. The Epilogue at the end of the book gives the details of my passage from sadness to joy.

After I had cured myself, I wondered: Could I use my new advances in cognitive therapy—Self-Comparisons Analysis, and Values Treatment—to help others, too? I proceeded to counsel with other persons who were depressed, and I found that these ideas could indeed help many of them get over their depressions and find new joy in life. Then I wrote a short version of this book, and leading psychiatrists and psychologists who read it agreed with me that the book—including Self-Comparisons Analysis, and the therapeutic approach derived from it—makes a new contribution not only to sufferers from depression but also to the theory of the subject. And people to whom I have given early copies, some of whose cases I'll mention later, have reported dramatic salvation from their own depressions—not in every case, but often.

I hope that there will soon be a smile on your face, too, and laughter bubbling inside you. I don't promise you instant cure. And you will have to work at overcoming the depression. You must exercise your intellect and will in outwitting the traps that your mind lays for you. But I *can* promise you that cure and joy are possible. . . .

A tip for the road: Try treating your fight to overcome depression as an adventure, and think of yourself as a valiant warrior. More power to you, and luck.

Afterword for Those Interested in the Scientific Evidence

The experimental evidence for the success of cognitive therapy in helping depression and other miseries has been mounting up. For 30 years now, a variety of studies have shown cognitive therapy to be helpful. And in 1986 the National Institute of Mental Health of the U.S. Department of Health and Human Services completed a tightly-controlled three-university study lasting six years (and costing ten million dollars!) comparing a) encouragement only, b) drug therapy, c) Beck's Cognitive Therapy, and d) Interpersonal Psychotherapy; both these latter psychotherapies emphasize the key element of altering one's own thinking and behavior. The results at the conclusion of treatment showed that the active psychotherapies were as successful as the standard drug imipramine in reducing the symptoms of depression and improving the patient's ability to function. Drug treatment produced improvement more rapidly, but the active psycho-therapies caught up later. Severely depressed and less-severely de-pressed patients both benefited from the active psychotherapies.[2]

These findings are extraordinarily impressive because drug thera-py has been the favorite of the medical establishment in recent years. And cognitive-behavioral therapy has none of the side-effect dangers, physical and psychological, that accompany drugs. Furthermore, as noted earlier, the drugs control rather than cure depression. Hence, even if drugs are to be used, psychotherapy is appropriate *in combination with the drugs* in order to root out the underlying causes and move toward real *cure.*

Afterword about Drug Therapy for Depression

Neither I nor anyone else can give you authoritative advice about whether drugs are right for you. It surely makes sense to hear what one or more physicians has to say to you about drugs. Finding a wise physician, however, is particularly difficult when the ailment is depression. The problem is, as two noted psychiatrists put it, that depression "may arise from a biological malfunction, from actual losses, deprivations, or rejections, or from personal limitation. The difficulty in sorting out such causal fact is a source of enormous confusion in the diagnosis and treatment of disorders of mood."[3] And as two other reliable psychiatrists put it, "depression is almost certainly caused by [many] different factors", and hence "there is no single best treatment for depression."[4] Your best bet is to listen to medical advice, and also advice from one or more psychologists, and then make your own decision about whether you want to try drugs first, or psychological therapy first, or both together.

Perhaps the most important piece of knowledge is that, contrary to what *some* physicians will tell you, drugs are *not* an all-purpose cure for depression. (Perhaps the only major exception is the case of a person who has suffered real tragedy from death or other great loss, and is slow in putting the tragedy behind her or him.) A sprained brain is very different from a sprained ankle. An out-of-order brain is very different from an out-of-order kidney or pituitary gland. Even if drugs relieve the depression while you are taking the medication, you almost surely need to straighten out your thinking so that the depression will not recur after you stop the drugs, and so that you will know how to fight off depression if it does recur.

Depression is not likely to be caused *only* by a biologically-induced chemical imbalance that a drug can neatly restore to balance. As Seligman[5] puts it, "Does the physiology cause the cognition, or does the cognition cause the physiological change? . . . the arrow of causation goes both ways." And as another psychiatrist has recently written, "Drugs do not cure the illnesses, they *control* them."[6]

Only psychotherapy offers true cure in most cases of depression. And as the official statement of the American Psychiatric Association judiciously puts it, "All depressed patients need and can benefit from psychotherapy,"[7] rather than relying upon medication alone. Patients treated with cognitive-behavioral psychotherapy as well as drugs have fewer recurrences than patients treated with drugs alone, in one study.[8]

I do *not* intend to suggest, however, that drug therapy may not be appropriate for you. Modern anti-depression drugs offer hope to some people who are otherwise doomed to misery for long periods of time. I myself probably would and should have tried such drugs during my long depression if they had been as well-established as they now are. Drugs are particularly indicated when the depression continues for a very long time, because "One thing seems sadly certain: the person who remains chronically depressed over time has a reduced chance of recovering."[9] What I *am* suggesting is that you should not *only* consider drugs, and that it might be wise to try cognitive therapy *first.* You can read more about antidepressant drug therapy in Chapter 4.)

THE NATURE OF THE TROUBLE AND THE FORMS OF HELP

WHAT DOES 'DEPRESSION' MEAN?

The term 'depression' means to psychiatrists and psychologists a *continued* state of mind with these central characteristics: 1. You are sad or 'blue'. 2. You have a low regard for yourself. In addition, 3. a sense of being helpless and hopeless is an integral part of the depression process. A variety of other symptoms such as poor sleep may or may not accompany these two core symptoms. They are not central to the depression.

Sadness is not equivalent to depression, and not all sadness is pathological. Everyone is sad from time to time, sometimes in response to genuinely sad events such as the loss of a loved one. The sadness that follows such a loss is natural and even necessary, and should be accepted as such. Unless the sadness continues un-normally—that is, continues so long that it disturbs a person's life, and the person feels that there is something wrong—the label 'depression' does not apply. But if the sadness does continue un-normally, and then picks up an accompanying feeling of worthlessness and turns into a prolonged state, the condition then becomes an enemy to be fought.

Very occasionally there may be some doubt about whether to call a person 'depressed', especially when sadness continues for a long time after a tragic death. In such a case, the person may not feel worthless. But almost always depression is clearcut, though the depth of depression may vary.

Sadness is caused by the mechanism which will be described

shortly. If you understand and manipulate the mechanism properly, you can get rid of the sadness. The depression mechanism does not by itself produce or explain low self-regard. But if you operate the mechanism appropriately, you are likely to get rid of the low self-regard, too, and at the least you will not be preoccupied with it and ravaged by it.

This is the mechanism which causes the sadness in depression: Whenever you think about yourself in a judgmental fashion—which most of us frequently do—your thought takes the form of a comparison between a. the state you think you are in (including your skills and capacities) and b. some other hypothetical 'benchmark' state of affairs. The benchmark situation may be the state you think you ought to be in, or the state you formerly were in, or the state you expected or hoped to be in, or the state you aspire to achieve, or the state someone else told you you must achieve. *This comparison between actual and hypothetical states* makes you feel *bad* if the state in which you think you are in is less positive than the state you compare yourself to. And the *bad* mood will become a *sad* mood rather than an angry or determined mood if you also feel *helpless* to improve your actual state of affairs or to change your benchmark.

We can write the comparison formally as a Mood Ratio:

$$\text{Mood} = \frac{\text{(Perceived state of oneself)}}{\text{(Hypothetical benchmark state)}}$$

If the numerator (perceived state of oneself) in the Mood Ratio is low compared to the denominator (hypothetical benchmark state)—a situation which I'll call a Rotten Ratio—your mood will be bad. If on the contrary the numerator is high compared to the denominator—a state which I'll call a Rosy Ratio—your mood will be good. If your Mood Ratio is Rotten *and* you feel helpless to change it, you will feel *sad*. Eventually you will be depressed if a Rotten Ratio and a helpless attitude continue to dominate your thinking. This precise formulation constitutes a new theoretical understanding of depression.

The comparison you make at a given moment may concern any one of many possible personal characteristics—your occupational success, your personal relationships, your state of health, or your morality, for just a few examples. Or you may compare yourself on several different characteristics from time to time.

If the bulk of your self-comparison thoughts are negative over a sustained period of time, and you feel helpless to change them, you will be depressed. Check yourself and you will observe in your mind such a negative self-comparison ('neg-comp' for short) when you feel bad, whether or not the sadness is part of a general depression.

Only with this Self-Comparisons Analysis can we make sense of such exceptional cases as the person who is poor in the world's goods but nevertheless is happy, and the person who 'has everything' but is miserable; not only do their actual situations affect their feelings, but so do the benchmark comparisons they set up for themselves.

The sense of *loss* which is often associated with the onset of depression can also be seen as a negative self-comparison (neg-comp)—a comparison between the way things were before the loss, and the way they are after the loss. A person who has never had a fortune does not experience the loss of a fortune in a stock market crash and therefore cannot suffer grief and depression from losing it. Losses that are irreversible, such as the death of a loved one, are particularly saddening because you are helpless to do anything about the comparison. But the concept of comparisons is a more fundamental logical element in thought processes than is loss, and therefore it is a more powerful engine of analysis and treatment.

The key element for understanding and dealing with depression, then, is the sadness-producing negative comparison between one's actual state and one's benchmark hypothetical situation, together with the attitude of helplessness as well as the conditions that lead a person to make such comparisons frequently and acutely.

Now we are ready to ask: How can you manipulate your mental apparatus so as to reduce the flow of negative self-comparisons about which you feel helpless? There are several possibilities for any given person, and any one method may be successful for you. Or perhaps some combination of methods will prove best for you. The possibilities include: changing the numerator in the Mood Ratio; changing the denominator; changing the dimensions upon which you compare yourself; making no comparisons at all; reducing your sense of helplessness about changing the situation; and using one or more of your most cherished values as an engine to propel you out of your depression. Sometimes a powerful way to break a logjam in your thinking is to get rid of some of your 'oughts' and 'musts', and recognize that you do not *need* to make the negative comparisons that have been causing your sadness. I'll say a few words about each possibility now, and I'll discuss each general tactic at length later in the book.

IMPROVING YOUR NUMERATOR

Are you actually in as bad shape as you think you are? If you have an *incorrect* unflattering picture of some aspects of yourself that you consider important, then your self-comparison ratio will be erroneously negative. That is, if you systematically bias your estimate of yourself in a manner that makes you seem to yourself objectively worse than you really are, then you invite needless negative self-comparisons and depression.

We are talking about assessments of yourself that can be checked objectively. An example: Samuel G. complained that he was a consistent 'loser' at everything he did. His counselor knew that he played ping pong, and asked him whether he usually won or lost at ping pong. Sam said that he usually lost. The counselor asked him to keep a record of the games he played in the following week. The record showed that Sam won a bit more often than he lost, which surprised Sam. With that evidence in hand, he was receptive to the idea that he was also giving himself a short count in other areas of his life, and hence producing fallacious negative self-comparisons and a Rotten Ratio. If you can raise your numerator—if you can find yourself really to be a better person than you now think you are—you will make your self-comparisons more positive. By so doing you will reduce sadness, increase your good feelings, and fight depression.

SWEETENING YOUR DENOMINATOR

When told that life is hard, Voltaire asked, "Compared to what?" The denominator is the standard of comparison that you habitually measure yourself against. Whether your self-comparison appears favorable or unfavorable depends as much upon the denominator you use as upon the supposed facts of your own life. Standards of comparison include what you hope to be, what you formerly were, what you think you ought to be, or others to whom you compare yourself.

'Normal' people—that is, people who do not get depressed frequently or for a long time—alter their denominators flexibly. Their procedure is: choose the denominator that will make you feel good about yourself. Psychologically-normal tennis players choose opponents who provide an even match—strong enough to provide invigorating competition, but sufficiently weak so you can often feel successful. The depressive personality, on the other hand, may pick an opponent so strong that the depressive almost always gets beaten. (A person with another sort of problem picks an opponent who is so weak that he or she provides no exciting competition.)

In the more important life situations, however, it is not as easy as in tennis to choose a well-fitting denominator as the standard of comparison. A boy who is physically weak and unathletic relative to his grammar-school classmates is stuck with that fact. So is the child who is slow at learning arithmetic, and the homely girl. A death of a spouse or child or parent is another fact with which one cannot deal as flexibly as one can change tennis partners.

Though the denominator that stares you in the face may be a simple fact, you are not chained to it with unbreakable shackles. Misery is not your inexorable fate. People can change schools, start new families, or retrain themselves for occupations that fit them better than the old ones. Others find ways to accept difficult facts as facts, and to alter their thinking so that the unpleasing facts cease causing distress. But some people—people we call 'depressives'—do not manage to free themselves from denominators that hag-ride them into depression, or even unto death by suicide or other depression-caused diseases.

Why do some people appropriately adjust their denominators while others do not? Some do not change their denominators because they lack experience or imagination or flexibility to consider other relevant possibilities. For example, until he got some professional career advice, Joe T. had never even considered an occupation in which his talent later enabled him to succeed, after failing in his previous occupation.

Other people are stuck with pain-causing denominators because they have somehow acquired the idea that they *must* meet the standards of those pain-causing denominators. Often this is the legacy of parents who insisted that unless the child would reach certain particular goals—say, a Nobel prize, or becoming a millionaire—the child should consider himself or herself a failure in the parents' eyes. The person may never realize that it is *not necessary* that she or he accept as valid those goals set by the parents. Instead, the person *musturbates*, in Ellis's memorable term (Ellis has good words to say about *masturbation*). Ellis emphasizes the importance of getting rid of such unnecessary and damaging 'oughts' as part of his Rational-Emotive variation of cognitive therapy.

Others believe that attaining certain goals—curing others of illness, or making a life-saving discovery, or raising several happy children—is a basic value in itself. They believe that one is not free to abandon the goal simply because it causes pain to the person who holds that goal.

Still others think that they *ought* to have a denominator so challenging that it stretches them to the utmost, and/or keeps them miserable. Just why they think that way is not usually clear to those persons. If they learn why they do so they often stop.

Chapter 13 describes a six-step procedure that can help you change your denominator to a more livable standard of comparison than the one which may now be depressing you.

NEW DIMENSIONS AND BETTER RATIOS

If you can't make the old Mood Ratio rosy or even livable, then consider getting a new one. Folk wisdom is indeed wise in advising us to forcefully direct our attention to the good things in our lives instead of the bad things. Counting one's blessings is the common label for focusing on dimensions that will make us happy: remembering your good health when you lose your money; remembering your wonderful loving children when the job is a failure; remembering your good friends when a false friend betrays you, or when a friend dies; and so on. What folk wisdom does not tell you is that counting your blessings often is not easy to do. It can require great effort to keep your attention focused on your blessings and away from what you consider your curse.

Related to counting blessings is refusing to consider aspects of your situation which are beyond your control at the moment in order to avoid letting them distress you. This is commonly called 'taking it one day at a time'. If you are an alcoholic, you refuse to let yourself be depressed about the pain and difficulty of stopping drinking for the rest of your life, which you feel almost helpless to do. Instead, you focus on not drinking today, which seems a lot easier. If you have had a financial disaster, instead of regretting the past you might think about today's work to begin repairing your fortunes.

Taking it one day at a time does not mean that you fail to *plan* for tomorrow. It does mean that after you have done whatever planning is possible, you then forget about the potential dangers of the future, and focus on what you can do today. This is the core of such books of folk wisdom as Dale Carnegie's *How to Stop Worrying and Start Living.*[1]

Finding personal comparisons which make your Mood Ratio positive is the way that most people construct an image of themselves which makes them look good. The life strategy of the healthy-minded person is to find a dimension on which he or she performs relatively well, and then to argue to oneself and to others that it is the most important dimension on which to judge a person.

A 1954 popular song by Johnny Mercer and Harold Arlen went like this: "You've got to accentuate the positive . . . Eliminate the negative . . . Latch on to the affirmative . . . Don't mess with Mister In-between." That sums up how most normal people arrange their views of the world and themselves so that they have self-respect. This procedure can be unpleasant to *other* people, because the person who accentuates his or her own strengths may thereby accentuate what in other people is less positive. And the person often proclaims intolerantly that that dimension is the most important one of all. But this may be the price of self-respect and non-depression for some people. And often you *can* accentuate your own strengths without being offensive to others.

A more attractive illustration: appreciating your own courage is often an excellent way to shift dimensions. If you have been struggling without much success for years to convince the world that your fish-meal protein is an effective and cheap way of preventing protein-deficiency diseases in poor children (an actual case), you may be greatly saddened if you dwell on the comparison between what you have achieved and what you aspire to achieve. But if you focus instead upon your courage in making this brave fight, even in the face of the lack of success, then you will give yourself an honest and respectable positive comparison and a Mood Ratio which will make you feel happy rather than sad, and which will lead you to esteem yourself well rather than poorly.

Because of childhood experiences or because of their values, depressives tend not to be flexible in choosing dimensions that will make them look good. Yet depressives *can* successfully shift dimensions if they work at it. In addition to the ways mentioned above, which will be discussed at length in Chapter 14, there is still another—and very radical—way to shift dimensions. This is to make a determined effort—even to *demand* of yourself—in the name of some other value, that you shift from a dimension that is causing you grief. This is the core of Values Treatment which was crucial in curing my 13-year depression; more about this shortly.

THE SOUND OF A NUMERATOR CLAPPING

No self-comparisons, no sadness. No sadness, no depression. So why don't we just get rid of self-comparisons completely?

A practicing Zen Buddhist with an independent income and a grown family can get along without making many self-comparisons. But for those of us who must struggle to achieve our ends in the workaday world, some comparisons between what we and others do are necessary to keep us directed toward achieving these ends. Yet, if we try, we can successfully reduce the number of these comparisons by focusing our minds on other activities instead. We can also help ourselves by judging only our *performances* relative to the performances of others, rather than judging our very *selves*—that is, our *whole persons*—compared to others. Our performances are not the same as our persons.

Work that absorbs your attention is perhaps the most effective device for avoiding self-comparisons. When Einstein was asked how he dealt with the tragedies he suffered, he said something like: "Work, of course. What else is there?"

One of the best qualities of work is that it is usually available. And concentrating upon it requires no special discipline. While one is thinking about the task at hand, one's attention is effectively diverted from comparing oneself to some benchmark standard.

Another way to shut off self-comparisons is to care about other people's welfare, and to spend time helping them. This old-fashioned remedy against depression—altruism—has been the salvation of many.

Meditation is the traditional Oriental method of banishing negative self-comparisons. The essence of meditation is to shift to a special mode of concentrated thinking in which one does not evaluate or compare, but instead simply experiences the outer and inner sensory events as interesting but devoid of emotion. (In a less serious context this approach is called 'inner tennis'.)

Some Oriental religious practitioners seek the deepest and most continuous meditation in order to banish physical suffering as well as for religious purposes. But the same mechanism can be used while participating in everyday life as an effective weapon against negative self-comparisons and depression. Deep breathing is the first step in such meditation. All by itself, it can relax you and change your mood in the midst of a stream of negative self-comparisons.

We'll go into details later about the pros and cons and procedures for various methods to avoid self-comparisons.

GETTING HOPE BACK

Negative self-comparisons (neg-comps) by themselves do not make you sad. Instead, you may get angry, or you may mobilize yourself to change your life situation. But a helpless, hopeless attitude *along with* neg-comps leads to sadness and depression. This has even been shown in rat experiments. Rats that have experienced electric shocks which they cannot avoid later behave with less fight and more depression, with respect to electric shocks that they *can* avoid, than do rats that did not experience unavoidable shocks. The rats that experienced unavoidable shocks also show chemical changes like those associated with depression in humans.[2]

It behooves us, then, to consider how to avoid feeling helpless. One obvious answer in some situations is to realize that you are *not* helpless

and you *can* change your actual state of affairs so that the comparison
will be less negative. Sometimes this requires gradual relearning
through a graded series of tasks that show you that you can be
successful, eventually leading to success in tasks that at the beginning
seemed overwhelmingly difficult to you. This is the rationale of many
behavioral-therapy programs that teach people to overcome their fears
of elevators, heights, going out in public, and various social situations.

Indeed, the rats mentioned in the paragraph above, which learned
to be helpless when given inescapable shocks, were later taught by
experimenters to learn that they could escape the later shocks. They
showed diminished chemical changes associated with depression after
they had 'unlearned' their original experiences.

Mitigating the helpless and hopeless attitude is discussed at greater
length in Chapter 17.

A NEW HOPE: VALUES TREATMENT

Let's say that you feel you're at the end of your rope. You believe
that your numerator is accurate, and you see no appealing way to
change your denominator or your dimensions of comparison. Avoiding all comparisons, or drastically reducing the quantity of them, does
not attract you or does not seem feasible to you. You'd prefer not to be
treated with anti-depression drugs or shock treatment unless there is
absolutely no alternative. Is there any other possibility open to you?

Values Treatment may be able to rescue you from your end-of-the-
rope desperation. For people who are less desperate, it may be
preferable to other approaches to their depressions. The central
element of Values Treatment is discovering within yourself a value or
belief that conflicts with being depressed, or conflicts with some other
belief (or value) that leads to the negative self-comparisons. That is
how Bertrand Russell passed from a sad childhood to happy maturity
in this fashion:

> Now [after a miserably sad childhood] I enjoy life; I might almost
> say that with every year that passes I enjoy it more. *This is due partly
> to having discovered what were the things that I most desired, and having
> gradually acquired many of these things.* Partly it is due to having
> successfully dismissed certain objects of desire—such as the acqui-

sition of indubitable knowledge about something or other—as essentially unattainable.[3]

Values Treatment does exactly the opposite of trying to argue away the sadness-causing value. Instead it seeks a more powerful countervailing value to dominate the depression-causing forces. Here is how Values Treatment worked in my case: I discovered that my highest value is for my children to have a decent upbringing. A depressed father makes a terrible model for children. I therefore recognized that for their sake it was necessary to shift my self-comparisons from the occupational dimension that led to negative comparisons and sadness, and focus instead on our health and the enjoyment of the day's small delights. And it worked. I also discovered that I have an almost religious value for not wasting a human life in misery when it can possibly be lived in happiness. That value helped, too, working hand-in-hand with my value that my children not grow up having a depressed father.

That description makes the process seem much easier than it really is, of course. Focusing your mind upon your chosen values requires effort, often very great effort. Sometimes the required effort is so great that you cannot will yourself to make it, and instead you let yourself remain in the slough of despond. But the method of Values Treatment teaches you what has to be done, and gives you a reason for making the effort to do what must be done.

The depression-fighting value may be (as it was for me) the direct command that life should be joyful rather than sad. Or it may be a value that leads indirectly to a reduction in sadness, such as my value that my children should have a life-loving parent to imitate.

The discovered value may lead you to accept yourself for what you are, so that you can go on to other aspects of your life. A person with an emotionally-scarred childhood, or a polio patient confined to a wheelchair, may finally accept the situation as fact, cease railing at fate, and decide not to let the handicap dominate. The person may decide to pay attention instead to what he can contribute to others with a joyful spirit, or how he can be a good parent by being happy.

Values Treatment need not always proceed systematically. But a systematic procedure may be helpful to some people, and it makes clear which operations are important in Values Treatment. In Chapter 18 I'll describe such a systematic procedure for Values Treatment.

IS THIS MAGIC?

Please let's get this straight: This book, and cognitive therapy in general, do not offer you an instantly-working formula that will transport you from misery to bliss without the slightest effort or attention on your part. In order to transform yourself from being sad to being joyful you'll have to give the problem your attention and some hard work—whether you do the work alone, or with Kenneth Colby's computer program, *Overcoming Depression*, available free to purchasers of this book, or with the help of a professional counselor. The work includes writing down and analyzing your thoughts, a tedious but invaluable exercise. If you picked up this book looking for a while-you-wait no-sweat miracle, put it right back down again.

Nevertheless I do offer you 'magic'. I offer you a new analytic way of understanding your depression, upon which you can build a rational, successful procedure for extricating yourself from your unhappy jam. And the cure need not wait for long years of psychotherapy, dredging up the details of your past life and reliving it all. If you do choose to get outside help, ten or twenty sessions with a therapist are par for the course, and insurance often pays most of the cost.

This is not a guarantee that you will succeed with this method. But it is a promise that a speedy cure—faster than nature's usual regenerative processes—is possible for a large proportion of depression sufferers. Understanding aspects of your past life may be helpful in figuring out how to reconstruct your present mental life. But cognitive therapy focuses on the present structure of your thinking, and on changing that structure so that you can live with it joyfully, rather than simply proceeding to examine your history in the faith that such an examination will eventually produce a cure.

Though I believe that this book offers the most powerful methods for overcoming your depression, I recommend as strongly as I can that you read other books as well. The more you learn, the greater the chances that you will stumble across sentences or thoughts or anecdotes which will be just the right triggers for you to understand and cure your own depression. The best books for laymen, in my opinion, are David Burns's *Feeling Good* and Albert Ellis's and Robert Harper's *A New Guide to Rational Living*. Both contain lots of practical suggestions, as well as dialogues between therapists and depression sufferers which demonstrate the processes involved in dealing with depressed thinking. Your reading of those books will be even better if you bring to them the Self-Comparisons Analysis discussed in this book. It will render the ideas in the other books more specific, and easier to understand and put to work. And after you have worked your way through one or both of those books, you might like to study some of the other books, including some intended for professionals, named in the reference at the end of their book.

You may also find crucial nuggets of wisdom in the aphorisms and anecdotes which fill popular self-help books. The commonsense ideas in those books would not live on from generation to generation if they did not help a substantial number of people from time to time.

Making yourself happy when you have been depressed is a great achievement. That achievement can make you proud of yourself in addition to the relief from pain and the new joy it brings. I wish you the same success and joy that I have had in using this method.

SUMMARY

The term 'depression' means a *continued* state of mind with these central characteristics: 1. You are sad or 'blue'. 2. You have a low regard for yourself. In addition, 3. a sense of being helpless and hopeless is an integral part of the depression process.

This mechanism causes the sadness in depression: Whenever you think about yourself in a judgmental fashion, your thought takes the form of a comparison between a. the state you think you are in (including your skills and capacities) and b. some other hypothetical 'benchmark' state of affairs. The benchmark situation may be the state you think you ought to be in, or the state you formerly were in, or the state you expected or hoped to be in, or the state you aspire to achieve, or the state someone else told you you must achieve. *This comparison between actual and hypothetical states* makes you feel *bad* if the state in which you think you are in is less positive than the state you compare yourself to. And the *bad* mood will become a *sad* mood rather than an angry or determined mood if you also feel *helpless* to improve your actual state of affairs or to change your benchmark.

If you understand and manipulate the mechanism properly, you can get rid of the sadness. The depression mechanism does not by itself produce or explain low self-regard. But if you operate the mechanism appropriately, you are likely to get rid of the low self-regard, too, and at the least you will not be preoccupied with it and ravaged by it.

We can write the comparison formally as a Mood Ratio:

$$\text{Mood} = \frac{\text{Perceived state of oneself}}{\text{Hypothetical benchmark state}}$$

If the numerator (perceived state of oneself) in the Mood Ratio is low compared to the denominator (hypothetical benchmark state)—a situation which I'll call a Rotten Ratio—your mood will be bad. If on the contrary the numerator is high compared to the denominator—a state which I'll call a Rosy Ratio—your mood will be good. If your Mood Ratio is Rotten *and* you feel helpless to change it, you will feel *sad*. Eventually you will be depressed if a Rotten Ratio and a helpless attitude continue to dominate your thinking. This precise formulation constitutes a new theoretical understanding of depression.

The comparison you make at a given moment may concern any one of many possible personal characteristics—your occupational success, your personal relationships, your state of health, or your morality, for just a few examples. Or you may compare yourself on several different characteristics from time to time.

If the bulk of your self-comparison thoughts are negative over a sustained period of time, and you feel helpless to change them, you will be depressed.

There are several ways to manipulate your mental apparatus so as to prevent the flow of negative self-comparisons about which you feel helpless. The possibilities include: changing the numerator in the Mood Ratio; changing the denominator; changing the dimensions upon which you compare yourself; making no comparisons at all; reducing your sense of helplessness about changing the situation; and using one or more of your most cherished values as an engine to propel you out of your depression. Sometimes a powerful way to break a logjam in your thinking is to get rid of some of your 'oughts' and 'musts', and recognize that you do not *need* to make the negative comparisons that have been causing your sadness.

This book, and cognitive therapy in general, do not offer you an instantly-working formula that will transport you from misery to bliss without the slightest effort or attention on your part. In order to transform yourself from being sad to being joyful you'll have to give the problem your attention and some hard work—whether you do the work alone or with the help of a professional counselor.

The book does offer you a new analytic way of understanding your depression, upon which you can build a rational, successful procedure for extricating yourself from your unhappy jam. And the cure need not wait for long years of psychotherapy, dredging up the details of your past life and reliving it all. If you do choose to get outside help, ten or twenty sessions with a therapist are par for the course.

This is not a guarantee that you will succeed with this method. But it is a promise that a speedy cure—faster than nature's usual regenerative processes—is possible for a large proportion of depression sufferers.

Note

Chapter 1 has summarized ideas found in Part II of the book, Chapters 2–9. If you are impatient to get to the self-help procedures in Part III, Chapters 10–19, you can go directly from here to there, without pausing now to read further about the nature of depression and its elements. But if you have the patience to study a bit more before moving on to the self-help procedures, it may be worth your while to read through Part II first. Or you can come back to Part II later.

The discussion in this book is pitched at a higher level of abstraction than are most self-help books. Partly this is because cognitive therapy requires somewhat more mental discipline, and more willingness to be introspective, than behavioral and other therapies.[4] But the higher level is partly due to the fact that the book is also aimed at psychiatrists and psychologists, to present to them these new ideas and methods that render more powerful some theories and procedures with which they are already familiar. And these ideas can only be presented effectively to the professions in the context of working therapy rather than in a more rarefied and abstract context.

PART TWO

The Nature of Depression

WHAT IS DEPRESSION? HOW DOES IT FEEL TO BE DEPRESSED?

Let's be sure that you and I are talking about the same state of mind when we use the word 'depression'. People sometimes say 'I'm depressed' when they refer to a state of mind quite different from the established psychological meaning of the term.

The rock-bottom element in depression is the feeling of sadness. The term 'sad' includes without distinction the feelings and moods one might call 'melancholy', 'the blues', 'being down', 'misery', 'grief', 'despair', and similar descriptions of negative feeling. The prolonged feeling of sadness, plus the thought 'I'm worthless', constitute depression; these two elements are the hallmarks of the depressed person.

A variety of other symptoms are also found in some depressed persons—inability to sleep, disinterest in sex, inability to work, for example. But these other symptoms are by no means universal. If we stick to a definition of depression as sadness plus low self-esteem, we will be clear and unconfused about the subject of this book. And you will find it easy to check yourself against that definition, with the aid of the detailed descriptions of sadness and the sense of worthlessness in the definitions and case histories that follow.

A sense of helplessness, often with a sense of hopelessness, accompanies (or is part of) the sadness and lack of self-regard in depression. The helpless attitude might be considered part of the core of depression. A rigid set of 'oughts' and 'musts', and an absence of pleasurable experiences, are frequently important constituents, too.

Prolonged sadness and depression felt to me—and others have used similar language—like living in a pool of pain, feeling helpless to escape from it.

Some sadness is inescapable and normal, of course; life without sadness would not be human. But the subject of this book is the state of sadness which does not pass as fast as it 'ought' to, and the person who stays sad longer than is 'reasonable'. The words 'ought' and 'reasonable' are troublesome, and we'll come to them later. For now let us simply think of depression as a state of sadness sufficiently intense and persistent that the depressed person might consider seeking help to get less sad. And in depression, thoughts of personal worthlessness ('low self-esteem') are more frequent and intense than most people experience.

Similar descriptions of depression—or 'melancholia'—have been given at least since ancient Roman times.[1]

TYPICAL DEPRESSIVES AND SYMPTOMS

Here are some depression cases as seen and described in capsule by psychotherapists: The depressions are mostly much more severe than you are likely to suffer, but they should be instructive nevertheless.

A young housewife:

Margaret . . . was young, about 25 and married, as she said, to a very fine man. She held a job which she found fairly interesting and about which she voiced no complaints. In fact there was nothing about her life that displeased her, yet she said she suffered from chronic depression. I would not at the outset have said that Margaret was depressed, because when she came into my office, she always smiled and talked about herself very excitedly in a high-pitched voice. No one meeting her for the first time would guess the nature of her problem unless he was astute enough to see that her manner was a mask. If you observed her carefully or caught her off guard, you would notice that at times she became very quiet, and as the smile faded, her face grew blank.

Margaret knew she was depressed. It required an effort of will simply to get up in the morning and go to work . . . There was an inner emptiness and a lack of real pleasure . . . Her smile, her volubility and her manner were a facade pretending to the world that everything was all right with her. When she was alone, the facade crumbled and she experienced her depressed state.[2]

A 25-year-old engineer, who said:

> I feel as though I'm dragging myself down as well as my family. I have caused my parents no end of aggravation. The best thing would be if I dug a hole and buried myself in it. If I would get rid of myself, everybody would be upset for a time but they would get over it. They would be better off without me. . . .
>
> After graduating from college, he had had a succession of jobs and had started a small business that failed. He was not doing well in his current position and was certain that he would be fired within a few days. He experienced a gradual loss of self-confidence as his work did not seem to measure up to the expectations of his employer. Two days before his psychiatric consultation he received notice that he would be fired. He became very discouraged and experienced a complete loss of appetite and considerable difficulty in sleeping. He thought of various ways of killing himself, such as taking an overdose of pills or throwing himself from a high building.[3]

A middle-aged single woman:

> Anne was an intelligent woman who had been successful alike in her career and her creative pursuits. With the collapse of her morale, work became difficult and her creative urge diminished. Several other factors contributed to her collapse, but all were related to the loss of the feeling of femininity and womanhood.
>
> When I first saw Anne, she *looked* collapsed. Her body was flabby, her muscles lacked tone, the skin of her face sagged, her color was poor. She lacked the energy to breathe deeply and her constant comment was 'It's no use'. When a patient utters these words, what he generally means is, 'It's no use trying. I can't make it'. But I had the impression that Anne was saying, 'It's no use *living*. I simply can't make it'.[4]

And another woman:

> [A]lmost continuously depressed for more than 20 years . . . That was the story Joan told me when she first consulted me. She was in her early forties, twice married and twice divorced. She had a child from her first marriage who was now away at college. Joan lived alone, but this didn't trouble her. She *was* disturbed, however, by a lack of desire to do anything and by the loss of interest in her friends. She found it painful to be with people, even those she had

known for many years. She felt that her life was empty and meaningless.[5]

A mother whose children have grown up:

Recently a middle-aged woman presented herself . . . Every day, she says, is a struggle just to keep going. On her bad days she cannot even bring herself to get out of bed, and her husband comes home at night to find her still in her pajamas, with dinner unprepared. She cries a great deal; even her lighter moods are continually interrupted with thoughts of failure and worthlessness. Small chores such as shopping or dressing seem very difficult and every minor obstacle seems like an impassable barrier. When I reminded her that she is a good-looking woman and suggested that she go out and buy a new dress, she replied, "That's just too hard for me. I'd have to take the bus across town and I'd probably get lost. Even if I got to the store, I couldn't find a dress that would fit. What would be the use anyway, since I'm really so unattractive?" . . .

Up until last fall she had been vivacious and active, the president of her suburban PTA, a charming social hostess, a tennis player, and a spare-time poet. Then two things happened: her twin boys went away to college for the first time, and her husband was promoted to a position of much greater responsibility in his company, a position that took him away from home more often. She now broods about whether life is worth living, and has toyed with the idea of taking the whole bottle of antidepressant pills at once.[6]

A college girl who 'had everything':

Nancy entered the university with a superb high-school record. She had been president and salutatorian of her class, and a popular and pretty cheerleader. Everything she wanted had always fallen into her lap; good grades came easily and boys fell over themselves competing for her attentions. She was an only child, and her parents doted on her, rushing to fulfill her every whim; her successes were their triumphs, her failures were their agony. Her friends nicknamed her Golden Girl.

When I met her in her sophomore year, she was no longer a Golden Girl. She said that she felt empty, that nothing touched her any more; her classes were boring and the whole academic system seemed an oppressive conspiracy to stifle her creativity. The previous semester she had received two F's. She had 'made it' with a succession of young men, and was currently living with a dropout. She felt exploited and worthless after each sexual adventure; her current relationship was on the rocks, and she felt little but contempt for him and for herself . . .

She was majoring in philosophy, and had a marked emotional attraction to Existentialism: like the existentialists, she believed that life is absurd.[7]

PERSONAL ACCOUNTS OF DEPRESSION

Now here are some autobiographical descriptions of depressive states and personalities. If you have become frustrated by people who have never been depressed pooh-poohing the pain you are suffering—which often happens—show them these descriptions.

Perhaps the most famous depression is that of Hamlet:

Oh . . . that the Everlasting had not fixed
His canon 'gainst self-slaughter! Oh, God! God!
How weary, stale, flat, and unprofitable
Seem to me all the uses of the world!

The Psalms contain some of the most affecting cries of pain that have been written. Consider Psalm 22, lines 2 and 3:

My God, my God, why has Thou forsaken me,
And art far from my help at the words of my cry?
O my God, I call by day, but Thou answerest not;
And at night, and there is no surcease for me.

Psalm 22, lines 7 and 8:

But I am a worm, and no man;
A reproach of men, and despised of the people.
All they that see me laugh me to scorn;
They shoot out the lip, they shake the head.

Psalm 22, lines 15, 16, 17, 18, and 19:

I am poured out like water,
And all my bones are out of joint;
My heart is become like wax;
It is melted in mine inmost parts.
My strength is dried up like a potsherd;

And my tongue cleaveth to my throat;
And Thou layest me in the dust of death.
For dogs have encompassed me;
A company of evil-doers have inclosed me;
Like a lion, they are at my hands and my feet.
I may count all my bones;
They look and gloat over me.
They part my garments among them,
And for my vesture do they cast lots.

Psalm 102, lines 4, 5, and 6:

For my days are consumed like smoke,
And my bones are burned as a hearth.
My heart is smitten like grass, and withered;
For I forget to eat my bread.
By reason of the voice of my sighing
My bones cleave to my flesh.

And Psalm 13, lines 2, 3, and 4:

How long, O Lord, wilt Thou forget me for ever?
How long wilt Thou hide Thy face from me?
How long shall I take counsel in my soul,
Having sorrow in my heart by day?
How long shall mine enemy be exalted over me?
Behold Thou, and answer me, O Lord my God;
Lighten mine eyes, lest I sleep the sleep of death;

Bertrand Russell described his youthful depression:

I was not born happy. As a child, my favorite hymn was: 'Weary of earth and laden with my sin'. At the age of five, I reflected that, if I should live to be 70, I had only endured so far, a fourteenth part of my whole life, and I felt the long-spread-out boredom ahead of me to be almost unendurable. In adolescence, I hated life and was continually on the verge of suicide, from which, however, I was restrained by the desire to know more mathematics.[8]

Abraham Lincoln:

I am now the most miserable man living. If what I feel were equally distributed to the whole human family, there would not be one cheerful face on earth. Whether I shall ever be better, I cannot tell; I awfully forebode I shall not. To remain as I am is impossible. I must die or be better, it appears to me.[9]

An English novelist who had made two serious attempts at suicide:

I don't know how much potential suicides *think* about it. I must say, I've never really thought about it much. Yet it's always there. For me, suicide's a constant temptation. It never slackens. Things are all right at the moment. But I feel like a cured alcoholic: I daren't take a drink because I know that if I do I'll go on it again. Because whatever it is that's there doesn't alter. It's a pattern of my entire life. I would like to think that it was only brought on by certain stresses and strains. But in fact, if I'm honest and look back, I realize it's been a pattern ever since I can remember.

My parents were very fond of death. It was their favorite thing. As a child, it seemed to me that my father was constantly rushing off to do himself in. Everything he said, all his analogies, were to do with death. I remember him once telling me that marriage was the last nail in the coffin of life. I was about eight at the time. Both my parents, for different reasons, regarded death as a perfect release from their troubles. They were very unhappy together, and I think this sunk in very much. Like my father, I have always demanded too much of life and people and relationships—far more than exists, really. And when I find that it doesn't exist, it seems like a rejection. It probably isn't a rejection at all; it simply isn't there. I mean, the empty air doesn't reject you; it just says, 'I'm empty'. Yet rejection and disappointment are two things I've always found impossible to take . . . When I'm not working, I'm capable of sleeping through most of the morning. Then I start taking sleeping pills during the day to keep myself in a state of dopiness, so that I can sleep at any time. To take sleeping pills during the day to sleep isn't so far from taking sleeping pills in order to die. It's just a bit more practical and a bit more craven. You only take two instead of two hundred . . .

In the afternoons my mother and father both retired to sleep. That is, they retired to death. They really died for the afternoons . . . But during those afternoons I used to be alive and lively. It was a great big house but I never dared to make a sound. I didn't dare pull a plug in case I woke one of them up. I felt terribly rejected. Their door was shut, they were absolutely unapproachable. Whatever terrible crisis had happened to me, I felt I couldn't go and say, 'Hey, wake up, listen to me'. And those afternoons went on a long time. Because of the war I went back to live with them, and it was still exactly the same. If I ever bumped myself off, it would be in the afternoon. Indeed, the first time I tried was in the afternoon. The second time was after an awful afternoon. Moreover, it was after an afternoon in the country, which I hate for the same reasons as I hate afternoons. The reason is simple: when I'm alone, I stop believing I exist.[10]

A California woman:

I am 49 years old. All my life I've been a very functional, active person, totally community-involved. I have three children, aged 20, 23 and 29. I was married for five years and divorced, then married 20 years and divorced and remarried once more.

I was a dancer, an Arthur Murray instructor. I did stitchery. I did mosaics. I attended night courses—psychology, architecture and theater classes, I was totally involved and doing.

In April, 1976, I was employed selling real estate in an office where my husband, Eddie, was boss. I was totally functioning and happy. But he hated his job so he resigned. When he resigned they said, "Take Gloria with you. You're a team." That was a blow to my self-esteem at the time. I think that's where the clinical depression, the illness itself, was setting in . . .

I totally lost myself during this clinical depression. I didn't know who this other person was and felt I was going crazy. Where was Gloria? Where was this once-confident person? . . .

. . . The worst for me was sleep disturbance—the inability to get any rest at all, not even one hour's sleep at night. In regular life, I'm not an eight-hour sleeper; I only need four hours of good sleep.

During the clinical depression I thought my husband should get a divorce and marry a young woman and live in a tract house and raise little children. So that's what I told him to do . . .

As my depression wore on, I stopped talking to my friends. I didn't want to tell them I was depressed because I didn't want them to worry about me.[11]

An English writer:

My wife, who visited me nobly at least twice a week for the whole eleven months of my confinement . . . was the only person to whom I dared confide my horrors, and I tried hard to show my train of reasoning. Roughly it was that I was a sort of opposite of Jesus Christ. Satan's job had been to catch a man, get him to sell his soul to him completely and utterly, like Faust, and then take him down alive into the pit. That was a sort of necessary counterweight to the resurrection of Jesus and the elect. I was the man. But if I could only kill myself, it might blow up the whole Universe, but at least I would get out of eternal torture and achieve the oblivion and nothingness for which my soul craved. I did in fact make three attempts at suicide, the most serious of which was when I tore myself from my attendant and threw myself in front of a car, with my poor wife, who was visiting me, looking on.

Although my attempts at suicide failed, they had one satisfactory effect; the doctors increased my drugs. As long as I was able to attain unconsciousness at night (with the aid of three or four doses of paraldehyde), and to maintain a fairly soporific state during the day (with anything up to four tablets of allonal), I could just keep the horrors at bay. My whole conscious effort was now directed towards the aim of putting off the moment when I would disappear finally into Hell . . .

By this time, say four or five months after my arrival, I had evolved a definite technique to help me in this effort of getting through the days and nights. I had frankly admitted my position. God had turned His back on me and left me to Satan, but perhaps I could persuade Satan to put off the evil day a bit. That was all I asked for, and it seemed to me I stood a chance of getting some postponement if I could worship Satan really properly. So I evolved my own little rituals—they incidentally have little to do with genuine Satanism, which is obviously much more closely associated with my manic periods.

Every night I said the Lord's Prayer backwards, letter by letter, smoking three ritual cigarettes as I did so. By that time the drug I had taken used to begin to work, and I always got to sleep before I had finished the prayer . . .[12]

A Massachusetts teacher after he voluntarily went to a hospital community for two weeks:

For weeks I had been coming awake every morning with a sick, empty feeling, with a dread of the long hours before I could crawl back in bed. How could I endure yet another day when life seemed so meaningless, so tasteless, that there was nothing I looked forward to doing? This day was the worst yet: I was still the captive of my depression, and I realized where I was. What would I do with myself all day, confined within this tiny hospital ward? Would I ever get well again, or was this just the first of an endless succession of empty days? I writhed under the covers, I groaned; I crouched in a fetal position, I pounded my fists on the pillow.

Van Wyck Brooks:

There came a time . . . when my own bubble burst, when the dome under which I had lived crumbled into ruin, when I was

consumed with a sense of failure, a feeling that my work had all
gone wrong and that I was mistaken in all I had said or thought . . .
    I could no longer sleep. I scarcely sat down for a year . . .
when I napped for an hour or so I dreamed that I was about to be
hanged . . . All my affections and interests fell into abeyance, and
it seemed to me that, where normal depressions occasionally sank
to zero, mine sank from zero indefinitely down . . .
    I was possessed now with a fantasy of suicide that filled my
mind as the full moon fills the sky. It was a fixed idea. I could not
expel this fantasy that shimmered in my brain and I saw every knife
as something with which to cut one's throat and every high
building as something to jump from. A belt was a garotte for me, a
rope existed to hang oneself with, the top of a door was merely a
bracket for the rope. Every rusty musket had its predestined use
for me and every tomb in a graveyard was a place to starve in. I
could see an axe only as lethal and every bottle meant for me
something to be swallowed in splinters or to slash one's wrists with,
while even the winter snow fell in order to give one pneumonia if
one spent a night lying on the ground. Meanwhile, every morning,
when I began to sleep again, I awoke with my arms folded over my
breast. I had been dreaming that I was dead at last and uncon-
sciously arranged my limbs in the posture of a mummy . . .
    In my *crise a quarante ans* I shrank from all human
relations . . .[13]

Leo Tolstoy:

It had come to this, that I, a healthy, fortunate man, felt I could no
longer live: some irresistible power impelled me to rid myself one
way or other of life. I cannot say I *wished* to kill myself. The power
which drew me away from life was stronger, fuller, and more
widespread than any mere wish. It was a force similar to the former
striving to live, only in a contrary direction. All my strength drew
me away from life. The thought of self-destruction now came to me
as naturally as thoughts of how to improve my life had come
formerly. And it was so seductive that I had to be wily with myself
lest I should carry it out too hastily. I did not wish to hurry, only
because I wanted to use all efforts to disentangle the matter. 'If I
cannot unravel matters, there will always be time.' And it was then
that I, a man favoured by fortune, hid a cord from myself, lest I
should hang myself from the crosspiece of the partition in my
room, where I undressed alone every evening, and I ceased to go
out shooting with a gun, lest I should be tempted by so easy a way
of ending my life. I did not myself know what I wanted: I feared
life, desired to escape from it; yet still hoped something of it.

And all this befell me at a time when all around me I had what is considered complete good fortune. I was not yet fifty; I had a good wife who loved me and whom I loved, good children, and a large estate which without much effort on my part improved and increased, I was respected by my relations and acquaintances more than at any previous time. I was praised by others, and without much self-deception could consider that my name was famous. And far from being insane or mentally diseased, I enjoyed on the contrary a strength of mind and body such as I have seldom met with among men of my kind; physically, I could keep up with the peasants at mowing, and mentally I could work for eight and ten hours at a stretch without experiencing any ill results from such exertion. And in this situation I came to this—that I could not live, and fearing death, had to employ cunning with myself to avoid taking my own life.[14]

Sylvia Plath's fictionalized autobiographical account of a young author who had already tried suicide and who would soon kill herself (Plath too was to die by her own hand):

I was still wearing Betsy's white blouse and dirndl skirt. They drooped a bit now, as I hadn't washed them in my three weeks at home. The sweaty cotton gave off a sour but friendly smell.

I hadn't washed my hair for three weeks, either.

I hadn't slept for seven nights.

My mother told me I must have slept, it was impossible not to sleep in all that time, but if I slept, it was with my eyes wide open, for I had followed the green luminous course of the second hand and the minute hand and the hour hand of the bedside clock through their circles and semicircles, every night for seven nights, without missing a second, or a minute, or an hour.

The reason I hadn't washed my clothes or my hair was because it seemed so silly.

I saw the days of the year stretching ahead like a series of bright, white boxes, and separating one box from another was sleep, like a black shade. Only for me, the long perspective of shades that set off one box from the next had suddenly snapped up, and I could see day after day after day glaring ahead of me like a white, broad, infinitely desolate avenue.

It seemed silly to wash one day when I would only have to wash again the next.

It made me tired just to think of it.

I wanted to do everything once and for all and be through with it . . .

That morning I had tried to hang myself.

I had taken the silk cord of my mother's yellow bathrobe as soon as she left for work, and, in the amber shade of the bedroom, fashioned it into a knot that slipped up and down on itself. It took me a long time to do this, because I was poor at knots and had no ideas how to make a proper one.

Then I hunted around for a place to attach the rope.

The trouble was, our house had the wrong kind of ceilings.

The ceilings were low, white and smoothly plastered, without a light fixture or a wood beam in sight. I thought with longing of the house my grandmother had before she sold it to come and live with us, and then with my Aunt Libby.

My grandmother's house was built in the fine, nineteenth-century style, with lofty rooms and sturdy chandelier brackets and high closets with stout rails across them, and an attic where nobody ever went, full of trunks and parrot cages and dressmakers' dummies and overhead beams thick as a ship's timbers.

But it was an old house, and she'd sold it, and I didn't know anybody else with a house like that.

After a discouraging time of walking about with the silk cord dangling from my neck like a yellow cat's tail and finding no place to fasten it, I sat on the edge of my mother's bed and tried pulling the cord tight.

But each time I would get the cord so tight I could feel a rushing in my ears and a flush of blood in my face, my hands would weaken and let go, and I would be all right again.

Then I saw that my body had all sorts of little tricks, such as making my hands go limp at the crucial second, which would save it, time and again, whereas if I had the whole say, I would be dead in a flash.

I would simply have to ambush it with whatever sense I had left, or it would trap me in its stupid cage for fifty years without any sense at all. And when people found out my mind had gone, as they would have to, sooner or later, in spite of my mother's guarded tongue, they would persuade her to put me into an asylum where I could be cured.

Only my case was incurable.[15]

There is a happy conclusion to the grim reports quoted above. Modern psychology and medicine provide rapid relief to most people who develop the sorts of depressions described in those reports. No more does a sufferer simply have to wait until nature takes its course, or until you can yourself invent a way to successfully reshape your thinking patterns. Cognitive-behavioral therapy can promise relief to most people within a few months, accompanied by long-run protection against relapse by teaching you how to avoid depressing modes of thought. Drug therapy often provides fast relief of the symptoms, too, though without promising that your depression has been cured.

In view of the large number of depression sufferers—a larger proportion of the population nowadays than ever before—these advances must rank as among the most beneficial contributions of science to human welfare.

SUMMARY

The chapter describes a variety of cases of depression, often in their own words. The fundamental element is the feeling of sadness. The term 'sad' includes without distinction the feelings and moods one might call 'melancholy', 'the blues', 'being down', 'misery', 'grief', 'despair', and similar descriptions of negative feeling. The prolonged feeling of sadness, plus the thought 'I'm worthless', constitute depression; these two elements are the hallmarks of the depressed person.

Other symptoms are also found in some depressed persons— inability to sleep, disinterest in sex, inability to work, for example. But these are by no means universal.

A sense of helplessness, often with a sense of hopelessness, accompanies or is part of the sadness and lack of self-regard in depression. The helpless attitude might be considered part of the core of depression. A rigid set of 'oughts' and 'musts', and an absence of pleasurable experiences, frequently are important constituents, too.

NEGATIVE SELF-COMPARISONS, COMBINED WITH A HELPLESS FEELING, ARE THE PROXIMATE CAUSE OF DEPRESSION

Roadmap Note

The book is organized so that you can go directly from the overall summary in Chapter 1 to the get-to-work self-help procedures in Part III (Chapters 10–20), without pausing to read further about the nature of depression and its elements in Part II (Chapters 3–9). But if you have the patience to study a bit more before moving on to the self-help procedures, it will be worth your while to first read through Part II, which expands greatly on Chapter 1. Or, you can come back and read the rest of Part II later.

When you are depressed you *feel sad;* this is the basic fact about the condition called 'depression'. The *feeling* of sadness is accompanied by the *thought* 'I'm worthless'. An attitude of 'I'm helpless' is a precursor of the sadness, and the belief 'I ought to be different from the way I am' usually helps keep the person locked into sadness. Our first task, then, is to understand sadness—to learn what causes sadness, what relieves sadness, and what prevents sadness.

THE IMPORTANCE OF NEGATIVE
SELF-COMPARISONS

Attempts to distinguish 'normal' from 'abnormal' sadness have not proven useful. Apparently there is but a single sort of sad feeling; the pain is the same whether it follows upon the loss of a friend (a 'normal' event) or, say, the keenly-felt loss of an honor which it was not reasonable for you to expect but which you had nevertheless set your heart on. This makes sense when we notice that one does not distinguish between the *pain* from a finger that got cut in an accident, and the pain of a self-inflicted cut on the finger. The *contexts* are very different, however, in the cases of the two sorts of loss mentioned above, and it is those contexts that distinguish between the depressed person and the person who suffers from a 'normal' sadness.

We must know, then: Why does one person respond to a particular negative event in his/her life with short-lived sadness after which normal cheerful life reappears, whereas another responds to a similar event with persistent depression? And why does a trivial or almost nonexistent blemish in life trigger sadness in some people and not in others?

The answer in brief is as follows: Some people acquire from their personal histories: 1. *a tendency to make frequent negative self-comparisons,* and therefore a tendency to have a Rotten Mood Ratio; 2. *a tendency to think one is helpless to change the events that enter into the Rotten Ratio;* and 3. *a tendency to insist that one's life should be better than it is.*

Concerning the first of these elements, the tendency to make frequent negative self-comparisons: This does not mean quite the same as 'thinking poorly of yourself' or 'having low self-esteem'. The differences will be explained later.

There are many possible interacting elements in the development of a propensity to make neg-comps (negative self-comparisons), conceivably including a genetic element, and the elements differ from person to person. Understanding this mechanism is a necessary forerunner to designing the appropriate cure as discussed in Part III. The neg-comp is the last link in the causal chain leading to sadness and depression, the 'common pathway', in medical parlance. If we can remove or alter this link, we can relieve depression.

To repeat, the central element in your sadness and depression, and the key to your cure, is as follows: You feel sad when a. you compare your actual situation with some 'benchmark' hypothetical situation, and the comparison appears negative; and b. you think you are helpless to do anything about it. This analysis may seem obvious to you after you reflect on it, and many great philosophers have touched on it. But this key idea has had little or no place in the psychological literature on depression, though the negative self-comparison is the key to understanding and treating depression.

The element of 'negative thoughts' has been mentioned by just about every writer on depression through the ages, as has been the more specific set of negative thoughts that make up low self-evaluation. And controlled laboratory experiments have recently shown that depressed people remember fewer instances of being rewarded for successful performance than do non-depressed subjects, and remember more instances of being punished for unsuccessful performance. Depressed subjects also reward themselves less frequently when told to decide which responses were successful and which were not.[1]

Negative thoughts have not, however, been previously discussed in a *systematic* fashion as comprising *comparison,* as every evaluation is by nature a comparison. Nor has the *interaction* between the neg-comps and the sense of helplessness, which converts neg-comps into sadness and depression, been described elsewhere as it is here. It is the conceptualization of the negative thoughts as *negative self-comparisons* which opens up the wide variety of theoretical and curative approaches discussed here.

After you grasp this idea, you see its traces in many places. For example, notice the casual mention of self-comparisons in these remarks of Beck that "the repeated recognition of a gap between what a person expects and what he receives from an important interpersonal relationship, from his career, or from other activities, may topple him into a depression",[2] and "The tendency to compare oneself with others further lowers self-esteem".[3] But Beck does not *center* his analysis on the self-comparisons. It is the *systematic development* of this idea which provides the new thrust in Self-Comparisons Analysis as offered here.

The State of Your Life as You Perceive It to Be

Your 'actual' state is what you *perceive* it to be, of course, rather than what it 'really' is. If you *think* you have failed an examination, even though you will later learn you passed it, then your perceived actual state is that you have failed the test. Of course there are many facets of your actual life that you can choose to focus upon, and the choice is very important. The accuracy of your assessment is important, too. But the actual state of your life usually is not the controlling element in depression. How you *perceive* your life is not *completely* dictated by the actual state of affairs. Rather, you have considerable discretion as to how to perceive and assess the state of your life.

The Benchmark to Which You Compare Yourself

The 'benchmark' situation to which you compare your actual situation may be of many sorts:

a) The benchmark situation may be one that you were *accustomed to* and liked, but which no longer exists. This is the case, for example, after the death of a loved one; the consequent grief-sadness arises from comparing the situation of bereavement with the benchmark situation of the loved one's being alive.

b) The benchmark situation may be something that you *expected* to happen but that did not materialize, for example, a pregnancy you expected to yield a child but which ends in miscarriage, or the children you expected to raise but never were able to have.

c) The benchmark may be a *hoped-for* event, a hoped-for son after three daughters that turns out to be another daughter, or an essay that you hope will affect many people's lives for the good but that languishes unread in your bottom drawer.

d) The benchmark may be something you feel you are *obligated* to do but are not doing, for example, supporting your aged parents.

e) The benchmark may also be the *achievement of a goal* you aspired to and aimed at but failed to reach, for example, quitting smoking, or teaching a retarded child to read. Betty Ford (wife of former president Gerald Ford) wrote: "I was always measuring myself against impossible ideals—Martha [famous dancer Graham], or my mother—and coming up short. That's a good recipe for alcoholism"—or depression (*Washington Post Book World*, March 1, 1987, 5).

The expectations or demands of others may also enter into the benchmark situation with which you negatively compare your actual situation. And, of course, the benchmark state may contain more than one of these overlapping elements.

The best proof that sadness is caused by the unfavorable comparison of actual and benchmark situations is self-inspection of your thoughts. If you observe in your thinking, when you are sad, such a negative self-comparison along with a sense of helplessness about changing the situation—whether the sadness is part of a general depression or not—this should convince you of the key role of negative self-comparisons in causing depression.

THE ROLE OF NEGATIVE SELF-COMPARISONS

Only the concept of negative self-comparisons makes sense of a person's being bereft of life's good things yet happy anyway, or having everything a person could want but being miserable nevertheless.

The author of Ecclesiastes—traditionally considered to be King Solomon—tells us how useless and helpless he felt despite all his riches:

> So I hated life, because the work that is wrought under the sun was grievous unto me; for all is [in vain] and a striving after wind. (2–17, my language in brackets)

The sense of loss—which is often associated with the onset of depression—is a negative comparison between the way things *were* and the way they are *now*. The American poet John Greenleaf Whittier (in *Maud Muller*) caught the nature of loss as a comparison in these lines: "For of all sad words of tongue or pen, the saddest are these: It might have been!" Whittier makes it clear that sadness arises not just because of what *actually* happened, but also because of the counterfactual benchmark which "might have been".

Notice how, when we suffer from what we call 'regret', we harp on the counterfactual benchmark—how an inch more to the side would have won the game which would have put the team into the playoffs which would have led to a championship, how but for one horse's nail the war was lost, how—if not for the slaughter by the Germans in World War II, or the Turks in World War I—the Jews and Armenians would be so much more numerous and their cultures would be strengthened, and so on.

The basis for understanding and dealing with depression, then, is the negative comparison between your actual and hypothetical bench-mark situations that produces a bad mood, together with the condi-tions that lead you to make such comparisons frequently and acutely, and combined with the helpless feeling that makes the bad mood into a sad rather than angry mood; this is the set of circumstances constitut-ing the deep and continued sadness that we call depression.

Why Do Negative Self-Comparisons Cause a Bad Mood?

But *why* do negative self-comparisons and a Rotten Ratio produce a bad mood?

There is a biological connection between negative self-comparisons and physically-induced pain. Psychological trauma such as a loss of a loved one induces some of the same bodily changes as does the pain from a migraine headache, say. When people refer to the death of a loved one as 'painful', they are speaking about a biological reality and not just a metaphor. It is reasonable that more ordinary 'losses'—of status, income, career, and of a mother's attention or smile in the case of a child—have the same sorts of effects, even if milder. And children learn that they lose love when they are bad, unsuccessful, and clumsy, as compared to when they are good, successful, and graceful. Hence negative self-comparisons indicating that one is 'bad' in some way are likely to be coupled to the biological connections to loss and pain. It also makes sense that the human's need for love is connected to the infant's need for food and being nursed and held by its mother, the loss of which must be felt in the body.[4]

Indeed, research cited later shows a statistical link between the death of a parent and the propensity to be depressed, in both animals and humans. And much careful laboratory work shows that separation of adults and their young produces the signs of depression in dogs and monkeys.[5] Hence lack of love hurts and makes one sad, just as lack of food makes one hungry.

Research shows chemical differences between depressed and undepressed persons. Similar chemical effects are found in animals which have learned that they are helpless to avoid painful shocks.[6] Taken as a whole, then, the evidence suggests that negative self-comparisons, together with a sense of helplessness, produce chemical effects linked to painful bodily sensations, all of which results in a sad mood.

A physically-caused pain may seem more 'objective' than a negative self-comparison because the jab of a pin, say, is an *absolute* objective fact, and does not depend upon a *relative* comparison for you to have a painful perception of it.[7] The bridge is that neg-comps are connected to pain through *learning* during your entire lifetime. You *learn* to be sad about a lost job or an examination failure; a person who has never seen an exam or a modern occupational society could not be made sad by those events. Learned knowledge of this sort always is relative, a matter of comparisons, rather than involving only one absolute physical stimulus.

All this represents therapeutic opportunity: It is because the causes of sadness and depression are largely learned that we can hope to remove the pain of depression by managing our minds properly. This is why we can conquer psychologically-induced pain with mental management more easily than we can banish the sensation of pain from arthritis or from freezing feet. With respect to a stimulus that we have learned to experience as painful—lack of professional success, for example—we can relearn a new meaning for it. That is, we can change the frame of reference, for example, by altering the comparison states that we choose as benchmarks. But it is impossible (except perhaps for a yogi) to change the frame of reference for physical pain so as to remove the pain, though one can certainly reduce the pain by quieting the mind with breathing techniques and other relaxation devices, and by teaching ourselves to take a detached view of the discomfort and pain.

To put the matter in different words: Pain and sadness which are associated with mental events can be prevented because the meaning of the mental events was originally learned; relearning can remove the pain. But the impact of physically-caused painful events depends much less on learning, and hence relearning has less capacity to reduce or remove the pain.

The Nature of Comparisons

Comparison and evaluation of the present state of affairs *relative to* other states of affairs is fundamental in all planning and businesslike thinking. The relevant cost in a business decision is the 'opportunity cost'—that is, the cost of what else you might do rather instead of the opportunity being considered. Comparison is also part of judgments in all other endeavors. As the book's front note says: "Life is hard". But compared to what?

Indeed, comparison-making is central to all our information processing, scientific as well as personal:

> Basic to scientific evidence (and to all knowledge-diagnostic processes including the retina of the eye) is the process of comparison of recording differences, or of contrast. Any appearance of absolute knowledge, or intrinsic knowledge about singular isolated objects, is found to be illusory upon analysis. Securing scientific evidence involves making at least one comparison.[8]

A classic remark illuminates the centrality of comparisons in understanding the world: A fish would be the last to discover the nature of water.

Just about every evaluation you make boils down to a comparison. 'I'm tall' must be with reference to some group of people; a Japanese who would say 'I'm tall' in Japan might not say that in the U.S. If you say 'I'm good at tennis', the hearer will ask, 'Whom do you play with, and whom do you beat?' in order to understand what you mean. Similarly, 'I never do anything right', or 'I'm a terrible mother' is hardly meaningful without some standard of comparison.

The psychologist Helson put it this way: "[A]ll judgments (not only judgments of magnitude) are relative." Without a standard of comparison, you cannot make judgments.[9]

An example of how one cannot communicate factual knowledge without making comparisons is my attempt in the Epilogue to describe to you the depth of my depression. It is only by comparing the depression to something else that you might understand from your own experience—time in jail, or having a tooth pulled—that I can give you any reasonable idea of how my depression felt. And communicating factual knowledge to *oneself* is not basically different from communicating with others; without comparisons you cannot communicate to yourself the information (true or false) that leads to sadness and eventually to depression.

THE OLD AND NEW VIEWS OF DEPRESSION

Now the difference between this view of depression and that of traditional Freudian psychotherapy is clear: Traditional psychotherapists, from Freud on, believe that negative self-comparisons (or rather, what they call 'low self-esteem') and sadness *are both symptoms* of the underlying causes, rather than the negative self-comparisons causing the sadness; their view is shown in Figure 1. Therefore, traditional psychotherapists believe that you cannot affect depression by directly altering the kinds of thoughts that are in your consciousness, that is, by removing negative self-comparisons. Additionally, they believe that you are not likely to *cure yourself* or ameliorate your depression in any simple direct way by altering the contents of your thoughts and ways of thinking, because they believe that unconscious mental elements influence behavior. Rather, they believe that you can only remove the depression by reworking the events and memories in your early life that led you to have a propensity to be depressed.

In direct contrast is the cognitive viewpoint of this book as shown in Figure 2. Negative self-comparisons operate between the underlying causes and the pain, which (in the presence of a sense of being helpless) cause sadness. Therefore, if one can remove or reduce the negative self-comparisons, one can then cure or reduce the depression.

The rest of this chapter is rather technical, and intended mainly for

Figure 1
The Traditional Psychotherapeutic View

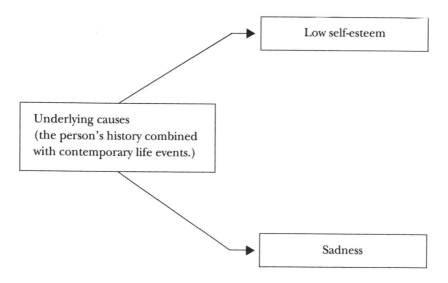

Figure 2
Self-Comparisons Analysis and Cognitive Therapy

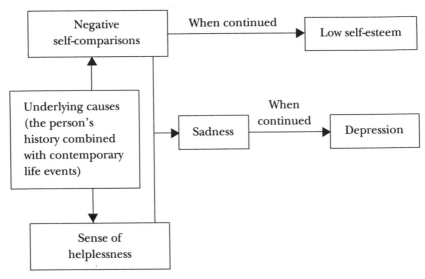

professionals. Laypersons may well skip to the next chapter. Professionals will find additional technical discussion in the Postscript for the Professional Reader at the end of the book.

Freud pointed in the right direction when he talked about people avoiding pain and seeking pleasure. Nor was this purely a tautology in which what people chose to do is simply *called* pleasurable; painful events can be connected to chemical events within the body, as discussed in Chapter 2. This idea is helpful here because it helps us understand the relationship of a variety of mental illnesses to negative self-comparisons and the pain they cause.

Some of the possible responses to negative self-comparisons and the consequent pain are as follows:

1. One can sometimes avoid pain by *changing the real circumstances* involved in the neg-comp; this is what the 'normal', active, undepressed person does, and what the normal rat does who has not previously been subjected to shocks that it cannot escape.[10] The absence of such purposive activity with respect to neg-comps because of a sense of *helplessness* to improve the situation is a crucial characteristic of sufferers from depression.

2. One can deal with the pain by *getting angry*, which tends to make you forget about the pain—until after the rage subsides. Anger can also be useful in changing the circumstances. Anger arises in a situation where the person has not lost hope but feels frustrated in attempting to remove the source of the pain.

3. You can *lie to yourself* about the existing circumstances. Distortion of reality can avoid the pain of a neg-comp. But this can lead toward schizophrenia and paranoia.[11] A schizophrenic may fantasize that his actual state is different than it really is, and while believing that the fantasy is true the painful neg-comp is not in the person's mind. The irony of such distortion of reality to avoid the pain of a neg-comp is that the neg-comp itself may contain a distortion of reality; making the neg-comp more realistic would avoid the need for schizophrenic distortion of reality.[12]

4. Still another possible outcome is that the person *assumes that he or she is helpless* to do anything about it, and this produces sadness and eventually depression.

Other states of mind which are reactions to the psychological pain of neg-comps fit well with this view of depression.[13]

1. The person suffering from *anxiety* compares an *anticipated* and *feared* outcome with a benchmark counterfactual; anxiety differs from depression in its uncertainty about the outcome, and perhaps also about the extent to which the person feels helpless to control the outcome.[14] People who are mainly depressed often suffer from anxiety, too, just as people who suffer from anxiety also have symptoms of depression from time to time.[15] This is explained by the fact that a person who is 'down' reflects on a variety of neg-comps, some of which focus on the past and present whereas others focus on the future; those neg-comps pertaining to the future are not only uncertain, but may sometimes be altered, which accounts for the state of arousal that characterizes anxiety, in contrast to the sadness that characterizes depression.

Beck differentiates the two conditions by saying that 'In depression the patient takes his interpretation and predictions as facts. In anxiety they are simply possibilities.'[16] I add that in depression an interpretation or prediction—the negative self-comparison—may be taken as fact, whereas in anxiety it is not assured but is only a possibility, *because of the depressed person's feeling of helplessness to change the situation.*

2. *Mania* is the condition in which the comparison between actual and benchmark states seems to be very large and *positive,* and often it is a condition in which the person believes that she or he is able to control the situation. It is especially exciting because the person is not accustomed to positive comparisons. Mania is like the wildly-excited reaction of a poor kid who has never before been to a professional basketball game. In the face of an anticipated or actual positive comparison, a person who is not accustomed to making positive comparisons about his life tends to exaggerate its size and be more emotional about it than people who are accustomed to comparing themselves positively.

3. *Dread* refers to future events just as does anxiety, but in a state of dread the event is expected for sure, rather than being uncertain as in anxiety. One is *anxious* about whether one will miss the plane, but one *dreads* the moment when one finally gets there and has to perform an unpleasant task.

4. *Apathy* occurs when the person responds to the pain of neg-comps by giving up goals, so that there is no longer a neg-comp. But when this happens the joy and the spice go out of life. This may still be thought of as depression, and if so, it is a circumstance when depression occurs without sadness—the only such circumstance that I know of.

The English psychiatrist John Bowlby observed a pattern in children, aged 15–30 months of age and separated from their mothers, that fits with the relationships between types of responses to neg-comps outlined here. Bowlby labels the phases "Protest, Despair, and Detachment".

First the child "seeks to recapture [his mother] by the full exercise of his limited resources. He will often cry loudly, shake his cot, throw himself about. . . . All his behaviour suggests strong expectations that she will return."[17]

Then, "During the phase of despair . . . his behaviour suggests increasing hopelessess. The active physical movements diminish or come to an end. . . . He is withdrawn and inactive, makes no demands on people in the environment, and appears to be in a state of deep mourning."[18]

Last, in the phase of detachment, "there is a striking absence of the behaviour characteristic of the strong attachment normal at this age . . . he may seem hardly to know [his mother] . . . he may remain remote and apathetic. . . . He seems to have lost all interest in her."[19] So the child eventually removes the painful neg-comps by removing the source of the pain from his thought.

5. Various *positive feelings* arise when the person is hopeful about improving the situation—changing the neg-comp into a more positive comparison—and is actively striving to do so.

This book confines itself to depression, leaving these other topics for treatment elsewhere.

People we call 'normal' find ways to deal with losses and the consequent neg-comps and pain in ways that keep them from prolonged sadness. Anger is a frequent response, and can be useful, partly because the anger-caused adrenaline produces a rush of good feeling. Perhaps any person will eventually be depressed if subjected to many very painful experiences, even if the person does not have a special propensity for depression; consider Job. And paraplegic accident victims judge themselves to be less happy than do normal uninjured people. On the other hand, consider this exchange reported between Walter Mondale, who ran for president of the United States in 1984, and George McGovern, who ran in 1972: Mondale: "George, when does it stop hurting?" McGovern: "When it does, I'll let you know." But despite their painful experiences, neither McGovern nor Mondale seems to have fallen into prolonged depression because of the loss. And Beck asserts that survivors of painful experiences such as concentration camps are no more subject to later depression than are other persons.[20]

Let's close this chapter on an upbeat topic: love. Requited youthful romantic love fits nicely into this framework. A youth in love constantly has in mind two deliciously positive elements—that he or she 'possesses' the wonderful beloved (just the opposite of loss, which often figures in depression) and that messages from the beloved say that in the eyes of the beloved he or she is wonderful, the most desired person in the world. In the unromantic terms of the mood ratio this translates into numerators of the perceived actual self being very positive relative to a range of benchmark denominators that the youth compares him/herself to at that moment. And the love being returned—truly the greatest of successes—makes the youth feel full of competence and power because the most desirable of all states—having the love of the beloved—is not only possible but is actually being realized. So there is a Rosy Ratio and just the opposite of helplessness and hopelessness. No wonder it feels so good!

And of course it makes sense that unrequited love feels so bad. The youth is then in the position of not having the most desirable state of affairs one can imagine, and believing her/himself incapable of bringing about that state of affairs. And when one is rejected by the lover, one loses that most desirable state of affairs which the lover formerly had. The comparison is between the actuality of being without the beloved's love and the former state of having it. No wonder it is so painful to believe that it really is over and nothing one can do can bring back the love.

SUMMARY

The basis for understanding and dealing with depression is the negative comparison between your actual and hypothetical benchmark situations that produces a bad mood, together with the conditions that lead you to make such comparisons frequently and acutely, and combined with the helpless feeling that makes the bad mood into a sad rather than angry mood; this is the set of circumstances constituting the deep and continued sadness that we call depression.

Negative self-comparisons and a Rotten Ratio produce a bad mood because there is a biological connection between negative self-comparisons and physically-induced pain. Psychological trauma such as a loss of a loved one induces some of the same bodily changes as does the pain from a migraine headache, say. When people refer to the death of a loved one as 'painful', they are speaking about a biological reality and not just a metaphor. It is reasonable that more ordinary 'losses'—of status, income, career, or of a mother's attention or smile in the case of a child—have the same sorts of effects, even if milder. And children learn that they lose love when they are bad, unsuccessful, and clumsy, as compared to when they are good, successful, and graceful. Hence negative self-comparisons indicating that one is 'bad' in some way are likely to be coupled to the biological connections to loss and pain.

Because the causes of sadness and depression are largely learned, we can remove the pain of depression by managing our minds properly. With respect to a stimulus that we have learned to experience as painful—lack of professional success, for example—we can relearn a new meaning for it. That is, we can change the frame of reference, for example, by altering the comparison states that we choose as benchmarks.

Traditional psychotherapists, from Freud on, believe that negative self-comparisons (or rather, what they call 'low self-esteem') and sadness *are both symptoms* of the underlying causes, rather than the negative self-comparisons causing the sadness. Therefore, traditional psychotherapists believe that one cannot affect depression by directly altering the kinds of thoughts that are in one's consciousness, that is, by removing negative self-comparisons. Additionally, they believe that you are not likely to *cure yourself* or ameliorate your depression in any simple or direct way by altering the contents of your thoughts and ways of thinking, because they believe that unconscious mental elements influence behavior. Rather, they believe that you can only remove the depression by reworking the events and memories in your early life that led you to have a propensity to be depressed.

In direct contrast is the cognitive viewpoint. Negative self-comparisons operate between the underlying causes and the pain, which (in the presence of a sense of being helpless) cause sadness. Therefore, if one can remove or reduce the negative self-comparisons, one can then cure or reduce the depression.

THE MECHANISMS THAT MAKE A DEPRESSIVE

Why do some people stay 'blue' and 'down' for a *long time* after something bad happens to them, whereas others snap out of it quickly? Why do some people *frequently* fall into a blue funk whereas others suffer sad moods only infrequently?

Chapter 3 presented the general framework for the understanding of depression. Now this chapter proceeds to discuss why a *particular person* is more predisposed to depression than are other people who are closer to 'normal'.

Figure 3 presents an overview of the depression system. It shows the main elements that influence whether a person is sad or happy at a given moment, and whether one does or does not descend into the prolonged gloom of depression. Starting at the left, these numbered elements are as follows: 1. Experiences in childhood, both the general pattern of childhood as well as traumatic experiences, if any. 2. The person's adult history; the recent experiences have the greatest weight. 3. The actual conditions of the individual's present life—relationships with people as well as such objective factors as health, job, finances, and so on. 4. The person's habitual mental states, plus her view of the world and herself. This includes her goals, hopes, values, demands upon herself, and ideas about herself, including whether she is effective or ineffective and important or unimportant. 5. Physical influences such as whether she is tired or rested, and anti-depression drugs she is taking, if any. 6. The machinery of thought which processes the material coming in from the other elements and produces an evaluation of how the person stands with respect to the hypothetical situation taken for comparison. 7. A sense of helplessness.

The main lines of influence from one element-set to another are

Figure 3
The Mechanisms of Depression
For a more detailed diagram, see Appendix C.

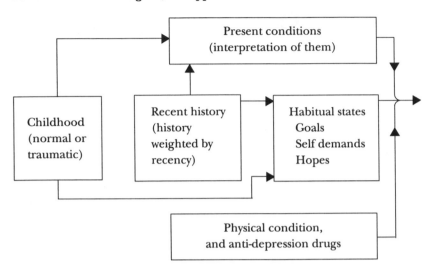

also shown in Figure 3. The question we ask is: how may a person, alone or with a counselor, alter these elements or their effects to produce fewer negative self-comparisons and a greater sense of competence—hence less sadness—and by that means pull the person out of depression?

Now we proceed in greater detail, considering the elements within these various element-sets and how they influence one another. Those who want still more details on the relationships between these various elements may wish to consult Appendix C, where all these specific ideas are linked graphically.

THE NORMAL PERSON

A few definitions to start with: A 'normal' person is someone who has never suffered from serious depression, and whom we have little reason to think will suffer serious depression in the future. A 'depressed' person is someone now suffering from serious depression. A 'depressive' is someone who is now depressed or in the past has

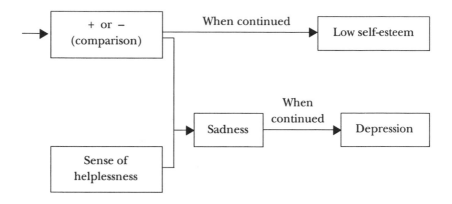

suffered serious depression, and is subject to depression again unless it is prevented. A depressive who is not now depressed is like an alcoholic who does not now drink, that is, he is a person with a dangerous propensity that requires careful control.

A normal person has 'realistic' expectations, goals, values, and beliefs that 'normally' keep him feeling good. That is, the normal person's view of the world and himself interacts with his actual state in such a way that the comparisons he makes between actual and hypothetical are usually positive, on balance. Normal people may also have a higher tolerance for negative self-comparisons when they do occur, compared to depressives.

Bad fortune may befall the normal person—perhaps death in the family, injury, marriage breakdown, money problems, loss of job, or a disaster to the community. The person's actual situation then is worse than before, and the comparison between actual and benchmark-hypothetical becomes more negative than before. The unfortunate event must be understood and interpreted in the context of the person's entire life situation. The normal person eventually perceives and interprets the event without distorting it or misinterpeting it to make it seem more terrible or permanent than it really is. And the normal person may suffer less pain and "accept" the event more easily than the depressive.

What then happens? There are several possibilities including: a) Circumstances may change of themselves. Bad health may improve or the individual may purposely alter the circumstances—find a new job, or another spouse or friend. b) The person may 'get used to' his health disability or being without the loved one. That is, the person's expectations may change. This affects the hypothetical situation to which he compares his actual situation. And after the expectations of the normal person change in response to the change in circumstances, the hypothetical-comparison state again comes into balance with the actual state in such fashion that the comparison is not negative, and sadness no longer occurs. c) The normal person's goals may change. A basketball player who aimed to make the college team may suffer a spinal injury and be confined to a wheelchair. A 'healthy' person's reaction is, after a time, to shift his goal to being a star on the wheelchair basketball team. This restores the balance between the hypothetical state and the actual state, and removes sadness.

David Hume, as great as any philosopher who ever lived, as well as a person of cheerful 'normal' temperament, describes how he reacted when his first great book had a very disappointing reception:

> I had always entertained a notion that my want of success in publishing the *Treatise of Human Nature,* had proceeded more from the manner than the matter, and that I had been guilty of a very usual indiscretion, in going to the press too early. I therefore cast the first part of that work anew in the *Enquiry concerning Human Understanding,* which was published while I was at Turin. But this piece was at first little more successful than the *Treatise of Human Nature.* On my return from Italy, I had the Mortification to find all England in a ferment, on account of Dr. Middleton's *Free Enquiry,* while my performance was entirely overlooked and neglected. A new edition, which had been published at London of my *Essays, moral and political,* met not with a much better reception.
>
> Such is the force of natural temper, that these disappointments made little or no impression on me.[1]

'Normal' people do *not*, however, respond to misfortune by adapting so readily that their spirits are unaffected. A study that compared paraplegic accident victims to persons who had not suffered paralysis from accident found that the paraplegics remained less happy than the uninjured persons months after the accident.[2] Normal people may be flexible in adapting their thinking to their circumstances, but they are not *perfectly* flexible.

THE DEPRESSIVE

The depressive differs from the normal person in having a propensity for prolonged sadness; this is the stripped-down minimum definition of a depressive. This propensity, caused by some mental baggage or biochemical scar carried over from the past, interacts with contemporary events to maintain a state of negative self-comparison.

Much of this Part II is devoted to describing this special mental baggage of the depressive. In preview, here are several important cases:

1. The depressive may, because of her intellectual or emotional training in childhood, misinterpret actual current conditions in a negative direction so that the comparison between actual and hypothetical is perennially negative, or so that after a bit of bad fortune the return to a balanced or positive comparison is much slower than for a person who is not a depressive.

2. The depressive may have a view of the world, herself, and her obligations such that her actual conditions will necessarily always be below the hypothetical. An example is a person whose talents are not extraordinary but who was brought up to believe that her talents are such that she ought to win a Nobel prize. Hence, all her life she will feel a failure, her actual state below the hypothetical, and she will therefore be depressed.

3. The depressive may have a mental quirk which forces all comparisons to be seen as negative even if his actual conditions compare well with his counterfactual condition. For example, he may believe that all people are basically sinful, as Bertrand Russell was afflicted in his youth. Or the perennial negative self-comparison may be caused by biochemical factors to be discussed shortly.

4. The depressive may feel more acute pain from a given negative

self-comparison than does the normal person. For example, the depressive might have memories of severe punishment in childhood each time his performance fell below the parental norm. Those memories of the pain from childhood punishment may intensify the pain of negative self-comparisons later on.

5. Still another difference between depressives and non-depressives is that depressives—almost invariably while they are depressed, and in many cases also when they are not depressed—have a conviction of personal worthlessness and incompetence and *lack of self-esteem.* This sense of worthlessness is general and persistent in depression, compared to the specific and transient sense of worthlessness everyone experiences from time to time. The person who is not depressed says, 'I did badly on the job this month'. The depressed person says, 'I *always* do badly on jobs', and he thinks that he will continue to do badly in the future. The depressed person's 'I'm no good' judgment seems permanent and refers to all of him, whereas the 'I did badly' of the nondepressed person is temporary and refers to one part of him alone. This is an example of *overgeneralizing,* which is typical of many depressives and a source of much pain and sadness.

Perhaps depressives tend to overgeneralize as a general habit, and to be more absolutistic in their judgments than do normal people in most of their thinking. Or perhaps depressives confine these damaging habits of thought to self-evaluative areas of their life, which cause depression. Whichever is the case, these habitual modes of inflexible thinking can cause prolonged sadness and depression.[3]

Habitual Negative Self-Comparisons Produce A Sense of Worthlessness

A single negative self-comparison does not imply a general sense of worthlessness and lack of self-esteem. A single negative self-comparison is like a single frame of a movie that is in your consciousness at a single moment, whereas a lack of self-esteem is like an entire movie full of negative self-comparisons. In addition to the specific negative self-comparison impressions you receive from each of the movie's frames, you also take away a general impression from the movie as a whole—personal worthlessness. And when later reflecting on the movie, you may at a given moment remember either a single frame or your general impression of the movie as a whole, and both the specific and the general views give you the impression of worthlessness.

A depressive reviews so many thoughts of individual negative self-comparisons that she develops the general impression of lack of personal value—worthlessness—which reinforces the individual negative self-comparisons. The never-ending flow of neg-comps also contributes to the sense that the person is helpless to stop the flow, and causes the person to lose hope that the painful neg-comps will ever cease. The general impression of worthlessness then combines with a sense of helplessness to cause sadness. The relationship between negative self-comparisons, lack of self esteem, and sadness may be diagrammed as in Figure 4.

Additional evidence that self-comparisons are crucial in depression comes from a series of studies reported by Oatley (1992, 293), in which the occurrence of depression was examined in connection with the occurrence of stressful life situations. "[W]omen who had made self-deprecatory remarks about themselves at the first interview before they were depressed were two and a half times more likely to break down if they suffered a severe event than those who also suffered events but had not made such remarks."

SELF-EVALUATION AND YOUR 'LIFE REPORT'

Put the above discussion another way: At any given moment you have in your mind something like a school report card—call it your 'Life Report'—with grades on it for a variety of 'subjects'. You write the grades for yourself, though taking into account how other people judge you, of course, to a greater or lesser degree. The 'subjects' include both life conditions, such as the condition of your love life or marriage, and activities, such as your professional achievements and your behavior toward your grandfather.

Another category of 'subjects' on the Life Report are future occurrences that matter to you and which are related to your 'success' or 'failure'—on the job, in your relationships with others, even religious experiences. These are marked 'High hope' or 'Low hope'.

The 'subjects' are marked 'important' (for example, professional achievement) or 'unimportant' (for instance, behavior toward grand-uncle). Again, other people's judgments influence you, but probably less so than their judgments about how you are doing in specific activities.

The over-all state of your Life Report—the larger proportion of those 'important' matters that are of your own doing are marked positive or negative—constitutes your self-esteem or 'self-image'. If there are many important matters marked 'bad', the composite constitutes low self-esteem and a poor self-image of yourself.

Then along comes some unpleasant event, minor or major, that leads to a negative self-comparison between, on the one hand, what you think about yourself in light of the event, and on the other hand, the standard which you take as your benchmark for comparison. The consequent sadness will be only temporary when the event is not seen as all-important or is surrounded by a lot of other negative indications; the effects of the death of a loved one upon a person with generally high self-esteem is such an example. But if your Life Report is predominantly negative in the categories marked 'important', then any negative event will be reinforced by the overall sense of worthlessness, and will in turn contribute to your feeling worthless. This gives extra strength to each particular negative self-comparison. And when (or if) the thought of that particular negative self-comparison leaves you, the generalized negative self-comparison of being worthless keeps you feeling sad. When that state continues for a time, we call it depression.

When talking of his own depressed thoughts, Tolstoy put the matter this way: "[L]ike drops of ink always falling on one place they ran together into one big blot."[4]

How does one happen to have a negative Life Report? These are possible contributing factors: a. one's childhood training and upbringing; b. one's present life situation, including the recent past and the expected future; and c. an innate predisposition to react fearfully or otherwise negatively toward events. The last of these possibilities is pure speculation; no evidence has yet been shown for its existence.

The role of the present is straightforward: it provides evidence that you interpret about how well you are doing with various matters, and how well you can hope to do in the future.

The past has a multiple role; it provided—and still provides—evidence about how well you usually do on some matters.[5] But it also taught you methods—sound or unsound—to interpret and evaluate the evidence that the world provides to you about your activities and life condition. And, perhaps most important, your childhood training influences which categories you mark as 'important' and 'unimportant'. For example, one person may consider relationship with one's family or work success as very important, whereas another person may consider neither important because of (or in reaction to) childhood experience.

Those are some of the ways in which a depressive may differ from a normal person, differences that may cause the depressive to suffer prolonged sadness in the face of a set of external conditions whereas they cause only fleeting sadness to the normal person.

Many of the above tendencies can be summarized as a propensity for seeing a half-empty glass instead of a half-full glass. This propensity is neatly demonstrated by an experiment that showed people two images at the same time—a positive and a negative, one in each eye—with a special viewing device. Depressed persons 'saw' the unhappy image and did not 'see' the happy image more frequently than persons who were not depressed.[6] And other research shows that even after a siege of depression is over, the former sufferers have more negative thoughts and biases than do normal persons.

There are many possible reasons *why* depressives differ from other persons. For example, depressives may have experienced especially strong pressure from parents to set and achieve high goals, and in response have come to rigidly believe that those goals must be sought. They may have suffered traumatic loss of parents or others as children. They may have genetically-caused biological makeups, such as a low energy level, that may easily make them feel helpless. And there are many other possible causes. But we need not further consider the matter, because it is the *current* thinking and behavior patterns that must be changed.

BIOLOGY AND DEPRESSION

Earlier, it was mentioned that biological factors—genetic origins, physical constitution, state of your health—may influence your propensity for depression. A word about them seems appropriate here.

Biological factors can apparently operate directly upon the emotions of sadness-happiness, and/or upon the comparison mechanism to make a comparison seem more negative or positive than it otherwise would be perceived. This is consistent with such observed facts as that:

1. Being sad often comes with being tired. Being tired also makes depressives judge that endeavors will fail, that they are helpless as well as worthless, and so on. This makes sense because when one is tired it is objectively true that one is less competent to control the circumstances of one's life than when one is fresh. And the tiredness also typically makes depressives project into the future that they will not be successful. Hence the bodily state of being tired affects the person's self-comparisons and hence her sadness-happiness state.

2. Postpartum depression follows a whole series of biological changes, and seems to have no psychological explanation.

3. Mononucleosis and infectious hepatitis tend to cause depression.[7]

4. Some geneticists have concluded that there is "strong evidence in favor of considering manic-depressive psychosis to be genetically influenced in good part, [but] we are unable to come to any conclusions regarding its mode of inheritance."[8] And some researchers believe that there is evidence for a 'biochemical scar' which remains from past depression and which continues to influence feelings in the present; a deficiency of the chemical norepinephrine is commonly implicated by the biochemists. Recent research (*Science*, volume 254, 6 December, 1991, p. 1450, reporting work of Robert Post at the National Institute of Mental Health) provides some evidence that episodes of depression or stress may 'imprint' traces on the brain that predispose one to further depression, as earlier speculated by Kline (1974, 63). (This need not contradict the observation mentioned earlier that survivors of catastrophes such as concentration-camp experience do not suffer unusual amounts of depression. It is entirely possible that depression with a manic phase is not genetically caused.)

There is clear biological evidence that depressed people have differences in body chemistry from non-depressed people.[9] There also is a direct biological connection between negative self-comparisons and physically-induced pain. Psychological trauma such as a loss of a loved one induces some of the same bodily changes as does the pain from a migraine headache, say. When people refer to the death of a loved one as 'painful', they are speaking about a biological reality and not just a metaphor. And it is reasonable that more ordinary 'losses'—of status, income, career, and of a mother's attention or smile in the case of a child—have the same sorts of effects even if milder.

The Appendix to this chapter discusses the role of drugs in treating depression.

FROM UNDERSTANDING TO CURE

Ultimately we are interested in the mechanism of depression so that we can manipulate it to treat depression. Let's say that you have a Life Report which is predominantly negative, and it causes you to be sad and depressed. As noted in many places in this book, there are several ways to get rid of your sadness at any given moment. These include putting the Life Report out of your mind by pushing it out; changing some of the negative categories from important to unimportant; changing the standards by which you grade yourself on particularly important negative matters; learning how to interpret the external evidence more accurately, if you now do not interpret the evidence well; and involving yourself in work or creative activity that pulls your mind away from the Life Report.

The advantages and disadvantages of these and other methods of preventing depression depend upon your own psychology and your life situation. The pros and cons of each are discussed later in this book.

SUMMARY

This chapter discusses why a *particular person* is more predisposed to depression than are other people who are closer to 'normal'.

The main elements that influence whether a person is sad or happy at a given moment, and whether one does or does not descend into the prolonged gloom of depression are as follows: 1. Experiences in childhood, both the general pattern of childhood as well as traumatic experiences, if any. 2. The person's adult history: the recent experiences have the greatest weight. 3. The actual conditions of the individual's present life—relationships with people as well as such objective factors as health, job, finances, and so on. 4. The person's habitual mental states, plus her view of the world and herself. This includes her goals, hopes, values, demands upon herself, and ideas about herself, including whether she is effective or ineffective and important or unimportant. 5. Physical influences such as whether she is tired or rested, and anti-depression drugs she is taking, if any. 6. The machinery of thought which processes the material coming in from the other elements and produces an evaluation of how the person stands with respect to the hypothetical situation taken for comparison. 7. A sense of helplessness.

The depressive differs from the normal person in having a propensity for prolonged sadness; this is the stripped-down minimum definition of a depressive.

There are many possible reasons *why* depressives differ from other persons. For example, depressives may have experienced especially strong pressure from parents to set and achieve high goals, and in response have come to rigidly believe that those goals must be sought. They may have suffered traumatic loss of parents or others as children. They may have genetically-caused biological makeups, such as a low energy level, that may easily make them feel helpless. And there are many other possible causes. But we need not further consider the matter because it is the *current* thinking and behavior patterns that must be changed.

APPENDIX

ON DRUG THERAPY FOR DEPRESSION

Why not simply prescribe anti-depression drugs—several of which are in the armamentarium of physicians—for all cases of depression? The fact that bodily states may be related to depression suggests the use of drugs to artificially remove neurochemical imbalances, that is, to alter bodily states in such manner as to relieve depression. Indeed, Kline suggested that "physical repair through drug therapy is probably useful even in cases in which the original problem was primarily psychological."[10]

The word "repair" seems overly strong. The most important reason not to rely on drug therapy is that, in the words of one psychiatrist, "The drugs do not cure the illnesses; they *control* them."[11] As noted earlier, one long-term follow-up study shows that patients treated with cognitive-behavioral therapy in addition to drugs have fewer recurrences than do patients treated with drugs alone.[12]

There are also several other persuasive reasons why one should continue to seek psychological understanding of depression, and psychological methods for its treatment:

1. It is not clear in most cases whether depressed thinking caused the chemical imbalances, or the chemistry caused the depression. If the former is true, though drugs may help temporarily, it is reasonable to expect a recurrence of the depression when drugs are stopped. If so, it seems more reasonable to attack the depression by working on the bad thinking first, rather than by starting with drugs.

2. Physical treatment can have side-effects years after their use, as too many tragic examples (such as improperly-prescribed birth-control pills and x-ray radiation) have shown too well. Since there is an inherent unknown danger in the use of drugs, non-drug treatment that promises equal success must be preferable.

3. There are some immediate physically dangerous side-effects from the common anti-depressant drugs.[13]

4. There may be immediate mental side-effects destructive to creativeness and other thinking faculties, though there is little discus-

sion of such side-effects by psychiatric drug enthusiasts. A reasonable conclusion drawn from the studies that have been made on this issue suggest that anti-depressant drugs reduce the creativity of some writers (and presumably, other artists) while increasing the creativity of others by enabling them to work. The crucial dosage is "delicate" and "complex", according to physicians who have studied the matter.[14]

5. Drugs do not work in some cases.

6. For at least some people the process of conquering depression without drugs can lead to valued states of ecstasy, self-knowledge, religious experience, and so on: Bertrand Russell is one such example:

> [T]he greatest happiness comes with the most complete possession of one's faculties. It is in the moments when the mind is most active and the fewest things are forgotten that the most intense joys are experienced. This indeed is one of the best touchstones of happiness. The happiness that requires intoxication of no matter what sort is a spurious and unsatisfying kind. The happiness that is genuinely satisfying is accompanied by the fullest exercise of our faculties, and the fullest realization of the world in which we live.[15]

7. There can be damaging *psychological* side-effects of drug treatment. According to a physician, the anti-depressant drug may become "a nagging reminder that something within is not working as it should . . . [and] has the potential for decreasing one's sense of self-worth"[16]. . . . "It is not uncommon for patients to go off the medications a number of times, testing their limitations. This often (but not always) results in further episodes. . . . This returns the patient to square one and further disturbs his sense of self-worth".[17]

"Some patients are very upset by the idea that it is not their own will but a medication that is responsible for preserving control over their behavior, mood, or judgment . . . as a weakness. These feelings can lead to a rather negative attitude. . . ."[18]

8. Understanding depression as part of human psychology is of interest for its own sake. Hence the existence of effective anti-depression drugs is not a good reason to cease searching for psychological understanding of depression.

There are a variety of anti-depressant drugs and a variety of side-effects. A convenient up-to-date summary of them is in Chapter 5 of the book by Papalos and Papalos referred to in the bibliography.

THE HAND OF THE PAST IN DEPRESSION

Skip this chapter about the effect of your history upon your depressive tendencies if you are impatient to get on to practical methods for overcoming your sadness. But come back later if you do skip now; this material should help you understand yourself better, and therefore help you deal with yourself.

Childhood experiences are the colors with which the adult draws pictures of life. A typical case: M.'s father gave M. the impression that he never expected much of M. So M. spent the years until age 50 so hungry for achievement that he kept learning new occupations, and giving chunks of himself to the needy, while at the same time deriding all his achievements as those of an 'overachiever'.

The child builds patterns of behavior on her experiences as she lives them, even if the childhood experiences are not relevant to adult life. In the lingo of scientific research, the adult sees her latest experience as one observation in her lifetime sample of experiences.

A single traumatic childhood experience can leave a lasting imprint and predispose a person to adult depression. Or, none of the experiences may be traumatic yet their effect may be cumulative.

The early experiences may influence the adult's perceptions and interpretations of the adult's actual situation. Or they may work directly upon the self-comparison mechanism. They may also affect the adult's sense of being competent or helpless to improve her life situation.

The non-traumatic experiences which gain their force by accumulation can be repeated punishments, or parental directions about which self-comparisons the child should make, or which companions to associate with, or—perhaps most deeply rooted in the adult—goals and values implanted in the young child by the parent or other persons, or by his own reactions to people and environment. These matters will now be discussed one by one.

CHILDHOOD EXPERIENCES

Death or Loss of a Parent

The classical Freudian explanation of depression is the death or disappearance of a parent, or the lack of parental love. Though it is probably incorrect that such an event has occurred to all depressives, it is likely that children who have suffered the loss of a parent are especially predisposed to depression.[1]

There are several ways that loss of a parent can cause depression. Children whose parents die often believe that they themselves *caused* the parents to die by some bad behavior or failure. Therefore, bad behavior or failure as an adult brings back the depressing feelings associated with great loss.

A child who loses a parent to death or divorce may re-experience the pain and sadness whenever, as an adult, the person suffers a loss in the widest sense—loss of job, loss of a lover, and so on.

Still another way in which loss of a parent may predispose a person toward depression is simply by making the person sad for a prolonged time after the event. That is, the child continually makes a negative comparison between a. his present parentless situation, and b. his former situation when the parent was alive (or to the situation of other children who still have parents). In this way the child develops a pattern of making neg-comps, and being depressed from time to time, which may simply continue into adulthood.

Another theory of why early separation can cause depression is that attachment to the mother is biologically programmed just as are mating behavior and parenting behavior in animals. If the bond is absent, pain is caused, says that theory.[2]

What is important for us is that if the attachment is broken by separation, temporary depression may occur immediately, and the chance of adult depression goes up.

Punishment for Failure as a Child

Some parents punish their children severely for actions inside or outside the home which the parents do not approve. The punishment may be straightforward, such as spanking or loss of rights; or the punishment may be more subtle, such as withdrawal of the parent's love. Many children who are severely punished by their parents learn to punish themselves for lack of achievement, and they continue to do so in adulthood. This self-punishment increases the pain suffered from a negative self-comparison, and hence it intensifies a depression. This was my case until I realized what was happening and decided to change: When I was a child my mother would say to me, no matter how well I did in school or other test situations: 'That's fine, but you can do better.' I then felt (rightly or wrongly) that I was being reprimanded for not doing well enough. And as an adult, I cursed myself for each minor fault, feeling painful sadness at my perennial failure to reach perfection.

It was this pattern which—after a precipitating event—kept me in constant depression for 13 years. One day I realized that there was no good reason why I should punish myself on my mother's behalf, no reason why I should speak her reprimands to myself. This was a major breakthrough in lifting my 13-year depression.

Though my sense of well-being came in a sudden rush, there had been hard work going on for weeks and months, along the lines of the program described in this book. And there is nothing miraculous about my continuing to stay free of depression; it is a matter of diligent effort which is sometimes so demanding that it seems too much to be worthwhile. I have trained myself to say, whenever the impulse to do so arises, 'Don't criticize'. And whenever I catch myself saying to myself 'You idiot!', I have trained myself to smile at the nuttiness of the abuse that I heap on myself for the silliest reasons. So even though I am a depressive with a propensity to sadness which I must constantly fight in this and other ways to be described below, I live a life that is free of prolonged sadness and which includes joy and contentment, as described at length in the Epilogue.

My story also points up the importance of building new habits to counter the habits of self-criticism and low self-esteem that have worn their ways into one's thinking over the years since childhood, as wheels wear ruts into soft roads.

Childhood punishment for failure may also make you fear failure so much that the threat of failure panics you to the point that you do not think clearly. This may cause you to reach wrong conclusions because you misinterpret relevant information, which can lead to neg-comps and sadness. As one salesman put it, "Every time I was a minute late for an appointment I'd be scared that the customer would think I am irresponsible and lazy, which would make me so nervous that I couldn't sell effectively. And I also immediately reminded myself that I never manage to do anything right." This was a fellow whose mother set very high standards of reliability for him even as a four-year-old child, and chided him when he failed to meet those standards.

Childhood-Formed Expectations about Adult Accomplishment

Experiences in childhood and adolescence influence your expectations about professional and personal accomplishments.

> Each violinist in any [symphony orchestra's] second chair started out as a prodigy in velvet knickers who expected one day to solo exquisitely amid flowers flung by dazzled devotees. The 45-year-old violinist with spectacles on his nose and a bald spot in the middle of his hair is the most disappointed man on earth.[3]

Sometimes changes in one's capacities trigger the depression. A 39-year-old amateur athlete's present expectations were formed both by his relative excellence as a youth and by his absolute excellence as an adult. And when age curbed his performance and he compared his performance with those expectations, he began to feel sad and depressed.

The 'normal' person revises his expectations so that they fit his possible accomplishment reasonably well. The middle-aged violinist may reassess his abilities and arrive at a more realistic assessment of the future. The aging athlete chooses to play in an over-40 tennis league. But some adults do not respond to a gap between expectations and performance by revising their expectations. This may result from heavy parental emphasis on certain expectations such as 'Of course you'll win a Nobel prize if you work hard.' Such a person carries expectations beyond actual possibilities, and depression ensues.

An interesting but troublesome set of expectations that many of us form as children concerns 'happiness'. As young people we get the idea that we can hope for (and even expect) a life of care-free ecstatic bliss, a perennial walking on air, as seen in movies and magazine articles about celebrities. Then, when in our youth or young adulthood we do not attain golden bliss—and at the same time we think that other people *have* attained it—we feel let down and sad. We must learn that continued bliss is not an attainable goal for anyone, and instead aim at the best that one can realistically expect from life as a human being.

Persistent Criticism by Parents

If your parents continually tell you that your acts are clumsy, foolish, or naughty, you are likely to draw the general conclusion that you are clumsy, foolish, or naughty. Hence as an adult you may have the habit of making negative self-comparisons. For example, a social act that may *or may not* be clumsy immediately evokes the inner response, 'I'm an idiot', or 'I'm a klutz'. This habit acts like a prejudiced judge who always finds the person guilty, and hence produces frequent negative self-comparisons and consequent prevailing sadness.

The habit of comparing oneself negatively and thinking 'I'm a klutz' arises from some combination of experiences in early childhood and throughout the rest of one's life. Each event in one's *adult* past is probably less important the longer ago it occurred, so that it is not only the sum of such experiences but also their recent timing which matters; if one has recently been down-and-out and unsuccessful, this probably matters more than being down-and-out for a similar length of time ten years earlier. In contrast, *childhood* experiences may have relatively heavy weight because the events involved interpretation by the parent. That is, if every time a child does poorly in school the parent says, 'See, you'll never be smart like your big brother', the effect is likely to be greater than a school failure after the child has left the house.

Furthermore, the habit of comparing oneself negatively is

strengthened by each additional negative self-comparison the person makes.

In addition to directly biasing the person's self-comparisons, this habit of self-criticism may act cumulatively to produce the sort of 'biochemical scar' mentioned in Chapter 4. Or, such a biochemical scar may result from the feedback effect of negative self-comparisons and the sadness itself upon the nervous system.

THE CHILD AS A FAILURE

If a child *strives unsuccessfully,* and hence develops a record of failure to achieve encouragement and affection, this record is likely to leave a heavy mark on the adult. A special case is the infant or young child who had no parent to *respond* to the child's strivings. One can view the lack of a parent as a separation or deprivation which by itself predisposes the adult to depression. Alternately, one may see this as the child not being able to successfully induce its environment to respond positively to its efforts to obtain the gratifications it seeks, leading to a sense of being helpless.

Such unsuccessful striving evokes the emotion of sadness. It also may produce the general conclusion about one's life that there is a negative balance between what one seeks and what one gets. It is reasonable that this leads to the disposition to evaluate oneself negatively relative to one's aspirations, hopes, and obligations.

Rigid Goal-Setting in Childhood

By 'goal' I mean an aim that is broad and deep. For example, it is a *goal* to be the greatest tennis player in the world or to win a Nobel prize. And a goal is often abstract—for example, to make a contribution to humanity or to contribute something important to culture. Goals can be fixed rigidly in childhood in at least three ways: 1. Parents may stress that the child can and must make great achievements, and the parents may suggest to the child that the parents' love depends upon the child accepting those goals. 2. Children who lack love during their childhood may conclude that by achieving great successes as adults they can win the admiration and love from the world that they do not receive as children. 3. Children may decide on their own that they must achieve greatly or else they are worthless.

Goals and goal-setting are very complex. If your goals are too high, you will fail to reach them; negative self-comparisons and sadness will ensue. But if your goals are not high enough, you may not stretch your capacities to the fullest and thereby deny yourself full and satisfying self-realization. But you cannot know in advance which goals are reasonable and which are not. Furthermore, your goals are interwoven with your values and beliefs, which—if they are really values and beliefs—are not chosen simply on the basis of what will be most comfortable for you. We can be sure, however, that parents who press high goals on their children, and condition their love on the achievement of those goals—thereby creating a situation in which the adult cannot alter his goals to fit his capacities—may predispose the child both to adult depression *and* to significant accomplishment. That's complex! One more complication: Some people will, as adults, more frequently be in the coping-evaluating mode than will others because of more competitiveness and pressure applied to them as children.

Values, which are closely related to goals, get special treatment in the following chapter.

SUMMARY

This chapter discusses the relationship of earlier learning and experiences, and especially those in childhood, upon the propensity to be depressed. Understanding the various mechanisms can sometimes throw light upon one's present make-up in a manner that can help one alter one's self-comparisons to overcome depression.

THE COLLAPSE AND CREATION OF VALUES

Values and beliefs play an even more complex role in depression than do ordinary goals. For example, Warren H. believes that it is very important that each person dedicate himself or herself to the welfare of the community. But unfortunately he lacks the talent and energy to make a large contribution to the community. When he compares his *actual* contribution to the contribution he believes one *should* make, his self-comparison is negative, leading to sadness and depression.

Values are more fundamental than ordinary goals. We can think of values as goals that are based on the individual's deepest beliefs about human life and society—assessments of what is good and what is evil. Even if a person's values are obviously implicated in a depression—for example, the soldier who refuses to kill during a battle, and is therefore judged by other soldiers and himself as unpatriotic and worthless—no one would suggest that he should simply alter for convenience his belief that life is good and killing is bad.

There is nothing *irrational* about the soldier's thinking or that of Warren H. Nor is there any logical flaw in the thinking of the English cabinet minister John Profumo who courted danger for his country by consorting with prostitutes who were also consorting with a Soviet spy. For his actions, Profumo did penance for ten years in charity work; that choice is not irrational.

Nor is a person irrational who kills a child in an avoidable auto accident and then judges himself harshly because he has contravened his highest value by destroying human life. There is nothing irrational about the subsequent negative self-comparisons between his behavior and his ideal self which result in depression. Indeed, the guilt and depression may be seen as an appropriate self-punishment, similar to punishment of a person that society may inflict by sending that person to jail. And the acceptance of the punishment may be part of a process of doing penance which may result in the person finding a new and better life. In such a situation some clergymen say 'Judge the sin but not the sinner', but that may not be psychologically or morally appropriate.

These are the kinds of cases that take us beyond psychology and into philosophy and religion.

VALUES AND THE CHOICE OF COMPARISONS

Values present harder-than-usual questions about whom you should compare yourself to. Should you compare your moral behavior to a saint, or to an ordinary sinner? To Albert Schweitzer, or to the fellow next door? You cannot be as casual about this choice for comparison as when you choose a level of competitive tennis to set as your standard.

The value of meeting one's felt obligations to family, community, and society according to prevailing standards is often involved in depression. (The prevailing standards usually are, however, far more demanding than is the norm of other people's actual conduct!) Another troublesome value is the *relative* importance of various aspects of life, for example, of devotion to family versus community, or devotion to success in one's profession versus family. Sometimes, even if you are very successful in many aspects of your life, your values may focus your attention on dimensions on which you do not excel, which can result in negative self-comparisons.

The development of a person's values and beliefs is complex, and differs from person to person. But it is clear that childhood experiences with parents and the rest of society influence one's values. And it seems likely that if your childhood was rigid, pressure-filled, and traumatic, you will be more rigid in your values, and less flexible in choosing a new set of values upon adult reflection, than a person who had a more relaxed childhood.

In particular, loss of love, or loss of a parent, must heavily influence one's fundamental view of the world and oneself. Loss of a parent or parental love is likely to make one feel that success, and the ensuing approval and love, are not automatic or easy to get. The loss probably makes one believe that it takes very high achievement, and the attainment of very high standards, to obtain such approval and love from the world. A person with such a view of the world is likely to conclude that her actual and potential achievements are, and will be, less than they must be to achieve love and approval; this implies hopelessness, sadness, and depression.

Of course childhood experiences persist in the adult not only as the objective experiences they were, but as the memory and interpretation of those experiences—which are often far from the objective facts.

COLLAPSE OF VALUES

Sometimes a person suddenly thinks, 'Life has no meaning'. Or to put it differently, you come to think that there is no meaning to, or value in, the activities which you had formerly thought were meaningful and valuable to yourself and the world. For one reason or another, you may come to cease accepting the values you had formerly accepted as the foundation of your life. This is Tolstoy's famous description of his 'loss of meaning' and collapse of values, his subsequent depression, and his later recovery.

> [S]omething very strange began to happen to me. At first I experienced moments of perplexity and arrest of life, as though I did not know how to live or what to do; and I felt lost and became dejected. . . . Then these moments of perplexity began to recur oftener and oftener, and always in the same form. They were always expressed by the questions: What's it for? What does it lead to? . . . The questions . . . began to repeat themselves frequently, and to demand replies more and more insistently; and like drops of ink always falling on one place they ran together into one black blot.
>
> Then occurred what happens to everyone sickening with a mortal internal disease. At first trivial signs of indisposition appear to which the sick man pays no attention; then these signs reappear more and more often and merge into one uninterrupted period of suffering. The suffering increases and, before the sick man can look round, what he took for a mere indisposition has already

become more important to him than anything else in the world—it is death!

That was what happened to me. I understood that it was no casual indisposition but something very important, and that if these questions constantly repeated themselves they would have to be answered. And I tried to answer them. The questions seemed such stupid, simple, childish ones; but as soon as I touched them and tried to solve them I at once became convinced, first, that they are not childish and stupid but the most important and profound of life's questions; and secondly that, try as I would, I could not solve them. Before occupying myself with my Samara estate, the education of my son, or the writing of a book, I had to know *why* I was doing it. As long as I did not know why, I could do nothing and could not live. Amid the thoughts of estate management which greatly occupied me at that time, the question would suddenly occur: 'Well, you will have 6,000 *desyatinas* of land in Samara Government and 300 horses, and what then?' . . . And I was quite disconcerted and did not know what to think. Or when considering plans for the education of my children, I would say to myself: 'What for?' Or when considering how the peasants might become prosperous, I would suddenly say to myself: "But what does it matter to me?' Or when thinking of the fame my works would bring me, I would say to myself, 'Very well; you will be more famous than Gogol or Pushkin or Shakespeare or Molière, or than all the writers in the world—and what of it?' And I could find no reply at all. The questions would not wait, they had to be answered at once, and if I did not answer them it was impossible to live. But there was no answer.

I felt that what I had been standing on had collapsed and that I had nothing left under my feet. What I had lived on no longer existed, and there was nothing left.

My life came to a standstill. I could breathe, eat, drink, and sleep, and I could not help doing these things; but there was no life, for there were no wishes the fulfillment of which I could consider reasonable. If I desired anything, I knew in advance that whether I satisfied my desire or not, nothing would come of it. Had a fairy come and offered to fulfill my desires I should not have known what to ask. If in moments of intoxication I felt something which, though not a wish, was a habit left by former wishes, in sober moments I knew this to be a delusion and that there was really nothing to wish for. I could not even wish to know the truth, for I guessed of what it consisted. The truth was that life is meaningless. I had as it were lived, lived, and walked, walked, till I had come to a precipice and saw clearly that there was nothing . . . ahead of me but destruction. It was impossible to stop, impossible to go back, and impossible to close my eyes or avoid seeing that there was nothing ahead but suffering and real death—complete annihilation.[1]

Some writers use the term 'existential despair' to describe the same phenomenon.

A collapse in values often results from philosophical and linguistic misunderstanding of such key concepts as 'meaning' and 'life'. These concepts seem obvious at first thought. But they are in fact often obscure and misleading, both the concepts and the words which stand for them. Making clear the confusion often reveals the implicit values.

The sense of loss of meaning is usually followed by depression, though it sometimes is followed by uncontrolled elation or by a violent oscillation between the two poles. The basic idea of this book, negative self-comparisons, explains this phenomenon: Before the event, actuality and the person's values were in balance or positive most of the time. But with the removal of one's customary values there is no longer a basis of hypothetical comparison for one's activities. Hence the result of the comparison is indeterminate *but very large* in one direction or the other, because there is no boundary to the comparison. The comparison is more likely to be negative than positive because the former values are likely to have been a support for, rather than a constraint of, the person's activities and life style.

VALUES CAN CURE THE SICKNESS THAT VALUES CAUSE

The most interesting curative possibility for collapse of values is the discovery of new values, or the rediscovery of neglected old ones. This is what happened to Tolstoy, when he later came to believe that life itself is its own value, a belief which he also thought characterized peasant life.

Values Treatment for collapse of values will be discussed in detail in Chapter 18. We should here note, however, that though values are interwoven from childhood into the very foundations of a person's character and personality, they are nevertheless subject to change as an adult. That is, values can be accepted and rejected as a matter of personal choice, though one cannot do so lightly and casually.

Tolstoy and modern existential thinkers have thought that the 'despair' of loss-of-meaning depression is the educated person's common condition. It seems to me, however, that most 'educated' people's training, interests, and life circumstances do *not* lead them to question the values they accepted in childhood in such manner as to lead to loss of meaning.

SUMMARY

Values and beliefs play an even more complex role in depression than do ordinary goals. Values are more fundamental than ordinary goals. We can think of values as goals that are based on the individual's deepest beliefs about human life and society, assessments of what is good and what is evil.

The collapse of a person's values can lead to depression. The most interesting curative possibility for collapse of values is the discovery of new values, or the rediscovery of neglected old ones. These possibilities will be discussed in Chapter 18.

AND THE FINGER OF THE DAY

The hand of the past pushes a depressive toward depression. But it is usually the jab of a present event that triggers the pain—say, loss of your job, or being jilted by your lover. It is that contemporary happening that darkly dominates your thoughts when you are depressed. To get undepressed you must reconstitute your current mode of thinking so you can get rid of the black thoughts. Again—yes, the past causes you to be what you are now. But the main avenue out of your present predicament is by reconstructing the present rather than dealing with the past.

A crucial issue is whether you interpret contemporary events accurately, or instead distort them in such manner as to make them seem more negative than they 'really' are. We are here talking only of negatively-*perceived* current events. Positively-perceived current events which are persistently misperceived as even more positive than they 'really' are constitute part of the manic phase of a manic depressive cycle. (By the way, most depressives do not have extended manic periods after their depression becomes chronic.)

Usually there is little question about whether a current event has a negative or positive valence for a person. Almost all of us, almost all the time, agree about whether such events as loss of a job, death of a loved one, damage to health, financial distress, success in sports or education, are positive or negative. Sometimes, of course, a person's reaction is unexpected: You may conclude that loss of wealth or a job or a competition really is beneficial, by relieving you of a hidden burden or opening up new perspectives or changing your view of life. But such unusual cases are not our topic.

In many cases the knowledge of your fate reaches you along with knowledge of how others have done. And in fact, such outcomes as an examination score or a competitive sports outcome only have meaning relative to the performance of other people.

WHAT SHOULD BE YOUR STANDARDS FOR SELF-COMPARISONS?

The choice of whom to compare yourself with is one of the important ways that you structure your view of your life. Some choices lead to frequent negative comparisons and consequent unhappiness. A psychologically 'normal' seven-year-old boy will compare his performance in shooting a basketball to other seven-year-olds, or to his own performance yesterday. If he is psychologically normal but physically not talented, he will compare his performance today only to his performance of yesterday, or to other boys who are not good at basketball. But some seven-year-olds like Billy H., insist on comparing their performances to their eleven-year-old brothers; inevitably they compare poorly. Such children will bring unnecessary sadness and despondency upon themselves unless they change their standards of comparison.

Whose performance *should* you compare yourself to? People of the same age? Those with similar training? People with similar physical attributes? With similar skills? There is no general answer, obviously. We can say, however, that the 'normal' person chooses a standard for comparison in such manner that the standard does not cause very much sadness. A sensible 50-year-old jogger learns to compare his time for the mile to others' times in his age and skill class, not to the world record or even to the best 50-year-old runner in the club. (If the standard is so low that it provides no challenge, the normal person will move to a higher standard that offers some uncertainty and excitement and pleasure in achievement.) The normal person lowers too-high standards in the same manner that a baby learns to hold on when starting to walk; the pain of doing otherwise is an effective teacher. But some people do not adjust their standards in a sensible flexible fashion, and hence they open themselves to depression. To understand why this is so for a particular person, we must refer to his psychological history.

I am an example of a person with an unwise set of standards. I treat myself the way an engineer treats a factory: the goal is perfect deployment and allocation of resources, and the criterion is whether the maximum output is achieved. For example, when I wake at 8:30 a.m. on weekdays, I feel like a time thief until I hit my desk and start work. On a weekend day I may wake at nine—and then I think 'Am I cheating the children by sleeping too much?' Maximum productivity may be a reasonable goal for a factory. But one's life cannot be satisfactorily reduced to a striving to meet a single criterion. A person is more complex than a factory, and a person is also an end in himself or herself, whereas a factory is only a means to an end.

How We Distort Reality and Cause Negative Self-Comparisons

One may manipulate current reality in still other ways that produce frequent negative self-comparisons. For example, one may convince oneself that other people perform better than they really do, or are better off than they are. A young girl may believe that other girls really are prettier than she is, or that others have many more dates than she has, when this is not true. An employee may be wrongly convinced that other employees are being paid more than she is. A child may refuse to believe that other children share her difficulty in making friends. A person may think that all others have argument-free marriages, and never fail to cope with the demands of their children.

Another way that you may generate more negative self-comparisons than a 'normal' person is by inaccurately interpreting a single event as something other than what it really is. If you receive a reprimand from the boss, you may immediately leap to the conclusion that you will be fired, and if you are warned that you *may* be fired you may conclude that the boss *surely* intends to fire you, even when these conclusions are not warranted. A person who suffers a temporary physical disability may conclude that he is disabled for life when that is medically most improbable.

Still another way a person can produce many negative self-comparisons is by putting disproportionate weight on single negative instances. A non-depressive girl will react to the information that she has failed an exam or received a reprimand from the boss by combining this instance with her entire past record. And if this is the first failed test in her school history, or the first reprimand on this job, the non-depressive girl will see this instance as being somewhat exceptional and therefore not deserving of great attention. But some people (all of us do it sometimes) will, on the basis of this one instance, make a faulty generalization about their present conditions with respect to this dimension of the person's life. Or, one may make an inaccurate generalization about one's whole life on this dimension based on this one instance. The depressive carpenter who loses a job once may generalize, 'I can't hold onto a job', and the depressive basketball player may generalize, 'I'm a lousy athlete' after one poor game on the basketball court.

A person's judgment may also be inaccurate because he or she puts *too little* emphasis on a present event. A woman who has learned athletics late in life may continue to think of herself as unathletic, though her present achievements make the past irrelevant in this respect.

The Causes of Distortion

Why should some people's interpretations of their present conditions and life experiences be inaccurate or distorted in such manner that depression is brought on? There are several possible factors acting singly or together, including early training in thinking, extent of education, fears caused by present and past experience, and physical condition. These will now be discussed in turn.

Albert Ellis and Aaron Beck explain most depression as due to poor thinking and distorted interpretations of present reality. And they analyze the present operation of the mechanism without delving into the past causes of such bad thinking. They believe that just as a student can be taught to do valid social-science research in a university, and just as a child in school can improve his or her information-gathering and reasoning with guided practice, so can depressives be taught better information-gathering and processing, by education in the course of psychotherapy.

Indeed, it is reasonable that if you judge your situation in the light of a biased sample of experience, an incorrect 'statistical' analysis of your life's data, and an unsound definition of the situation, you are likely to misinterpret your reality. For example, anthropologist Molly H. was often depressed for long periods of time whenever one of her professional papers was rejected by a professional journal. She ignored all her acceptances and successes, and focused only on the present rejection. Ellis's and Beck's sort of 'cognitive therapy' trained Molly to consider a wider sample of her life experience after such a rejection, and hence reduced her sadness and shortened her depressed periods.

Poor childhood training in thinking, and subsequent lack of schooling, may be responsible for an adult's misinterpretation of reality in some cases. But the lack of strong relationship between, on the one hand, amount of schooling, and on the other hand, propensity to depression, casts doubt on poor mental training as a complete explanation in many cases. More plausible is that a person's fears co-operate with poor training. Few of us reason well in the midst of panic; when fire breaks out few of us think as clearly about the situation as if we were sitting quietly and coolly considering such a situation. Similarly, if a person greatly fears failure in school or profession or in an interpersonal relationship because the person was severely punished for such failure when young, then the fear may panic the person into poor thinking about such an occurrence when it happens. The genesis and cure of such poor thinking will be discussed in following sections.

Sometimes a current major catastrophe such as loss of a loved one, a physical disability, or a tragedy in the community, triggers depression. Normal people recover from grief, and find satisfying lives again, and in a 'reasonable' length of time. But a depressive may not recover. Why the difference? It is reasonable to think that experiences in the past predispose some people to remain in depression after a tragedy whereas others recover, as discussed in Chapter 5.

Grief deserves attention because, as Freud put it, the person's sad feelings in ordinary depression are *like* those in grief. And indeed, his observation is consistent with the view of this book that sadness results from a negative comparison of actual and benchmark states. The benchmark event in the grief after the loss of a loved one is the wish that the loved one is still alive. Grief in the normal person also resembles depression in that the sadness is more prolonged than the normal person suffers after less catastrophic events. But the depressive may not recover from his grief at all, in which case we properly call it depression. Freud's analogy of depression with grief is otherwise not helpful, however, because it is the *difference between* depression and grief—as between depression and all other sadness from which people recover quickly—that is important, rather than any special similarity between depression and grief.

Physical condition can affect one's interpretation of present circumstances. We have all had the experience of suffering a setback when tired, but after a rest realizing that we had overestimated the damage and the seriousness. And this is logical, because a tired person *is* less able to deal with a problem, and hence the setback is more serious and more negative relative to a desired or accustomed state of affairs than when one is fresh. Too much mental stimulation may have a similar effect by overloading and tiring the nervous system. (The role of too *little* stimulation in depression might be interesting, too.)

SUMMARY

A crucial issue in depression is whether you interpret contemporary events accurately, or instead distort them in such manner as to make them seem more negative than they 'really' are. We are here talking only of negatively-*perceived* current events.

The choice of whom to compare yourself with is one of the important ways that you structure your view of your life. Some choices lead to frequent negative comparisons and consequent unhappiness. This chapter discusses various mechanisms that can operate to cause one to view one's situation in a fashion that produces negative self-comparisons.

WHAT ARE YOUR DIMENSIONS?

Everyone knows the old saw about seeing the glass half empty or half full. Even truer is that you can often choose *which glass to look at,* a glass which is full or one which is empty. Sadness and depression usually are optional. That is, in most situations you can choose to be happy or you can choose to be miserable.

An enormous variety of stimuli bombard us. We pick-and-choose which of these stimuli to focus on. Some of the stimuli are more insistent than others—a stomach ache, for example, or a last-second defeat of our favorite basketball team. But we are free to choose among the majority of stimuli around us.

CHOOSING 'FULL GLASS' DIMENSIONS

The healthy-minded person picks out characteristics—let's call them 'dimensions'—on which she rates well, and then argues to herself and to others that those are the most important dimensions on which to judge a person. A slightly exaggerated example: University faculty members who teach well but do no research argue that teaching should be weighted most heavily in salary and promotion evaluations; those who do much research and teach poorly argue instead that research should be most influential in evaluations; people who are rather good but not outstanding on both dimensions argue the virtues of well-roundedness. (Those who are *very* good on both dimensions don't waste their time on arguments like this one.)

As Collingwood put it, "The tailless fox preached taillessness."[1] If a person cannot find some external objective dimension of performance by which she rates well, one can always fall back on piety and prayer-saying, in which any person can excel without talent or training.

All this sounds amoral or even immoral, and sometimes it is. Morality and intellectual honesty must constrain a decent person in valuing various dimensions. And I certainly do not advise ignoring all higher standards and proceeding solely on the basis of what is good for you alone, which would be most cynical. But let us put aside that thorny issue for now.

This, then, is how most people fight sadness and depression—by skillfully choosing the dimensions by which they judge themselves, together with wisely selecting the standards on particular dimensions against which they measure themselves. William James put the matter beautifully:

> [W]e have the paradox of a man shamed to death because he is only the second pugilist or the second oarsman in the world. That he is able to beat the whole population of the globe minus one is nothing; he has 'pitted' himself to beat that one; and as long as he doesn't do that nothing else counts. He is to his own regard as if he were not, indeed he *is* not. Yonder puny fellow, however, whom every one can beat, suffers no chagrin about it, for he has long ago abandoned the attempt to 'carry that line', as the merchants say, of self at all. With no attempt there can be no failure; with no failure, no humiliation. So our self-feeling in this world depends entirely on what we *back* ourselves to be and do. . . . To give up pretensions is as blessed a relief as to get them gratified; and where disappointment is incessant and the struggle unending, this is what men will always do. The history of evangelical theology, with its conviction of sin, its self-despair, and its abandonment of salvation by works, is the deepest of possible examples, but we meet others in every walk of life. There is the strangest lightness about the heart when one's nothingness in a particular line is once accepted in good faith. *All* is not bitterness in the lot of the lover sent away by the final inexorable 'No.' . . . How pleasant is the day when we give up striving to be young—or slender! Thank God! we say, *those* illusions are gone. Everything added to the Self is a burden as well as a pride. A certain man who lost every penny during our civil war went and actually rolled in the dust, saying he had not felt so free and happy since he was born.[2]

The Grant Study followed the adaptation of men to the vicissitudes of life for several decades after they began college, the first group starting in the 1930s. Those who seemed to have adapted well to their life circumstances frequently used a device the investigators called "suppression—a mature mechanism that includes looking for silver linings, minimizing acknowledged discomfort, keeping a stiff upper lip, and deliberately postponing, *but not avoiding,* conscious impulse or conflict".[3] This is cut from the same cloth as the count-your-blessings device.

CHOOSING 'EMPTY GLASS' DIMENSIONS

Some people, however, are less flexible in their choice of dimensions on which to compare themselves; they do not choose at will the best 'line' for them to carry. For some people this is a matter of basic values; they will not praise taillessness simply because it is psychologically convenient to do so. Some people get stuck with dimensions that cause them sadness because of destructive values implanted during childhood, for example, the value that one should get maximum formal education, or that one should not think bad thoughts. Other people purposely focus only on dimensions which make them look bad in their self-comparisons; all of us have met people who live exemplary lives in all apparent respects but flay themselves day and night because they think they don't do enough for the community or for their aged parents or relatives.

Sometimes I find myself thinking that tonight's dinner engagement, which I can find a way to break, probably will be a big drag at which I'll undoubtedly make a fool of myself, instead of focusing on next week's dinner engagement which will be lots of fun and where I will sound funny and wise. Or, I will focus on next week's lunch that will undoubtedly be a bore instead of today's lunch which will surely be delightful. With a little effort, however, I can switch my mind to the better event of each pair. And if you do that often enough, you build a habit of focusing on the full glass instead of the empty one.

If you can pry yourself loose from dimensions that draw you to negative self-comparisons, and shift to other dimensions of evaluation, you can thereby shake loose from your depression. Chapter 14, and also Chapter 18 on Values Treatment, show how this may be done.

SUMMARY

The healthy-minded person picks out characteristics on which she rates well, and then argues to herself and to others that those are the most important dimensions on which to judge a person. This is how most people fight sadness and depression—by skillfully choosing the dimensions by which they judge themselves, together with wisely selecting the standards on particular dimensions against which they measure themselves.

Some people, however, are less flexible in their choice of dimensions on which to compare themselves; they cannot choose at will the best 'line' for them to carry. For some people this is a matter of basic values. Some people get stuck with dimensions that cause them sadness because of destructive values implanted during childhood. Other people purposely focus only on dimensions which make them look bad in their self-comparisons.

An important tactic in battling depression is to choose dimensions that allow you to make positive self-comparisons and are consistent with your basic system of values.

THE REWARDS OF DEPRESSION

Do you *really* want to shake off your depression? Don't answer too fast, and don't be too sure. It is quite common that people get enough benefits from their depressions so that they prefer remaining depressed—despite all its unpleasantness—to being undepressed. So they stay depressed.

At first this assertion seems nonsensical. Doesn't everyone want to be happy rather than sad? But the word 'want' is a tricky one, because a person can have more than one 'want' at a given moment. By analogy, consider that you may 'want' a piece of chocolate, but you may also 'want' not to ingest additional calories or get fat. The resultant of these two forces may be that you do not eat the cake even though you 'want' it, *or* you may eat it even though you want not to get fat.

There are two kinds of conflicting wants that may be involved in depression: other wants which conflict with being free of depression, and the wish to stay depressed for its own sake. Here are a few examples of 'wants' that may keep you depressed:[1]

1. You may know that overwork causes you to be depressed, but you may want the fruits of the work sufficiently badly so that you overwork anyway. This is little different than the situation of the person who risks heart attack by working too hard.

2. You may have the 'magical' belief that if you punish yourself for your misdeeds by being sad, an authority (which may be God) will take note of your self-punishment and therefore refrain from punishing you further. We see this in children who, following misbehavior, put on a sad and apologetic face and thereby effectively avoid punishment. This connection may continue to exist within the adult's mind, even

though it no longer works. A person who violates a legal or moral code may punish himself with sadness in the hope that the law or his peers or God will thereby be foreclosed from punishing him in an even worse manner. Hence he chooses to remain depressed.

3. 'Experienced' depressives—that is, people who suffer depression from time to time—sometimes use depression as an excuse not to meet demands and do unpleasant chores.

4. An important 'benefit' of depression is that you can feel sorry for yourself because you are so miserable. Self-pity and depression are almost inseparable, wrapped up with each other like climbing vines. Some writers have even believed that self-pity is the origin of depression.

At the root of the adult depression of a child whose parents die may lie this mechanism involving self-pity: At the time of the death, other members of the family express their sorrow and pity for the child, together with their love for the child. This is relatively pleasant for the bereaved child, and it is the best substitute for the parent's love. It would be logical for a child to extend the period of seeming depressed in order to continue eliciting this expressed pity and love by others. And this pattern of depression to elicit pity and love may continue through the person's life—perhaps most strongly for a person who does not get enough of this pity and sorrow to surfeit her at the time of bereavement.

BENEFITS OF SELF-PITY

Self-pity is a pleasant substitute for pity from others. In turn another person feeling pity for you is pleasant because it is associated with the other person caring about you, and that caring is associated with loving you. Any lack of love of others may be the proximate cause of sadness, because of the close association between lack of parental love and neg-comps. (Notice how a parent expressing love for a child can banish the child's sadness. And a depressed adult is often conscious of the desire that a friend or spouse give comfort in the form of expressing sorrow.)

There is sound inner logic, then, in remaining depressed so that you can give yourself a reasonable substitute for the love of others that you crave. And this may act as a powerful attraction toward depression and a formidable obstacle to forsaking depression for happiness.

In this respect depression is similar to hypochondria, which elicits sympathy from others and provides an excuse not to exert oneself. Just as with hypochondria, the benefits of depression may seem greater than the costs.

The concept of self-comparisons is especially fruitful in analyzing self-pity. Consider these examples of external events upon which people fix their thoughts when they are in a self-pitying frame of mind:

Homely Sally pities herself because she does not have the advantages that come with being better-looking; men therefore don't appreciate her other virtues, she tells herself. Unsuccessful poet Paul pities himself because magazines never publish his poetry, though they publish others' poems that are nowhere near as good as those he writes. Five-foot-seven-inch Calvin pities himself because, though he was a hot-shot basketball player in high school, no college would give him a scholarship due to his height, and he therefore never went on with his studies. Mother Tamara pities herself because two of her five children died.

Earlier I said that people enjoy self-pity. They get so much benefit from it that they are unwilling to stop feeling sorry for themselves even if the price of the self-pity is continued depression. But why should this be? What is there so pleasant in the nature of the examples given above that would make the thought desirable? Why would anyone want to go on pitying herself for losing two children to death, or because his poetry doesn't get published? We need an explanation in terms of neg-comps.

The answer to this riddle is that in their self-pity people *also* make a *positive* self-comparison which gives them gratification. Poet Paul tells himself, while he is feeling sorry for himself, that he really is a *better* poet than many of those who *do* get their poetry published; that self-praise makes him feel good. At the same time, the thought that he is not getting what he *deserves*—a negative self-comparison, please notice—is making him feel sad. He flips back and forth from one thought and feeling to the other, getting pleasure from the self-praise and the positive self-comparison, and then getting sadness from the negative self-comparison.

Tamara tells herself that when her two children died, she got a worse deal from life and God than she deserves, a negative self-comparison which makes her sad. At the same time she reminds herself that she is a virtuous woman who did not deserve the blow, and she gets gratification from thinking of her virtue by comparison to other people.

Calvin gets pleasure from reminding himself what a hot-shot basketball player he was, while pitying himself for the opportunities he did not know. And Sally gets pleasure from thinking about her good mind and her fine character when pitying herself that because of her face men don't like her despite these virtues.

We can now understand how a person gets hooked on the self-pitying mechanism, just the way a person gets hooked on heroin, and why it is so hard to kick this habit. Self-pity exerts a fatal fascination. It is like the situations in experimental psychology called 'plus-minus stimuli', stimuli that are neither only positive nor only negative, but rather are both negative and positive. The fatal fascination arises because you cannot obtain the benefits without suffering the costs. Paul cannot think how he is a good poet without also coming to think how his poems do not get published. And he cannot stop thinking about his publishing failure without giving up the pleasure of self-praise of his poetry.

To test this analysis on yourself, inspect your thoughts the next time you are feeling sorry for yourself. Look for *both* a. the self-praise for being virtuous and good—the positive self-comparison between what you *are*, compared to the benchmark comparison of what you are *getting* from life; *and* b. the negative self-comparison between what you *get* and what you *deserve*. You may also test this analysis by listening to what you say to another person when you express pity for him or her. And pure logic also implies this behavior: Unless the gratifying element of the positive self-comparison is present in self-pity, why would anyone not simply kick the habit?

Please notice that you will not expect—nor usually get—pity unless you *deserve better* than you got. The rotten mother, the mediocre basketball player, the lazy poet will neither expect nor get pity for child death, non-scholarship, or publication rejection.

This analysis of the benefits of feeling sorry for yourself is described in Mike Royko's satire of the benefits of moaning when suffering from a New Year's day hangover.

The other part of a hangover is physical. It is usually marked by throbbing pain in the head, behind the eyes, back of the neck, and in the stomach. You might also have pain in the arms, legs, knees, elbows, chin, and elsewhere, depending upon how much leaping, careening, flailing and falling you did.

Moaning helps. It doesn't ease the pain, but it lets you know that someone cares, even if it is only you. Moaning also lets you know that you are still alive.

But don't let your wife hear you moan. You should at least have the satisfaction of not letting her have the satisfaction of knowing you are in agony.

If she should overhear you moaning, tell her you are just humming a love song the lady with the prominent cleavage sang in your ear while you danced.

Some people say that moaning gives greater benefits if you moan while sitting on the edge of your bathtub while letting your head hang down between your ankles. Others claim that it is best to go into the living room, slouch in a chair, and moan while holding a hand over your brow and the other over your stomach.[2]

Consider the example of Charley T., an obese depressive. Charley says to himself: 'I'm so miserable, and the world has been so terrible to me, that I might as well cheer myself up with a few chocolates. Why shouldn't I? No one else gives me any love or help or pleasure, so at least I can give myself some pleasure!' And there goes the whole box of bon-bons.

If Charley stops feeling depressed, he no longer has a handy excuse to munch chocolates by the handful. And this is an inducement for him to remain depressed. We might label this sort of ailment 'candy depression'.

The goodies that the rest of us give ourselves when we are depressed—relief from work, self-sympathy in feeling sorry for ourselves, excuses not to do things for others—are not so obvious. Yet they can be just as powerful a barrier to curing our depressions as is Charley's yearning for food. If we are to cure our depressions, we must face up to the fact that we must give up something in exchange. If we won't pay the price, we won't stop being depressed. That may be hard for you to hear, but in many or most cases it is a fact.

Some writers such as Bonime[3] view depression *only* as a way of obtaining its benefits. To Bonime depression is a "practice . . . a way of living", that is, a way of manipulating other people. Certainly this may be an element in the depression of some persons, maybe even most depressives, a carryover from childhood sulking that often does produce results. But to view adult depression *only* as a device to achieve the sympathetic response of other persons simply is far from the facts of the lives of, for example, many depressed recluses who are not even in contact with other persons who might be induced to respond to the depression; the explanation then becomes downright silly.

The question we shall tackle later is how to decide whether you want the pleasures of a. moaning for yourself in combination with depression, versus b. being undepressed.

BREAKING THE HABIT OF SELF-PITY

As to dealing with the self-pity habit: I said that poet Paul thinks of himself as a 'good poet'. Perhaps he should ask himself whether his *poems* are good or bad, and not whether the *maker* of the poems is a good or bad *person*. Ellis uses the term 'rating' for this tendency to label the person rather than the act, and he argues that reducing the amount of rating is an important way to attack depression. I agree, though noting that such rating is very much bound up with the daily living of most of us, and therefore hard to forswear.

SUMMARY

Strange as it may seem, a person sometimes gets enough benefits from her/his depression so that the person prefers remaining depressed—despite all its unpleasantness—to being undepressed. Possible benefits include a good excuse from work or other demands, the concern of others, or the justification for self-pity. Recognizing that this sort of mechanism may operate can help you face the matter squarely, and decide that the benefits of the depression are not worth the pain of the depression.

PART THREE

Ways of Overcoming Depression

INTRODUCING SELF-COMPARISONS COGNITIVE THERAPY

All of us hanker for instant magic, a quick fix for our troubles. And that's what the simple-minded variety of get-happy self-help books promise, which explains why so many people buy them. But in the end there seldom is a one-stroke magical cure for a person's depression.

The understanding of depression provided by cognitive therapy and Self-Comparisons Analysis is an exciting advance over the older ways of dealing with depression. But this new theory also shows that there is more to understanding depression than a single magical button. Instead, you must do some hard thinking about yourself. Whether you have the help of a psychotherapeutic counselor, or fight your depression by yourself—perhaps using the computer program available with this book—the battle takes effort and discipline.

Writing down and analyzing your depressed thoughts is a very important part of the cure. Some detailed suggestions are given below. Learning more about the nature of depression is worthwhile, too. I particularly recommend two excellent practical books, *Feeling Good,* by David Burns, and *A New Guide to Rational Living,* by Albert Ellis and Robert A. Harper, both of which are available in inexpensive paperback. Other works which have two or three stars in the reference list at the end of this book also are valuable for the depression sufferer; the more you read, the better your chances to find insights and methods which will fit your mind-set and your daily needs. When reading those books, you will quickly see how their general notion of negative thoughts can be translated into the more precise and useful notion of negative self-comparisons.

A bit later, this chapter discusses whether you should try to win the battle by yourself (perhaps with the help of the computer program, *Overcoming Depression,* which accompanies this book) or seek a counselor's aid, and whether you can expect to sail into a permanent harbor of total untroubled bliss. First we must discuss the first requirements of almost any successful battle against depression.

Before proceeding further, here is a nice tidbit for you which—even if it will not cure your depression by itself—every depression specialist agrees is valuable therapy. *Do some things which you enjoy.* If you enjoy dancing, go out and dance tonight. If you like to read the funny papers before you start work for the day, read them. If you delight in a bubble bath, take one this evening. There are plenty of pleasures in this world that are not illegal, immoral, or fattening. Let it be the first step in your program to overcome depression to brighten up your days with some of these pleasures. This advice may seem trivial; trust me (the only time in the book I ask you to do so) that it is important.

Pleasurable activities reduce the mental pain which causes sadness. And while you are enjoying pleasure you do not feel pain. The less pain and the more pleasure, the more value you find in living. This advice to find pleasure clearly is 'just' common sense, and I do not know of any controlled scientific studies proving it is curative. But this shows how the core of the contemporary scientifically-proven cognitive theory is a return to the commonsense wisdom known for ages, though systematic modern research has made large advances with new theoretical understanding of the principles and practical development of the accompanying methods.

YOU MUST MONITOR AND ANALYZE YOUR THINKING

The understanding of depression provided by cognitive therapy and Self-Comparisons Analysis is an exciting advance over the older ways of dealing with depression. But this new theory also shows that there is more to understanding depression than a single magical button. Instead, you must do some hard thinking about yourself. Whether you have the help of a psychotherapeutic counselor, or fight your depression by yourself (perhaps with the computer's help), the battle takes effort and discipline.

Writing down and analyzing your depressed thoughts is a very important part of the cure.

Self-Comparisons Analysis teaches that your negative self-comparisons, together with a sense of helplessness, cause your sadness. Obviously, then, you will have to eliminate or reduce those negative self-comparisons in order to banish depression and achieve a joyful life. But with the possible exception of drug therapy or electroshock, every successful anti-depression tactic requires that you *know which depressing thoughts you are thinking.* Cognitive therapy also requires that you monitor your thinking in order to *prevent* those self-comparisons from entering and remaining in your mind.

So there it is. Fighting depression requires the *work* and *discipline* of observing your own thoughts. Watching over anything—watching over a child lest it get into the fireplace, or taking notes on what is said at a meeting, or listening to a travel guide give you directions to your destination—requires the effort of paying attention. And it requires the discipline of paying attention often enough and long enough. Many of us are sufficiently short of such discipline so that without a counselor to hold our hands we certainly will not do it, and even with a skilled counselor we may not be willing and able to do it. On the other hand, if you decide to do it—and making that *decision* to break out of depression, to give up its benefits and to do the necessary work is a key step—if you decide to apply yourself to the task, you almost surely *can* do it. Most depressed people *do* succeed in overcoming depression.

The first step in every tactic we shall describe, then, will be to observe your thoughts closely when you are depressed, analyze which negative self-comparisons you are making, and *write them down* if you can make yourself do so. Later, when you have learned how to keep depression at bay, an important part of your continuing exercise will be to identify each negative self-comparison before it gets a firm foothold, and pitch it out of your mind with the devices we shall describe.

One useful trick is to watch your thoughts in a disengaged fashion, as if they were the thoughts of a stranger whom you were reading about in a book or hearing at the movies. You can then examine the thoughts and see how interesting they are, including the peculiar illogical tricks we all play with our thinking. Watching your thoughts in this way is like what happens in meditation, which is described in Chapter 15. Watching your thoughts at a distance desensitizes them; it removes the sting of neg-comps. You will be amazed at the fascinating stream-of-consciousness drama that goes on inside your head, how one thing leads to another in the most peculiar way, with astonishing emotional ups and downs within a minute or less sometimes. Try it. You'll probably like it.

Learning to monitor your thoughts also is like the first crucial step in stopping smoking: You must first be *aware* of what you are doing before you can intervene to change the behavior. Confirmed smokers often pull out and light cigarettes without being fully aware of the process, and do not make a conscious decision to do so.

Other hard thinking also is necessary to overcome depression. You may have to straighten out some misapprehensions or confusions that customarily depress you. You may need to rethink your priorities. It may even help to search your memory for some childhood experiences. Perhaps hardest of all, you may have to study how you misuse

Table 1

Uninvited thought	*Causal Event*	*Self-Comparison*
'I never do anything right.'	Late for a meeting	I do fewer things right than most people.

language, and how you fall into linguistic traps. For example, your vocabulary probably makes you think that you *must* do some things which, upon inspection, you will conclude you have no obligation to do, and which may have dragged you into depression.

Conquering depression is not easy—rather, it is *difficult*. But difficult

> does not mean impossible. Of course you will find it hard to think and to act rationally in an irrational world. Of course you will have trouble reasoning your way out of circumstances which have unreasonably bogged you down for many years. All right, so you find it difficult. But it also proves difficult for a blind man to learn to read Braille, a victim of polio to use his muscles again, or a perfectly normal person to swing from a trapeze, learn ballet dancing, or play the piano well. Tough! But you still can do it.[1]

HOW TO OBSERVE YOUR THOUGHTS

You should—I'd say 'must' except that I don't want to add any musts to your life, and besides, there always are exceptions—you

Analysis	*Response*	*Behavior you wish to change*
Numerator: Are you *usually* late for meetings?	Almost never.	Inappropriately generalizing from a single instance to your entire life.
Denominator: Do most other people do most things more 'right' than you do?	Not really	Biased assessment of what other people are like, making you look bad.
Dimension: Is your timeliness at meetings an important aspect of your life?	Of course not.	Focusing on a dimension which a) you need not attribute importance to, and b) does not reflect well upon you.

should observe your thoughts with pencil and paper in hand, and *write down the thoughts and their analysis.* Better yet, because it makes writing easier, use a computer when you are near one.

Let's take this idea further. It is crucial that you actually *take action* to fight your depression. Writing down and analyzing your thoughts is one such action. But other actions are important, too, such as getting out and participating in pleasurable activities so that you will enjoy life more, or, arriving at meetings on time if you know that getting there late will start you thinking depressing thoughts. Certainly, all this takes effort. But cranking yourself up to carry through with the actions is often a crucial part of the cure of depression. More about this below.

Now back to your thoughts. Ask yourself, 'What am I thinking right at this moment, as I am feeling so sad?' Record your thought in the format of Table 10–1. This table guides you from the raw 'uninvited thought' ('automatic thought', some writers call it) which floats into your mind and causes you pain, into and through an analysis of that thought which pinpoints the problems and the opportunities to intervene so as to get rid of the painful negative self-comparison you are making.

Let's follow through an example I have taken from Burns so that a reader who uses his book can expand this method (developed over many years by Aaron Beck) with Self-Comparisons Analysis. Let's call it the case of Ms. X, a woman who suddenly realizes that she is late for an important meeting. The thought then zips uninvited into her mind, 'I never do anything right'. Ms. X *writes down* this thought in column 1 of Table 10–1. She also *writes down* in column 2 the event that triggered the uninvited thought, being late for the meeting.

The thought in column 1 creates pain. Let's assume that X has a hopeless attitude, too. The uninvited thought then produces sadness.

The uninvited thought in column 1 translates logically into the negative self-comparison, 'I do fewer things right than does the average person'. So Ms. X *writes down* in column 3 this analysis of her uninvited thought. Now we may consider various aspects of this neg-comp. The methods for dealing with the various aspects of neg-comps are discussed in detail in the chapters to follow, but we shall now skim through the process briefly in order to focus on the process rather than upon the particular methods.

Look first at the numerator. Is the assessment of her actual situation correct? Is she 'always' late, or even *usually* late? She asks this question, and writes it in column 4. Now X realizes that she is *very seldom* late. She had told herself, 'I'm always late', and then 'I never do anything right', because she has a typical cognitive-distortion habit of depressives, generalizing to 'always' or 'everything' bad from just a single bad instance. She specifies this self-fooling device in the last column of the table.

Ms. X now can see how she has created a painful neg-comp unnecessarily. If she has any sense of humor she can laugh at how her mind plays silly tricks on her—but tricks that make her depressed—because of habits built up through the years, for reasons that are long in her past.

Notice how the pain of depression is removed by examining *present* thoughts. It might be interesting and useful to know how and why X developed the habit of overgeneralizing from a single bad instance, but it is usually *not necessary* to have that knowledge. (Freudian doctrine erred fundamentally in this matter.)

It is worth mentioning that if you *are* usually late for meetings, you should re-arrange your life so that you get there on time. Depressives often fail to do this because, even when they acknowledge that they could change the situation so as to remove the causal event, they say they are helpless to change. Often the effort to get things right seems worse than the pain and sadness that getting it wrong produces; as long as a person feels this way, the person will continue to be depressed.

The analysis of X's actual-state numerator may be sufficient to demolish this painful neg-comp. But perhaps Ms. X is not easily convinced that she is playing the self-depressing mind game with her numerator that is shown in the table. People's capacity to fool themselves by using additional plausible-sounding distorted arguments is almost limitless. Therefore, let us go on to a second possible way to deal with this neg-comp, the denominator.

Ms. X agrees that her statement 'I never do anything right' implies that others do better than she. Now she can ask herself, Do others *really* usually do things more right than I do? And is my benchmark comparison really appropriate? Hopefully she will see that this is *not* a correct assessment, and she is *not* on average a poor performer. Once more, she may come to see how her biased assessment of others is biased against herself, and hence will let go of the depressing neg-comp. And perhaps she will see the humor in this, too, which will help even more.

Table 10–1 shows still a third line of analysis. Is the dimension of Ms. X being late for meetings important and appropriate for her to rate herself on? When she asks herself that question, she answers "No". Even if she is late for meetings, this does not mean that she is an incompetent person. And having realized this to be true, she can focus on other aspects of her life which are more important and on which she looks good to herself.

The analysis above provides three different tactics to deal with the neg-comp. Any one of these strategies may be appropriate and effective for a given circumstance for a given person. Sometimes, however, using more than one tactic increases your effectiveness in combating the neg-comp.

There are still other ways to address the problem Ms. X causes herself by telling herself 'I never do anything right', and we will discuss them later. The important point emphasized now is *writing down the analysis,* as a way of forcing your thoughts out into the open so that you—perhaps together with a therapist—can analyze their logic and their factual support. The rest of Part III of the book expands on this advice.

The moment just after awakening in the morning commonly is the bleakest, blackest of the day, depressives commonly say. Therefore, this moment is one of the most interesting to observe, just as it is one of the most challenging to deal with. It takes a bit of time, usually, to get one's morning thoughts directed onto a non-depressing path. This makes sense when you realize that when you first awake your thoughts have just been in the less-consciously-directed sleep state, which tends to be negatively-directed for depressives.

CAN YOU DO IT ALONE?

Can you really conquer depression by your own efforts, or do you need the help of a professional counselor? Many of us *can* do it alone, and if you are able to, you will gain great satisfaction and renewed strength from doing so. And nowadays you can have the assistance of Kenneth Colby's computer program, *Overcoming Depression,* based on the principles of Self-Comparisons Analysis set forth in this book; experimental research shows that computer-based cognitive thera-py does as well as therapy with a counselor (Selmi et al. 1990) and avoids several possible dangers touched on below.

In the example above, Ms. X can conduct the analysis in Table 10–1 by herself. And if she does so, she will gain considerable satisfaction from it. But a trained therapist can be helpful in helping X unravel her patterns of thought, and may help her discipline herself to proceed through the analysis.

Lest you doubt that a person can cure himself of depression without assistance from a physician or psychologist, keep in mind the millions of people who have done just that, in our times and in earlier times. Religion has often been the vehicle, though this is clearer in Eastern religion than in Western religion. The continuation through 2,500 years of Buddhism, which aims to reduce suffering, should itself be proof enough that at least some people can successfully combat depression without medical help. Granted, there do not exist scientifically-controlled experiments measuring whether the passage of time alone would have induced as much improvement as Buddhist techniques, as we do have controlled experiments for cognitive therapy with the aid of a therapist (see Appendix D). But people's own experiments on themselves, sometimes using such depression-preventing methods and sometimes not, would seem to constitute rather reliable evidence.

People's power to radically change the course of their own lives has been quite underestimated in recent years, in large part because of the emphasis of Freudian psychology on childhood experience as determinants of the adult's psychological state. As Beck described the dominant view in psychotherapy prior to cognitive therapy: "The emotionally disturbed person is [said to be] victimized by concealed forces over which he has no control."[3] In contrast, cognitive therapy has found that "Man has the key to understanding and solving his psychological disturbance within the scope of his own awareness."[4]

Even delinquency and drug addiction can be 'kicked' by some people who simply decide to do so. Alcoholics Anonymous provides massive evidence that it can be done. Another example is the Delancey Street Foundation of San Francisco: When a reporter asked its director about his

"pioneering" new way of rehabilitation, he was told, with glee: "Yeah, you could say we have a 'new' way of fighting crime and drugs. It's a way that hasn't been tried lately. We tell 'em to stop."[5]

The simple fact is that all of us, all the time, make and carry out decisions about how our minds will act in the future. We decide to study a book, and we do so. We focus our attention on doing this or that, and we do it. We are not beyond our own control.

As interesting evidence that 'ordinary' people can willfully alter their own thinking so as to make themselves happier at some times than at others, consider the example of Orthodox Jews on the Sabbath. Jews are enjoined not to think sad or anxious thoughts on the Sabbath (not even when in mourning). And for roughly 26 hours each Sabbath they do just that. How? The way a housewife chases out cats when they come in—as if with a mental broom.

This raises the question: Why not perform the same simple trick all week long? The answer is that the world prevents it. A person cannot, for example, neglect thoughts of work all week; one must make a living, and the world of work inevitably implies strife as well as cooperation, losses as well as gains, failure as well as success.

The operational question is whether you are *better off* attacking your depression on your own, or getting the help of a professional counselor. The appropriate answer is—a definite maybe.

The help of a counselor clearly can be valuable, as even such self-help advocates as Ellis and Harper agree:

> One of the main advantages of intensive psychotherapy lies in its repetitive, experimenting, revising, practicing nature. And no book, sermon, article, or series of lectures, no matter how clear, can fully give this. Consequently, we, the authors of this book, intend to continue doing individual and group therapy and to train other psychotherapists. Whether we like it or not, we cannot reasonably expect most people with serious problems to rid themselves of their needless anxiety and hostility without some amount of intensive, direct contact with a competent therapist. How nice if easier modes of treatment prevailed! But let us face it: they rarely do . . .
>
> Our own position? People with personality disturbance usually have such deep-seated and longstanding problems that they often require persistent psychotherapeutic help. But this by no means always holds true.[6]

But a counselor will only help you if the counselor is well skilled, and has a point of view which fits your particular needs. The chances of finding such a skilled counselor are always uncertain. For one thing, therapists tend to be typecast by their training, and there have occurred "increasingly sharp disagreements among authorities regarding the nature and appropriate treatment."[7] What you get depends on the accident of where the therapist studied and which 'school' she therefore belongs to; too few are the therapists whose thinking is broad enough to give you what you need rather than what they have in stock. Additionally, many practicing therapists got their training before cognitive therapy had been shown to be clinically effective (as none of the earlier therapies had been).

There is real danger here. Two experienced therapists and teachers of therapists write: "Some people are hurt . . . by the wrong types of therapists for them . . . Most people really have no sound basis on which to choose . . . Most therapists are trained in and practice a particular type of therapy, and in general you will get what that person knows, which may not necessarily be what is best for you."[8]

Depression is a profoundly philosophical disease. A person's most basic values enter into depressive thinking. On the one hand, values can cause depression when they set up overdemanding and inappropriate goals, and therefore a troublesome denominator in a Rotten Mood Ratio. On the other hand, values can help overcome depression as part of Values Treatment, as discussed in Chapter 18. Helping you deal with such issues requires a depth of wisdom which is not learned in school, and which is too seldom in any of us. But without such wisdom, a therapist is useless or worse.

Depression is also a philosophical matter when it arises from disorder of logical thinking and misuse of language. And starting in the 1980s, professional philosophers have begin to work with depressed people, with some apparent success (Ben-David 1990). The participation of philosophers is quite reasonable given that cognitive therapy is seen by its creators as being "primarily educative", with the therapist being a "teacher/shaper", and the process as being a Socratic "problem-solving question-and-answer format" (Karasu 1990, 139).

The interesting dialogues in Ellis and Harper's *A New Guide to Rational Living* and in Burns's *Feeling Good* illustrate how a skilled therapist with a sound grasp of logic can help patients correct their thinking and thereby overcome depression. But few therapists—or anyone else, for that matter—have the necessary skill in manipulating logical concepts. All this makes it difficult to find a satisfactory therapist, and provides additional incentive for you to proceed without a therapist.

Furthermore, the computer is not subject to some failings of human therapists: The computer never wears out from fatigue late in the day, becoming inattentive and therefore useless. The computer never burns out from emotional overload, as is not uncommon with human therapists—because they are human. The computer never becomes involved with the client in a troubling sexual relationship—as occurs in a surprisingly large number of cases, recent reports indicate. And you never feel that the computer is exploiting you financially, which bothers some clients whether or not there is a real basis for the feeling.

The ill-effects of getting involved with a counselor who is unsympathetic to your particular needs, or is temporarily ineffectual, or does not understand how to deal with your particular mentality, can be great. The encounter can discourage you further, and drive you further into depression, compounded by the pain of having paid your good money in return for being made worse off. Given all this, it would at least make sense to try to work on yourself for a while before seeking out professional help. And even if you do eventually seek out a counselor, you will be better prepared to find one you like, and to work with that person, if you have studied your own psychology and the nature of depression beforehand.

CAN YOU REACH PERMANENT BLISS?

You can hope to get rid of your depression, and by your own efforts. You can hope to remain depression-free most of your life. But if your depression is more than a passing episode you should not expect that after learning to fight and overcome deep depression you will have the same psychological make-up as nondepressives.

Just as alcoholics who have stopped drinking are forever different from other people with respect to alcohol (though recently there has been some scientific question raised about this), depressives who pull out of deep depression are often different than other people. They must constantly reinforce the dikes and guard against the first incursions of depression in order to keep a trickle from becoming a flood. Consider John Bunyan and Leo Tolstoy. Bunyan wrote as follows: "I found myself in a miry bog . . . and was as there left by God and Christ, and the Spirit, and all good things . . . I was both a burthen and a terror to myself . . . weary of my life, and yet afraid to die."[9] Tolstoy's relevant description of his depression is in Chapter 3 above.

William James wrote as follows about the lives of Bunyan and Tolstoy after their depressions:

> Neither Bunyan nor Tolstoy could become what we have called healthy-minded. They had drunk too deeply of the cup of bitterness ever to forget its taste, and their redemption is into a universe two stories deep. Each of them realized a good which broke the effective edge of his sadness; yet the sadness was preserved as a minor ingredient in the heart of the faith by which it was overcome. The fact of interest for us is that as a matter of fact they could and did find something welling up in the inner reaches of their consciousness, by which such extreme sadness could be overcome. Tolstoy does well to talk of it as that by which men live; for that is exactly what it is, a stimulus, an excitement, a faith, a force that reinfuses the positive willingness to live, even in full presence of the evil perceptions that erewhile made life seem unbearable.[10]

Depressives less exceptional than Tolstoy and Bunyan share this condition:

> You rarely ever completely win the battle against sustained psychological pain. When you feel unhappy because of some silly idea and you analyze and eradicate this idea, it rarely stays away forever, but often recurs from time to time. So you have to keep re-analyzing and subduing repeatedly. You may acquire the ridiculous notion, for instance, that you cannot live without some friend's approval and may keep making yourself immensely miserable because you believe this rot. Then, after much hard thinking, you may finally give up this notion and believe it quite possible for you to live satisfactorily without your friend's approbation. Eventually, however, you will probably discover that you, quite spontaneously, from time to time revive the groundless notion that your life has no value without the approval of this—or some other—friend. And once again you feel you'd better work at beating this self-defeating idea out of your skull.[11]

But this does *not* mean that you are doomed to a constant and unrelenting struggle. As you learn more about yourself and your depression, and as you build habits to keep negative self-comparisons at bay, it gets easier and easier.

> Let us hasten to add that you will usually find the task of depropagandizing yourself from your own self-defeating beliefs easier and easier as you persist. If you consistently seek out and dispute your mistaken philosophies of life, you will find that their influence weakens. Eventually, some of them almost entirely lose their power to harass you. Almost.[12]

Furthermore, one often develops a commitment to remaining free of depression, just as a person who has stopped smoking has an investment in keeping a 'clean record' and sustaining his or her success. One then feels a justifiable pride that helps keep you on the rails and away from sustained depression.

ONE STROKE FOR ALL?

Self-Comparisons Analysis makes clear that many sorts of influences, perhaps in combination with each other, can produce persistent sadness. From this it follows that many sorts of interventions may be of help to a depression sufferer. That is, different causes—and there *are* many different causes, as most psychiatrists have finally concluded, call for different therapeutic interventions. Furthermore, there may be several sorts of intervention that can help any particular depression. Yet all these interventions may be traced to the 'common pathway' of negative self-comparisons.

In short, different strokes for different folks. In contrast, however, each of the various schools of psychological therapy—psychoanalytic, behavioral, religious, and so on—does its own thing no matter what the cause of the person's depression, on the assumption that all depressions are caused in the same way. Furthermore, each school of thought insists that its way is the only true therapy.

Self-Comparisons Analysis points a depression sufferer toward whichever is the most promising tactic to banish the depression. It focuses on understanding why you make negative self-comparisons, and then develops ways of preventing the neg-comps, rather than focusing on merely understanding and reliving the past, or on simply changing contemporary habits. With this understanding you can choose how best to fight *your own* depression and achieve happiness.

In a capsule: Your thoughts about yourself cause your depression, though of course your thoughts may be prompted by conditions outside you. To overcome your depression, you must think about yourself in ways different than your habitual patterns. Self-Comparisons Analysis systematically suggests many possible kinds of change.

There are also some unsystematic tactics that sometimes effectively change your thinking about yourself. One of these is humor—jokes about your situation, as well as humorous songs. (Albert Ellis is big on these).[13] The switch in perspective that is the heart of much humor causes you to view your situation less seriously, and in that fashion takes the sting out of the negative self-comparisons that the humor makes fun of.

Viktor Frankl uses a method he calls "paradoxical intention" which radically switches a person's perspective in a fashion akin to humor. Often this is akin to the Values Treatment discussed in Chapter 18. Consider this case of Frankl's:

> A young physician consulted me because of his fear of perspiring. Whenever he expected an outbreak of perspiration, this anticipatory anxiety was enough to precipitate excessive sweating. In order to cut this circle formation I advised the patient, in the event that sweating should recur, to resolve deliberately to show people how much he could sweat. A week later he returned to report that whenever he met anyone who triggered his anticipatory anxiety, he said to himself, 'I only sweated out a quart before, but now I'm going to pour at least ten quarts!' The result was that, after suffering from his phobia for four years, he was able, after a single session, to free himself permanently of it within one week.[14]

Frankl's procedure can be understood in terms of altering negative self-comparisons. Frankl asks the patient (who must have some power of imagination for the method to work) to imagine that his *actual* state of affairs is different than what it is. Then he leads the person to compare the actual with that imagined state, and to see that the actual state is *preferable* to the imagined state. This produces a positive self-comparison in place of the former negative self-comparison, and hence removes sadness and depression.

ARE THE BEST THINGS IN LIFE FREE?

"The best things in life are free", says the song. In money terms, that may be true. But the *real* best things in life—such as true happiness, and the end to prolonged sadness—are not free in terms of effort. Not to recognize this can be disastrous.

The failure of all popular remedies for depression arises from their unwillingness to recognize that every anti-depression tactic has its cost. As with a farmer, giving up the struggle to plant and raise a crop means not having a harvest and not making a living. To avoid going to parties or business meetings that lead to negative self-comparisons is to forego the pleasures or profits that may also be present there. Another misleading example is the popular recommendation to 'accept yourself as you are'.

Accepting yourself certainly can have its benefits. But there is also a drawback with simply *accepting*—either 'accepting yourself', in the popular sense, or making no comparisons, as in Eastern meditative practices. If one wants to *change* one's habits or personality in order to improve or remedy a difficulty, one cannot avoid making comparisons. You cannot conduct any program of self-improvement without comparing and evaluating various modes of behavior.

An example: Wanda L. does not get much affection or respect from people in her work or personal life, other than from her husband and children. There are no obvious objective facts to explain this; she is a productive and talented worker, a very decent person, and not personally unpleasant. But a wide variety of aspects of her personality and behavior apparently combine to lead others to distrust her or not seek her out or to choose her for positions of responsibility.

Wanda can accept the situation as it is, not dwell on it in her thinking, and hence reduce the amounts of negative self-comparisons and sadness. But if she does that, she will not be able to study and analyze herself to change her behavior so as to improve her relationships.

Which should Wanda choose to do? The decision is like that of a business investor who must guess at the chances that the investment will pay off. So there is a price for Wanda to 'accept' herself as she is. The price is foregoing the chance of changing her life. Which is the better choice in this trade-off? That is a tough decision—and a choice that is ignored in the usual self-help books. And this makes those simplistic books, and their promises of quick and free miracles, unrealistic and ultimately disappointing.

Whereas this book focuses mostly on changes in how you *think*, this example focuses on changing the actual state of affairs so as to produce a more Rosy Ratio. But the underlying principle is exactly the same: reduce the negative self-comparisons.

WHO CAN BENEFIT FROM COGNITIVE THERAPY?

As is reasonable to expect from the nature of cognitive therapy, persons who are not among the most intellectually disturbed respond relatively better to cognitive therapy than do the most disturbed patients; the NIMH Collaborative Research Program found that outpatients who can think reasonably clearly do particularly well with cognitive-behavioral therapy (Sotsky et al. 1991). The implication is that if you are the sort of person who feels comfortable reading a book like this one in search of alleviation of depression, the kind of therapy offered here is the kind that you need. However, another study (Thase et al. 1991) emphasized that even severely depressed persons can benefit from cognitive therapy: "the response of the more severe patients in the current study could hardly be considered poor" (784).

SUMMARY

This chapter begins the section of the book that discusses ways to overcome depression and the sadness-creating mechanisms that the earlier chapters discussed. The understanding of depression provided by cognitive therapy and Self-Comparisons Analysis is an exciting advance over the older ways of dealing with depression. But this new theory also shows that there is more to understanding depression than a single magical button. Instead, you must do some hard thinking about yourself. Whether you have the help of a psychotherapeutic counselor, or fight your depression by yourself, you must struggle. But you *can* succeed.

Self-Comparisons Analysis teaches that your negative self-comparisons, together with a sense of helplessness, cause your sadness. Obviously, then, you will have to eliminate or reduce those negative self-comparisons in order to banish depression and achieve a joyful life. But with the possible exception of drug therapy or electroshock, every successful anti-depression tactic requires that you *know which depressing thoughts you are thinking.* Cognitive therapy also requires that you monitor your thinking in order to *prevent* those self-comparisons from entering and remaining in your mind. Writing down and analyzing your depressed thoughts is a very important part of the cure.

The first step in every tactic is to observe your thoughts closely when you are depressed, analyze which negative self-comparisons you are making, and *write them down* if you can make yourself do so. Later, when you have learned how to keep depression at bay, an important part of your continuing exercise will be to identify each negative self-comparison before it gets a firm foothold, and pitch it out of your mind.

You may have to straighten out some misapprehensions or confusions that customarily depress you. You may need to rethink your priorities. It may even help to search your memory for some childhood experiences. Perhaps hardest of all, you may have to study how you misuse language, and how you fall into linguistic traps.

One may seek the help of a counselor or choose to tackle depression by yourself. Self-cure certainly is feasible. The simple fact is that all of us, all the time, make and carry out decisions about how our minds will act in the future. We decide to study a book, and we do so. We focus our attention on doing this or that, and we do it. We are not beyond our own control.

The help of a counselor clearly can be valuable. But finding a counselor who meets your needs is not easy. Depression is a philosophical disease. A person's most basic values enter into depressive thinking. On the one hand, values can cause depression when they set up overdemanding and inappropriate goals, and therefore a troublesome denominator in a Rotten Mood Ratio. On the other hand, values can help overcome depression. Helping you deal with such issues requires wisdom.

Self-Comparisons Analysis makes clear that many sorts of influences, perhaps in combination with each other, can produce persistent sadness. From this it follows that many sorts of interventions may be of help to a depression sufferer. That is, different causes—and there *are* many different causes, as most psychiatrists have finally concluded, call for different therapeutic interventions. Furthermore, there may be several sorts of intervention that can help any particular depression. Yet all these interventions may be traced to the "common pathway" of negative self-comparisons.

Self-Comparisons Analysis points a depression sufferer toward whichever is the most promising tactic to banish the depression. It focuses on understanding why you make negative self-comparisons, and then develops ways of preventing the neg-comps, rather than focusing on merely understanding and reliving the past, or on simply changing contemporary habits. With this understanding you can choose how best to fight *your own* depression and achieve happiness.

PLANNING AND EXECUTING A STRATEGY AGAINST YOUR DEPRESSION

To repeat: the sadness in depression is caused by a) making negative comparisons between i. your perceived actual circumstances, and ii. some hypothetical circumstances—for example, what you would like to be, or what you think you ought to be, or what you are accustomed to—in combination with b) a sense that you must do better and are helpless to change the actual or hypothetical circumstances. There is a variety of possible reasons for making such negative comparisons persistently.

This chapter outlines a step-by-step strategy for fighting depression. The first two steps inquire into the unfavorable self-comparisons, asking: Which particular negative self-comparisons are most frequently in your mind when you are depressed? and Why do you persistently make these negative comparisons between your actual state and your benchmark state? The third step examines whether there are side-benefits of depression you must deal with. Step 4 inquires into the sense of helplessness that converts your negative self-comparisons into sadness. Step 5 is the preparation of a plan of intervention into your thinking process. And step 6 swings you into action, both in dealing actively with your thinking processes and also in getting you off your depressed duff into a more active and pleasurable mode of life which helps counteract depression.

SIX STEPS IN FIGHTING THE DEPRESSION

Step 1: Find out which negative self-comparisons you are making, and in which ways you feel helpless to achieve what you think you must achieve.

As described in Chapter 10, you do this by writing down the neg-comps as in Table 10-1. A therapist can help by urging or encouraging. If you have trouble stating the neg-comps, a therapist can use the tools of the clinical art to learn the content of your consciousness—that is, what you think about while feeling sad.

This may require some probing. For example, you may immediately say that you are suffering because a beloved spouse has died. But instead, you may say (as many do) that you think poorly of yourself because you are depressed, in which case further inquiry is needed. This may lead to such negative self-comparisons as that you feel like a failure in your work, or you feel that your life has no meaning, or that you are guilty of dishonest conduct.

The particular negative self-comparisons you are making may not be of importance in themselves, and they may change over time. But inquiry into these self-comparisons can help you, or your counselor, trace the causes of your depression.

Notice how this first step requires observing yourself, and noting the thoughts that lie in your mind.

Concerning the sense of helplessness, notice your reactions when you contemplate your negative self-comparisons and ask yourself why you do not change your actual or hypothetical circumstances. Observe yourself saying that you cannot, must not, are unable to, are not allowed to, and so on—all manifestations of *feeling helpless* to do anything about your condition, and therefore hopeless about improving your life and mood.

Step 2: Try to learn the causes of the negative self-comparisons, and of the helpless attitude.

By self-inquiry, or in discussion with a counselor, try to trace the causes of your making the negative self-comparisons. Perhaps you (and your counselor, if you have one) can figure out, for example, whether as a child you were frequently rebuked by your parents, whether you have work goals which seem very difficult for you to attain, whether you interpret your everyday experiences in a reasonably objective fashion, whether it is reasonable for you to feel unable to improve your circumstances, and so on. In this diagnostic state, the categories discussed in earlier chapters (and portrayed in the various boxes in Appendix A) may serve as guides to the inquiry.

A systematic attempt to diagnose the causes of the depression using these categories—or any categories—was not part of traditional psychoanalysis. Freudians have assumed that the therapist knows in advance what the cause is—childhood loss of a parent or of parental love. But I hope that by now you are persuaded that there are many, rather than just one, possible causal elements involved in depression.

Cognitive-behavioral therapists tend not to seek the original causes of a person's depression. And I agree that depression can often be cured without knowing the original causes, by focusing only on the present thought patterns. But sometimes learning the original cause illuminates the present situation. For example, when I realized that my overdemanding work goals stemmed from the 'oughts' my mother urged on me, I immediately saw that I should not continue to enslave myself to them, and in that moment I gained a great sense of freedom which sent me on my way out of depression.

In this diagnostic stage you must use your entire store of wisdom, insight, and experience. Counselors have a store of experience that non-psychologists lack, and that is one way they can be helpful. Another way they can be helpful is to offer a less biased interpretation of events in the past and present than a person has himself.

Step 3: Check whether there are any 'beneficial' aspects of depression which act as obstacles to letting go of your depression (see Chapter 9).

If you derive benefits from your depression—for example, the fruit of depression-causing overwork, or the pleasantness of self-pity—then you must choose between staying depressed and giving up the benefits of depression.

If you discover such a benefit which presents an obstacle to the cure of your depression, you must be honest enough to acknowledge that you can't have it both ways; you can't have both the cure *and* the fruits of depression. With this acknowledgment may come some sensible compromises. In the case of the depressed adult who fears punishment for some actual deed, it may be possible to tackle the possibility of legal or moral punishment head-on to ascertain what (if any) punishment may really be warranted, and to get it over with if possible. In the case of overwork, understanding the obstacle to a cure may lead to a choice of work level that will be an optimal combination of work output and depression.

Giving up the state of depression, and fighting it off when it threatens to come back, has costs. I repeat this because it is important to understand that it is so. An important cost is the energy required to grapple with the depression, just as it takes work and energy to staunch the bleeding from a wound. It is often easier to let the blood flow, than to repair the wound—that is, easier to let the negative self-comparisons course through one's mind than to examine them and either rebut or repress them.

Depressives are not skilled at staunching their mental bleeding—their negative self-comparisons. Everyone gets battered and cut in the world of people and work, but the depressive tends to let the bleeding go on and on. And it takes much work to change one's habits in this respect. But it must be done; it is the price that must be paid if you are to escape from depression. More about this in the next section.

Step 4: Address your sense of helplessness and hopelessness.

It is an accompanying sense of helplessness that converts negative self-comparisons into sadness and eventually depression. Therefore, if you can acquire the attitude that you are capable of altering your life situation, rather than simply accepting it, you can reduce sadness. Tactics for dealing with helplessness are discussed in Chapter 17.

Step 5: Intervene in the depressed person's thinking with the aim of reducing negative self-comparisons and the sense of helplessness.

Let us assume that drug therapy will not be used for now. Yet something stronger than rest and distraction is necessary. The type of intervention must then be determined by the causes of the depression diagnosed in the previous steps. The chapters to come discuss specific ways of intervening for specific sorts of problems.

As a review and preview, here are the various ways of battling your depression: a. Improve the numerator in your happiness ratio by altering your perception of the facts of your life. b. Sweeten your ratio by changing the benchmarks you use for self-comparisons. c. Change the dimensions on which you evaluate yourself. d. Reduce the number of self-comparisons you make. e. Diminish the sense of helplessness and increase your sense of competence to change your actual circumstances and hypothetical benchmark states. f. Change aspects of your life that lead to negative outcomes. g. Use Values Treatment.

Several sorts of interventions may be useful for any particular sort of cause. For example, one might intervene entirely in the present by creating habits to shut off the past, or one could also delve into the past to help relieve the problem. But one mode of intervention may be more efficient and successful than others.

Your past history, and especially your childhood, is almost inevitably involved in your depression. But the influence of the past can be relatively great or relatively little, and it may be relatively difficult or relatively easy to pry you loose from the relevant aspects of the past. The other side of this coin is that changing your present conditions may have greater or less influence, depending on the strength of the influence of the past on your mood.

An analogy may help. Consider a building's plumbing. A faucet that was installed some years ago is leaking badly. If the faucet was weak at the time of installation, then past events influence the present leak. If one can replace the faucet and thereby resolve the problem, the present situation can be effectively separated from its past, just as some habits people have can be changed in the present without further influence by the past that created the habit. But it may be that a new faucet will also go bad quickly because the rest of the plumbing that was installed years ago is defective and will ruin the new faucet. If so, the present leaky faucet problem cannot be separated from the past in a simple way, but rather the entire system created in the past requires inspection and repair. Just so with some kinds of contemporary behavior: a person may take herself out of one depressing situation and invariably find her way into another depressing situation because of some general tendencies created in the past.

This suggests that therapeutic strategy depends upon the continuing role of the person's past. That is why it is often (though not always) useful for you to know the cause of the present negative self-comparisons before deciding whether to concentrate on your present or your past. To paraphrase Robert Frost, 'Find out why a fence was put up before you tear it down.'

Step 6: Get into Action.

Two kinds of action are important: carrying out our self-curative plan, and participating in the worlds of work and of pleasurable life activity. Let's talk about them in that order.

Excellent self-knowledge and terrific plans by themselves will do you no good. Your plan of action will help you *only if you carry it out.* More specifically, this means that you must WRITE DOWN your thoughts and the analysis of them, as in Table 10-1. In many cases, it also means carrying out actions that will liberate you from hang-ups with respect to other people or with respect to phobias such as fear of elevators.

Yes, writing out your thoughts requires effort. But this I guarantee you: If you don't make at least *some* effort, you will either remain mired in your depression for a long time, or at the least you will remain in it for longer than you need to.

Two wise therapists put it this way:

> We can't say this often enough: the major function of therapy is educational. To have therapy sessions or to read self-help books without practicing and without doing homework assignments is like attending lectures at school without reading or studying. It is like taking piano lessons without practicing. You may get something out of it but only a fraction of what you might otherwise have derived. Keeping a notebook, recording observations about your own thinking and behavior, and practicing new thinking and behavior are the best ways of *changing.*[1]

Again, writing your thoughts and carrying out other curative actions requires effort. This means laboriously hauling yourself uphill rather than sliding effortlessly downhill. Exerting effort requires expenditure of energy and will. It is a drag, a cost.

Now let's talk about the second type of action you must crank up: participating in the worlds of work and of pleasurable life activity. Even normal people do not readily expend the energy and will that they believe would be sensible for them in the long run—in exercising for fitness, for example. And depressives typically have an even greater propensity than do normal people for not swinging into action and doing the things that they believe they ought to do for their own well-being.

A few depressives, like me, are lucky enough to go in the opposite direction of working too much rather than too little. This has the benefit that when they finally come out of their depression, their lives are not blighted by the accumulation of problems caused by lack of work while they were depressed. I was lucky enough to enjoy my main work, writing and research, and to find it easy to do, and therefore it required little energy to stay at it. Indeed, the hours while I was writing were the only oasis in my life when I could concentrate on what I was doing and not be obsessed by my depressed thoughts. My too-strict work discipline, which is a problem for me in other ways, was also a benefit at this time.

Some people have said to me that my working meant that I was not 'really' depressed, because not working is a standard symptom of depression. All this proves is that not all depressives have the same auxiliary symptoms. Whether a person should be called 'depressed' properly depends only upon that person's thoughts and feelings, and on how long the sadness persists.

Why don't *non-depressives* get right at the tasks that they know they 'should' undertake for their own good? You know the answers: a. They prefer leisure to exertion. (We are talking here, of course, of work which is not so enjoyable that people have no difficulty getting themselves going.) b. They convince themselves that not doing the task really won't be very harmful, and doing it will not be very beneficial. c. They fool themselves that they are just postponing the task for a short time, and keep repeating the procrastination. d. They start the task and then give up because they lose patience.

Depressives share all these patterns of inactivity with non-depressives, but more so. They give themselves more excuses for not acting, they have less patience with which to continue a frustrating task, and so on. So whereas normal people are often too slow starting but eventually do start, and are too quick to quit but at least get most of the task done, depressives may *never* get started, or else stop when they have barely begun.

Depressives also have some special twists of their own. Among these specialties of depressives are: a) They are often afraid to get going because then they must give up the benefits of being depressed (see Chapter 9). b) They lack hope that the task will result in success, and therefore have a special excuse not to start. c) They often have ridiculously high standards for successful accomplishment of the task, and therefore have 'rational' grounds for believing that they will fail. d) They are experts at manufacturing logical reasons why it is not worthwhile getting into action.

The worst part of the depressive's inactivity hang-up is that inactivity breeds a greater propensity to remain inactive. The depressive first fails to act, then berates himself for being a worthless person because he fails to act, then fails to act because he knows he is so worthless that attempting action is useless and a waste of effort, and on and on and on. If ever there is a vicious circle, full of negative feedback, this is it. The circle becomes tighter and tighter until, like the famed boudini bird which flies in ever-narrowing arcs, it disappears into its own anus.

How to get out of the vicious circle? The theory is as simple as the execution is difficult: Get started in even the smallest way, enjoy some satisfaction and pleasure from successfully carrying out even a tiny task, and then use that experience as the basis to do something just a little bit bigger. Just DO SOMETHING.

It is here that the theory and skills of behavioral therapy are at their most effective. The idea is to get a *benign* circle going, with *positive* feedback. In that way the arcs gradually become greater and greater with self-reinforcing vigor, until—reversing the natural history of the boudini bird—you are in self-sustained flight and zoom out of your depressed inert state.

There are lots of practical tricks that can help you. The chapter on 'Do-Nothingism: How to Beat It' in David Burns's book *Feeling Good* contains a host of useful suggestions. Or, a counselor may be particularly useful in this role, especially if you and the therapist have a clear understanding that you want very specific help on the very specific problem of getting doing, doing something, and eventually carrying out your plan of action.

Judaism differs from Christianity in its belief that actions are more important than beliefs. If an orthodox Jew consults a rabbi about a crisis of belief, the usual advice is to carry out the daily routine of being a Jew, and not worry about the beliefs. Experience has shown that belief often follows after the actions. And even if the belief does not follow, the sense of crisis usually seems to disappear.

In the same way for a depressive, actions lead thoughts. If you start doing things, even the littlest things, and feel satisfaction about them, you will feel more capable of doing more, and you will think you are less worthless, and then you will do more.

Not only the world of work but the world of pleasure is also important. Here I'll merely repeat the important advice given earlier, advice which every competent therapist agrees with: *Do some things which you enjoy.* If you enjoy dancing, go out and dance tonight. If you like to read the funny papers before you start work for the day, read them. If you delight in a bubble bath, take one this evening. Let the very first move in your anti-depression program be some activities that will brighten your days with some of these innocent pleasures.

How can you be *sure* that what I tell you here is true? You can't know *for sure,* without thorough study of the large scientific literature, and even then you could hardly be sure. But I make these two suggestions: 1. Have a little faith in me and other writers on this subject, and do what we suggest. 2. If you cannot muster a bit of faith in us, at least have faith in the scientific method. That is, *try this plan out.* If the process works, you will gain. If the process fails, you can try something else. Right?

SUMMARY

This chapter describes the strategy for fighting depression. Steps one and two examine the unfavorable self-comparisons you are making. You ask: Which particular negative self-comparisons are most frequently in your mind when you are depressed? and, Why do you persistently make these negative comparisons between your actual state and your benchmark state? The third step examines whether there are side-benefits of depression you must deal with. Step 4 inquires into the sense of helplessness that converts your negative self-comparisons into sadness. Step 5 is the preparation of a plan of intervention into your thinking process. And step 6 moves to action, both in dealing actively with your thinking processes and also in getting you into a more active and pleasurable mode of life which helps counteract depression.

IMPROVING YOUR NUMERATOR

If you can prove to yourself that you are not as bad as you think you are—that is, if you learn that the facts show you measure up much better than you thought you did—you may take a short and effective route to overcoming sadness and depression. So it makes sense first to check whether you can improve the numerator in your self-comparison Mood Ratio.

People can and do distort the facts about any of the aspects of their lives that are important to them. Consider as an example the case of a

> woman who always had a great zest for life, had felt a great deal of pride in herself and in her achievements, and had cared for her children with obvious love and tenderness. [She] became morose and lost interest in everything that had previously excited her. She withdrew into a shell, neglected her children and became preoccupied with self-criticisms and wishes to die. At one point, she formulated a plan to kill herself and her children, but was stopped before she could carry out the plan.
>
> How can conventional folk wisdom explain this woman's remarkable change from her normal state? In common with other depressed patients, she appears to violate the most basic principles of human nature. Her suicidal wishes and her desire to kill her children defy the most hallowed 'survival instinct' and 'maternal instinct'. Her withdrawal and self-debasements are clearcut contradictions of another accepted canon of human behavior—the pleasure principle. Common sense is foiled in attempting to understand and to fit together the components of her depression. Sometimes the deep suffering and withdrawal of the patient is

explained away by conventional notions such as, 'He is just trying to get attention.' The notion that a person tortures himself to the point of suicide for the dubious satisfaction of gaining attention greatly strains our credulity and actually runs counter to common sense.

In order to understand why the depressed mother would want to end her own life and that of her children, we need to get inside her conceptual system and see the world through her eyes. We cannot be bound by preconceptions that are applicable to people who are not depressed. Once we are familiar with the perspectives of the depressed patient, her behavior begins to make sense. Through a process of empathy and identification with the patient, we can understand the meanings she attaches to her experiences. We can then offer explanations that are plausible—given her frame of reference.

Through interviewing this depressed mother, I discovered that her thinking was controlled by erroneous ideas about herself and her world. Despite contrary evidence, she believed she had been a failure as a mother. She viewed herself as too incompetent to provide even the minimum care and affection for her children. She believed that she could not change—but could only deteriorate. Since she could attribute her presumed failure and inadequacy only to herself, she tormented herself continuously with self-rebukes.

As this depressed woman visualized the future, she expected her children would feel as miserable as she. Casting about for solutions, she decided that since she could not change, the only answer was suicide. Yet, she was appalled at the notion that her children would be left without a mother, without the love and care she believed that only a mother could give. Consequently, she decided that in order to spare them the kind of misery she was experiencing, she must end their lives also. It is noteworthy that these self-deceptions dominated the patient's consciousness but were not elicited until she was carefully questioned about her thoughts and plans.

This kind of depressive thinking may strike us as highly irrational, but it makes sense within the patient's conceptual framework. If we grant her the basic (though erroneous) premise, namely that she and her children are irrevocably doomed as a result of her presumed deficiencies, it follows logically that the sooner the situation is terminated the better for everyone. Her basic premise of being inadequate and incapable of doing anything accounts for her complete withdrawal and loss of motivation. Her feelings of overwhelming sadness stem inevitably from her continuous self-criticisms and her belief that her present and future are hopeless.[1]

Imprecise use of language can produce severe numerator problems.

When clients state, 'I can't stop worrying', or 'I find it impossible to diet', we try to get them to change their sentences to 'I *can* stop worrying, but so far I haven't', and 'I find it exceptionally difficult to diet—but hardly impossible'.[2]

The steps toward improving your numerator are: 1. *Direct your attention* to negative self-comparisons arising from your numerator. 2. *Study* your numerator to learn how to bring it closer to the real facts. 3. If there arc ways to improve your actual situation that you have thought yourself helpless to bring about, consider whether you are *really unable* to bring about the improvement, or whether the helpless feeling that accompanies your depression is a *false impediment.* 4. If your study of your numerator indicates that your assessment is biased in a negative direction because of unsound judgment, *develop devices* to ensure that your corrected numerator, rather than a biased numerator, affects your mood. Let's consider these steps individually.

1. Aim to reduce negative self-comparisons. The first step in improving your numerator is to understand that you must *try to reduce negative self-comparisons,* and thereby improve your Mood Ratio.

2. Study your numerator in order to correct it. You are a journalist, say, and you think of yourself as sloppy and insufficiently disciplined. What are the facts? Are you *really* less careful and disciplined than others in the same work conditions, with the same talent? Or are you *really* quite careful and disciplined, and is your criticism of yourself in this respect not well-founded?

3. Improve your numerator if it can reasonably be improved, not letting a false sense of helplessness hold you back. You're still a journalist. After looking at a set of your articles as dispassionately as you can, you conclude that one more rewriting would improve your work considerably. Ask yourself why you don't give it that extra rewrite. If you tell yourself that you just can't do it, you just can't force yourself to rewrite one more time, that it is hopeless, the rewrite won't matter anyway, you just don't have the energy and discipline to rewrite again, blah, blah, ask: 'Is it really so? Maybe I'm *not* as helpless as that. Maybe I *can* force myself to the effort of rewriting again.' And if you do muster the resources to do the additional rewrite, you may be able to improve your numerator enough to have your self-comparisons no longer be negative.

If you can get yourself into this active mode and make improvements in the work, it will have the additional beneficial effect upon your mood that your activity will oppose your helplessness. And reducing the sense of helplessness reduces the sting of sadness, and the consequent pain, from self-comparisons. All this fits together with the discussion at the end of the last chapter about carrying out your plan of action.

4. Build the habit of assessing your numerator correctly. Here we may take full advantage of recent advances in cognitive therapy, which teaches you how to avoid misinterpretations and misconstructions of your situation that cause negative self-comparisons. A person may incorrectly gather or process the data about one's life, as for example, when I say 'My writings are lousy' in response to one of my writings being ignored, without trying to remember those of my writings that have been successful. Or a woman may say 'I'm a klutz' when she spills a bottle of beer, without remembering that she is actually a skilled professional ballet dancer. Or, after your suggestion for improving a machine is rejected by your boss, you may fail to analyze why the suggestion was rejected, and then take stock of further possibilities. That is, you may act like an unskilled and/or incompetent researcher into the facts of your situation, reaching unsound conclusions because of poor research habits or insufficient knowledge.

Simple habit-training, such as learning to say 'I'm really the greatest' every time the world pans your work, is not likely to succeed in cases like this one. But coming to see the flaws in your method of gathering and processing information about how good your work is, and how well it is received, can sometimes reduce unfavorable self-comparisons.

An important common problem is generalizing from a particular trait to your whole life situation. The person who is not good at school work generalizes to 'I'm no good at anything'. This misunderstanding is seen in the famous cartoon about Adlerian inferiority-complex psychotherapy. The psychiatrist is shown saying to the patient, 'I'm very sorry, Mr. Smith, but you really *are* inferior.' But there is no logical connection between a low relative standing in school work, or piety, or any other single dimension, and a person's relative worth as a *whole person*. Becoming aware of this logical error can remove the source of pain for many.

THINKING CLEARLY ABOUT YOUR 'NUMERATOR'

Errors in interpretation of depressives' numerators are similar to the fallacies that logicians have taught about for centuries, which are also similar to the biases that cause difficulties in scientific research. The problem is a universal one: how to think clearly.

Peter L. is a social scientist who does research which is usually ahead of the times. Sometimes a piece of his work is at first neglected, but later it usually catches on and is successful. But he always gets depressed when the research is first published and receives a cool reception. He would be depressed less if he would take into account the possible long-run effects of his work, even if those effects are now uncertain, rather than ignore them entirely and focus on the short-run neglect.

Cognitive therapy aims to teach Peter how to think more realistically in this regard. But if your past history continues to lay a heavy hand upon you in such manner that you feel that you *must* find negative self-comparisons for yourself, or you *must* choose dimensions of comparison which show you in a bad light, then cognitive therapy will not succeed.

Now let's exercise the theory. We begin with the same analysis of uninvited thoughts that was introduced in Chapter 10. Refer again to Table 10-1, and notice the first line of the analysis which refers to changing the numerator of the woman who says 'I never do anything right'.

Consider Nancy who says 'I am a bad mother'.[3] First she writes that uninvited thought in column 1 Table 12-1 below. Next she writes in column 2 the causal event just preceding that invited thought, a note from the teacher saying that one of her sons was having difficulty in school. Next she writes in column 3 the underlying self-comparison, which is that she is 'less effective than other mothers'.

Now Nancy is ready for the analysis in column 4, asking 'Is it true that I spend less time with my children, and less time working with them, than do most mothers?' Phrasing the question in this concrete fashion leads her to review her behavior. She also asks, 'Are all or most mothers more skilled and more attentive to their children than I am?'. This plus the first question lead her to do a mental survey of the mothers whom she knows, and to check out the statements. And as in so many cases, the facts that are known to her do not support the generalization that she had made in the absence of an examination of the data. If anything she spends *too much* time with her children, and she works with them on their schoolwork very actively—certainly as much as the average mother.

With the facts in hand, Nancy can laugh at her error in judgment, and respond 'The hell you say', when the uninvited thought 'I'm a bad

Table 2

Uninvited thought	*Causal Event*	*Self-Comparison*
'I am a bad mother.'	Note from teacher	I spend less time, and work less with the kids, than most mothers.

mother' floats into her mind. Getting rid of the Rotten Ratio makes her feel less pain, less sad, and less depressed.

This process is like scientific surveys such as a census, which check on casual generalizations such as that the death rate is going up, or people are getting poorer. If we could form valid generalizations without a census, we would not need to go to so much expense and trouble as we do. This is one more example of how a depressive's difficulty in thinking clearly is little different than our overall human problem of thinking clearly and arriving at sound conclusions.

Here is an example from Don F., a reader of an early draft of this book, about an event as he was emerging from a black depression following a breakup with his wife:

> That night I had terrible dreams, all concerning confronting Linna and her new husband as a couple, coming face to face with the fact that she prefers some abusive maniac to me. By the time I got to work I was well on the way to feeling worthless.
>
> Fortunately, that morning your manuscript was on my desk. As I read I began to see how I've distorted reality. Linna did not leave me for an abusive man because I am worthless. She became obsessed with an abusive man because she is a fruitcake. I do not have to feel depressed over that.

Analysis	*Response*
Numerator: 1. Do I spend relatively little time with kids, and working with them?	'The hell you say.'
Denominator: 2. Are most mothers really more effective and attentive than I am?	'It ain't so, Mo.'

Can You Always Improve Your Numerator?

Improving your numerator by assessing your life more realistically is not always a cure. Many of the negative self-comparisons that make one sad may be factually correct. You may indeed be in the bottom fifth of your class in high school, doing poorly relative to most of your classmates. You may really have lost a leg in an accident. It is no wonder that Beck finds that "It is often difficult for the patient to accept the idea that his interpretations are incorrect, or at least inaccurate." To assert that these conditions are distortions of reality is itself a distortion of reality which may later come home to roost with more pain. Distortions of reality in one's thinking process should be attacked with cognitive therapy. But factually-correct unfavorable self-comparisons that cause sadness should be attacked with another of the approaches described here.

Indeed, a solid body of research in recent years[4] suggests that depressives are *more accurate* in their assessments of the facts concerning their lives than are non-depressives, who tend to have an optimistic bias. This raises interesting philosophical questions about the virtue of such propositions as 'Know thyself' and 'The unexamined life is not worth living', but we need not pursue them here.

Cognitive treatment of the numerator is also not appropriate if the root of your problem is not illogic or misinformation but particular values and hopes. For example, Ruth Y. is a child psychologist who devotes her time and energy to doing research on depression in children from a totally new angle. For a long time she has had little success and no professional recognition, which saddens her. A cognitive therapist might tell her to stop fooling herself, and to turn her energies to something different. But she replies that even though the chances of success are small, the benefits to people will be very great if she does succeed. And if she could look back at age 80 and feel that she had made such a contribution to people she would feel that her life was well-lived.

If this child psychologist has a reasonable idea of the odds facing her, it would be most presumptuous for a therapist to try to 'straighten her out', or 'show her the errors in her thinking'. Rather, her best chance of cure may lie in Values Treatment of the sort described in Chapter 18.

Cognitive treatment of the numerator sometimes shades over into just plain lying to a person. 'You are bound to find a job if you keep on looking for another month', or 'There are lots of women who are less attractive than you who have made it in the movies', or 'You weren't really trying to hurt your wife when you broke her jaw, you were just trying to give her a love tap'. But such lying is likely to be disastrous with a depressed person, even aside from its ethics. Depressed people are experts in avoiding even true facts which would show them in a good light, and *a fortiori* they are even more effective at spotting falsehoods of that sort.

If a person is good at accepting self-supportive lies or half-truths in order to avoid the pain caused by negative self-comparisons, the person is unlikely to be a depressive; rather, schizophrenia or paranoia is the likely illness in such situations. And a depressive becomes even more depressed when he or she comes to feel that the truth as seen by other people is not flattering, and lying is necessary to construct an attractive picture.

Let's assume you understand that eliminating inaccurate self-assessments will reduce sadness and depression by improving the numerator in your Mood Ratio. Let's also assume that you have uncovered one or more ways in which you frequently bias your numerator against yourself. To benefit from this discovery you must develop the *habit* of correcting your biased assessments whenever they spring into your mind, or even better, adopt the habit of not even allowing such negatively-biased assessments into your mind at all. But how may this be done?

The recipe is simple—deceptively simple: By exerting effort, by practice, and by rewarding yourself for doing so, you build a habit of not making incorrect self-assessments. On the one hand this recipe is nothing more than everyday folk wisdom. On the other hand, this recipe is the staple of modern-day behavioral therapy, which uses various ingenious ways of rewarding people for repeating the desired behavior and for not repeating undesired behavior.

Our power to alter our thoughts by will and practice and suitable 'reinforcement' has come to be vastly underestimated, probably because of the rise of Freudian psychoanalysis which emphasizes the power of events in our earlier history to influence our behavior. Columnist Mike Royko conveyed the essence of the method humorously in a column on New Year's Day.

> This is the time of year when all sorts of advice is written about hangovers. . . .
> It should be remembered that part of a hangover's discomfort is psychological.
> When you awaken, you will be filled with a deep sense of shame, guilt, disgust, embarrassment, humiliation and self-loathing.
> This is perfectly normal, understandable and deserved.
> To ease these feelings, try to think only of the pleasant or amusing things that you did before blacking out. Let your mind dwell on how you walked into the party and said hello to everyone, and handed your host your coat, and shook hands, and admired the stereo system.
> Blot from your mind all memories of what you later did to your host's rug, what you said to that lady with the prominent cleavage that made her scream, whether you or her husband threw the first punch. Don't dredge up those vague recollections of being asleep in your host's bathtub while everybody pleaded with you to unlock the bathroom door.
> These thoughts will just depress you. Besides, your wife will explain it in detail as the day goes on. And the week, too. . . .[5]

Or consider the example of Peter F., a teacher who has difficulties in his relationship to his immediate institutional authorities. When he wants something—say, a new teaching assignment—he walks into the department office hat in hand, feeling like a beggar, because he feels that the department head knows just how much his achievements fall below some benchmark level and therefore he feels he has no right to make any request at all. Some people actually verbalize these feelings, saying something like 'I know you won't want to say yes to this, but. . . .' When a person makes a request feeling that way, the request has a much lower chance of being granted than if the request is made by a person who has confidence that his request should and will be granted. This sequence of events produces sadness after the request is denied, and also sadness in advance as he compares what is likely to happen (his numerator) with what he wants to happen (the denominator).

Peter could build the habit of entering such a meeting with confidence. And that might well produce positive results which would then help build the habit of behaving in that manner, and would actually improve his numerator. Certainly there are no disadvantages to this tactic, except for the effort involved in cranking up confidence in advance.

On the other hand, this particular habit-building might not be effective because Peter believes that he would be fooling the chairman with phony self-esteem, and that deception in itself would make him sad. Even more important, this sort of encounter is at most a partial cause of Peter's depression, and hence devoting much time and energy to this particular habit-building might miss the mark with him. For some other people, the first attempt at such habit-building may be so traumatic that they can't get started habit-building, as with a person who has been thrown off a horse. But for those people for whom interpersonal problems such as this one are at the root of their depression, such habit-building may successfully remove the cause of negative self-comparisons by improving their numerators, and hence alleviate their depression.

I often begin to get depressed thinking about an upcoming day or two during which there will be events that I think will be a burden upon me and in which I expect not to be very effective. I then get anxious about getting through the time, and with the anxiety comes a tightening of the stomach. I have trained myself to the habit that when I feel my stomach tightening I say to myself, 'Hold on, will the day really be a terribly great burden? And will it really be a terrible disaster—for myself and for others—if it does not go super-well? No. So relax.' The habit of responding to my stomach-tightening signal in this fashion works to modify my behavior and my self-comparisons, and hence improves my mood.

Behavior-modification therapy is a systematic approach to controlling one's behavior and thoughts by teaching oneself new habits, with the aid of positive and negative reinforcements—that is, rewards and punishments—with the emphasis on the reward. An ape can be taught to work a machine properly with rewards of food, and later with rewards of tokens which the ape has been taught to associate with food. The behavior of persons in insane asylums has been made more helpful and appropriate with a system that rewards good behavior with points that can be used to obtain various good things. This sort of behavioral training perfectly complements cognitive therapy. Both approaches aim to change how depressives think. Cognitive therapists have concentrated on improving people's logic by showing them how they can think better, and behavior therapists have concentrated on the use of rewards to stamp in the improved thinking habits.

Behavior-modification therapy can help people stop smoking by having a person reward himself with a treat each time the person skips smoking a cigarette, or even when the person avoids *thinking* about smoking for a period of time, perhaps together with keeping a diary of such thoughts and actions. Similarly, behavior-modification researchers claim that it is possible to reduce unfavorable self-comparisons and increase pleasant (favorable) self-comparisons by teaching you to do something you like—perhaps looking out the window—each time you have a positive thought. The pleasurable relaxed feeling that I get in my viscera and muscles when I say, 'Don't criticize. Breathe slowly, and relax your belly', is an example of such a reward.

But the rewards for habit-building need not be the short-term rewards of a lozenge or a work-break with a look out the window. Millions of people have broken the old habit of smoking and developed the new habit of refusing cigarettes, and not thinking about smoking, with the help of the long-run rewards of a longer life expectation and the feeling of better health. Behavioral therapy may help people overcome such problems as smoking, and it may help some who cannot succeed another way. But it clearly is not the *only* way in which to get that job done.

In the 1920s, a Frenchman named Coué claimed that one could heal oneself of mental sickness by repeating, a certain number of times per day, 'Every day, and in every way, I am becoming better and better'. And apparently this method had some successes.

But to claim too much for habit formation and behavior modification—that is, to claim that they can cure all aspects of all depression without any other methods—is dangerous. A depressive whose hopes are raised high by such claims, and then finds that the claims are not well-founded, can become even more depressed. This can lead to the conclusion that no therapy can work, and hence finish her attempts to cure the depression.

SUMMARY

Finding out that you are not as bad as you think you are—that is, learning that the facts show you in a better light than you usually see yourself in—may be a short and effective route to overcoming sadness and depression. People can and do distort the facts about any of the aspects of their lives that are important to them. So it makes sense first to check whether you can improve the numerator in your self-comparison Mood Ratio.

Some people induce negative self-comparisons and sadness because they incorrectly assess the actual states of their lives. If you are one of them, you can cut sadness and depression by identifying your patterns of incorrect self-assessments, and then train yourself to correct them, or not make such assessments at all.

SWEETENING YOUR DENOMINATOR

Remember that when told that life is hard, Voltaire asked, "Compared to what?" One's actual state, almost no matter how bad it is in objective terms, can only cause sadness when you compare it to some benchmark hypothetical state of affairs, the denominator in your self-comparisons Mood Ratio.

Whether a self-comparison is positive or negative depends on the benchmark standard of comparison as well as the perceived facts of your life. (The latter was discussed at length in Chapter 12.) Many cases of depression can best be attacked by changing the benchmark state. This chapter discusses how that may be done.

People we consider 'normal' tend to adjust their denominators flexibly in such fashion that they will feel good about themselves. They seem to do this almost automatically, but in fact they may give considerable thought to the process, and the change may require a fair amount of time and pain to accomplish. Nevertheless, non-depressive people do alter their denominators for their well-being when necessary. In contrast, depressives—people with a propensity for depression —usually have a tendency to hang onto their denominators even when afflicted by them.

People are not *wholly* free to alter their denominators for the sake of emotional comfort. A woman who has trained to be a professional tennis player cannot reasonably take much pleasure from entering local club tournaments and doing well. An even stronger case: a man who was paralyzed in an accident should not expect to have no unusual difficulty in maintaining a merry mood. A dog may be unaware of having lost a leg and hopping peculiarly on three legs, but humans almost surely have a consciousness of their situations that dogs do not have. One can try to use the facts as they are; the paraplegic may focus on his courage in meeting his terrible fate with fortitude. He may even get satisfaction from participating in wheelchair athletics. But this is not the equivalent of not being paralysed.

This is true in one's occupation as well. If one is striving to make a great scientific discovery but so far without success, it is almost impossible to maintain total serenity as the results continue to be negative, and as others are making better progress.

Depressives can use the following systematic procedure to alter their denominators: 1. First, grasp the importance of the denominator in the Mood Ratio as the standard of comparison. 2. Then, accept that your denominator *can* be changed, and that *you* can change it, though of course you may decide not to do so. 3. Next, consider whether you are *willing* to change your denominator, that is, whether you are willing to exert the effort as well as give up any rewards (including the benefits of depression) that you obtain for yourself from the old denominator.

This procedure for helping you change your denominator to one that will produce fewer negative self-comparisons is described in this chapter. Chapter 18 discusses Values Treatment, which is a more radical procedure for changing your denominators and other aspects of your Self-Comparisons Mood Ratio.

ALTERING YOUR GOALS AND ASPIRATIONS

The standard of comparison in a denominator may be a) your *former* state; or b) the state in which you think you *ought* to be; or c) the condition in which you *wish* to be; or d) what a *peer* is; or e) it may be a *goal* that you aspire to achieve. Because achievement goals and workaday failures are so commonly implicated in depression in our modern society, let us take them as our examples for discussion here.

William James vividly described how it feels to be depressed about such perceived failures:

> Failure, the failure! so the world stamps us at every turn. We strew it with our blunders, our misdeeds, our lost opportunities, with all the memorials of our inadequacy to our vocation. And with what a damning emphasis does it then blot us out! No easy fine, no mere apology or formal expiation, will satisfy the world's demands, but

> every pound of flesh exacted is soaked with all its blood. The
> subtlest forms of suffering known to man are connected with the
> poisonous humiliations incidental to these results.[1]

Aspirations and achievement goals have a particularly important place in the depressions commonly found in a modern society because success in one's occupation is so important in the evaluation of a person by others and by himself. Hence the comparison between, on the one hand one's actual achievements, and on the other hand the attainments to which one aspires, frequently results in negative self-ratings and consequent sadness. Even if an individual has no special reason to compare herself negatively in this way, but has some generalized need to compare herself negatively on *some* dimension, success is the dimension she will probably pick in a modern, mobile, profession-oriented society.

Therapists and medical doctors faced with depressed (and also anxious) patients have often advised the person to lower or change her goals, even though it has not been part of their theory. For example, psychoanalyst Rubin reports:

> My depressed patient eventually learned that her depression was
> always linked to personal dissatisfaction with herself, to seeming
> "failures." . . . She eventually also learned that her self-hate was
> connected to impossible standards, which required considerable
> reduction to realistic human levels and possibilities . . . She be-
> came aware that to block depression successfully she must realize
> first that she was depressing and putting down angry feelings and
> thoughts about herself and others.[2]

The tactic of changing one's standards derives directly from the view of depression embodied in the self-comparison Mood Ratio: Sadness and depression result from an unfavorable comparison between a person's actual and hypothetical states. The theory and the practice fit perfectly with each other.

Arbitrary Goals

Goals that are obviously arbitrary are the easiest to change, whereas those that are involved with basic values and philosophy of life are hardest to change. If I set a goal of 40 sit-ups a day for this week, that number obviously was selected for what I thought to be my own good, a number that would gradually increase my strength and improve my health, as well as perhaps giving me satisfaction in attaining it. If I cannot nearly achieve that goal and feel helpless to do better—which makes me sad—or if I achieve the 40 sit-ups only with painful effort, then the goal is clearly a poor choice; the goal chosen for my own good is bad for me. Of course I might argue to myself that the gain in strength is more important than the pain of sadness. But if I at least get this argument into the open, and if I recognize that goals are intellectual tools, and in this case the purpose of the goal is my own welfare, then I'm likely to revise the sit-up goal downwards.

Another example of how one arbitrarily chooses a goal—and with it the prospects of failure and sadness—is in a game such as tennis. As a sports psychologist says,

> If you compete with players of ability equal to yours, you are setting yourself up for disappointment about fifty percent of the time. If you compete with players who are more capable than yourself, you set yourself up for an even greater percentage of unsatisfactory games. If you seek out less skilled competitors, you could win all the time, but you wouldn't feel like a winner.[3]

If you are willing to struggle a bit for wisdom, alone or with a therapist, you should find it relatively easy to improve your choice of *arbitrary* goals of this sort, and hence reduce negative self-comparisons and sadness.

Let's work out a specific exercise, for convenience returning to Nancy in Chapter 12 who told herself 'I'm a bad mother'. And let's say that for one reason and another, Nancy is not convinced by the analysis of her numerator given there. And she now says, 'Eleanor is the kind of mother I should be'.

You respond to Nancy as follows: 'Is Eleanor an average mother? Does she have an outside job or do volunteer work?'

Nancy: 'She devotes herself entirely to her children'.

You: 'Is that ordinary behavior?'

Nancy: 'No, she's an unusually good mother, the best one I know.'

You: 'Why do you compare yourself to her?'

Nancy: 'Because I should be as good as I can be, and she shows how good a mother can be.'

(Notice how skilled a depressive like Nancy can be in making her comparisons seem logical.)

You: 'Does Eleanor bring home a paycheck the way you do? Does she serve as president of Mothers Against Drunk Driving as you do? Does she do anything else besides be a mother?'

Nancy: 'That's enough.'

You: 'Maybe it's enough for her, but what's that got to do with you? Remember, you said you are a *bad* mother, not less devoted a mother than Eleanor—if that is good for the kids, anyway. To whom is it reasonable to compare yourself as a mother?'

After considerable more argumentation, Nancy sees the point. (We assume so for brevity; the fact is that she might out-logic anyone on this point.) And when she does see that Eleanor is not an appropriate comparison, and she *truly* concedes the point, her denominator will become less harsh and her Mood Ratio will become more Rosy.

Goals That Are Not Arbitrary

Other goals are less arbitrary and hence more complex. If I set a goal of writing five pages of this book each day, it is obvious that that number was chosen relative to what I think I can do, and relative to what I have done in the past. But I might say to myself that I ought to set the goal so as to get the maximum output from my productive capacities. If I think that way, deeper values—a matter to which we shall come shortly—as well as my psychological history are then also involved. This is more complex and harder to deal with than the number of sit-ups that I do.

The person who never clearly chooses a single direction, or decides on an achievement goal, has another sort of goal-setting problem. As Montaigne said: "No wind favors him who has no destined port."[4] That sometimes describes me in my occupation. (The rest of this paragraph and the next one were written in 1977, and is less true as of 1993). I start with the value that a person should contribute to society what he can, and with the belief that I have some talent (for research and writing) that should be harnessed to make a noticeable social contribution. But beyond this I have no well-defined goal. And I always feel that what I do is not enough, not sufficiently good. I find fault with most or all the pieces of work I've done, even those that I believe are technically excellent, because they have not produced the social changes I hoped they might, or because they have not started more than a few people thinking in new ways, or because they did not persuade many of my colleagues. If I can't find anything wrong with the idea or the research itself, I criticize myself for having failed because I appear too unconventional, or did not write it simply enough (or complexly enough), or did not make it seem more interesting and palatable to others, or did not concentrate enough on it and spend enough extra time presenting new versions of it and giving talks and writing letters and buttonholing people, and so on and so on.

Clearly I have not succeeded in developing an appropriate denominator. A wiser person than I might revise her goals downward by telling herself that experience has proven these goals to be too high to attain. For my own welfare, and with little likely loss to society, I probably should aspire to do less, or at least try not to feel that it is *necessary* that I do as much as is humanly possible. Or, a wiser person in my situation might simply force herself to choose entirely new sorts of goals—say, spending most of her time advising student research, and writing only texts. But I have not been successful in operating on my goals with these approaches. (Perhaps a wise counselor could have led me to do so. Instead I dealt with the consequences of these goals with Values Treatment, to be discussed in Chapter 18.) But fortunately I

Table 3

Uninvited thought	Causal Event	Self-Comparison
'I'm a bad mother.'	Note from son's teacher	I should be like Eleanor A.

have found other ways of reducing neg-comps and thereby avoiding sadness and depression.

Wants and Oughts

A common cause of depression located in the denominator is the belief that one 'ought' to do or be something that one is not or does not do. Just as imprecise language can produce numerator problems, so it can sour your denominator, especially by turning statements of your tastes or desires into statements of more obligations. Albert Ellis coined the term 'musturbating' for the practice of telling yourself that you must do this or be that—make a lot of money, keep your temper under control, or go to church regularly. Depressives also believe that if they do *not* do what they believe that they 'must' do, something terrible will happen, perhaps a punishment of some sort. 'Awfulizing', 'horribilizing', and 'catastrophizing' are the terms Ellis uses for this belief in terrible consequences of not doing what one believes one must.

If you are afflicted with 'musturbating' and 'catastrophizing',

Analysis	*Response*
Denominator: Is Eleanor the appropriate person with whom I should compare myself?	Eleanor is atypical.

examine the basis of your beliefs about what you 'must' do, and the terrible consequences you believe will ensue if you don't do it.

As to the notion of 'must' or 'ought': Usually it is more correct to say that you *want* to do or be certain things. Any 'must' or 'ought' is just one of your wants, but converted into a command that turns the desire into a compulsion. Is it an important enough want to be sad about? And after you think about it as a 'want' rather than an 'ought', do you still feel as strongly about it as before? Are you as disturbed about not satisfying the 'must' as before?

As to the consequences of not doing what you think you 'must', ask yourself: Why must you finish college? Will you be unable to make a living if you don't? Will people you like refuse your company if you don't? Will you be a bad person if you don't? Or do you think you must finish college because a relative once told you that you 'must', when you were a child?

You may experience an extraordinary sense of relief when you suddenly conclude that you *don't* have to do something or be something you believed that you 'must'. You can feel free as a bird and light as a feather after feeling weighted down and overloaded by the unwelcome burden. Try for yourself! Ask yourself honestly: Why *must* I do——? And what will happen if I don't?

Ellis and Harper retrain people as follows:

> When clients (in individual or group therapy) state, 'I must work harder at the office', or 'I should not hate my mate', we frequently interrupt them with: 'You mean, "It would prove better if you worked harder at the office", or "You preferably should not hate your mate".'[5]

When you shed these unnecessary oughts and musts, you lighten and sweeten your denominator, and remove the sources of much sadness and depression.

SWEETENING YOUR DENOMINATOR BY COUNTING YOUR BLESSINGS

There is a long and honorable tradition of writers who reduce sadness by inspiring people to 'think positively', ranging from Bertrand Russell[6] to Norman Vincent Peale, with lots of lesser writers in between them intellectually.

This method is simple: you remind yourself how well off you are compared to the situation you *might* be in. The mechanism works this way: you shift to a radically different standard of comparison than you begin with. Instead of comparing your minor arthritis with perfect and painless freedom of movement, you shift to comparing yourself with a paralytic. Instead of comparing your daughter who just threw a stone through the neighbor's window with a kid that never gets into trouble, you compare her against a really delinquent child, or a child that lacks vitality enough even to get into trouble. Instead of comparing your third-highest salary raise to that of the person in your office who gets the biggest raise, you compare it to the average or the lowest raise.

Different people use different devices to shift their denominators to those that make their present situations seem blessed. My own practice is that whenever I feel myself sinking into unfavorable self-comparisons in work or family situation, I ask myself 'Compared to what?' This usually serves to jolt me into seeing the absurdity of considering myself as ill-served by life when so many people that I can think of are much worse-served in that particular respect. Then I'm amused at myself, and sadness is behind me (if the device happens to be working that day).

Does this anti-depression tactic seem more like philosophy than psychology? Choose the label you like. But more and more, the wisest psychologists have come to view many (though not all) depressions as philosophical in origin, and therefore as requiring a change of philosophy for a cure; some philosophers have known this for thousands of years. William James made this very clear when he talked of the depressive as a "sick soul". And Ellis and Harper put the matter bluntly: "For effecting *permanent* and *deep-seated* emotional changes, philosophic changes appear virtually necessary."[7]

Certainly there is nothing wrong with the technique of counting your blessings. Professional counselors often use it to good effect. And it often works for all of us when we are sad in a mild or transient way. Why, then, is it not a sufficient cure for all depression?

There are several reasons why 'count your blessings' therapy alone is often insufficient to pull a person out of deep depression. 1. Much mental energy is required to focus on your blessings, just as it is hard work to keep one's eye fixed firmly on the ball in tennis or golf; depressed persons often lack the necessary energy. 2. Pain from a particular source—physical or mental—may be sufficiently intense to prevent concentration on something else. (Remember your lack of complete success in distracting yourself when the dentist is drilling?) Furthermore, you must believe that your blessings are important relative to other aspects of your life in order to focus on them, and many depressives have mechanisms that systematically act to devalue their objective blessings.

James put it this way:

> The method of averting one's attention from evil, and living simply in the light of good is splendid as long as it will work. It will work with many persons; it will work far more generally than most of us are ready to suppose, and within the sphere of its successful operation there is nothing to be said against it as a religious solution. But it breaks down impotently as soon as melancholy comes; and even though one be quite free from melancholy one's self, there is no doubt that healthy-mindedness is inadequate as a philosophical doctrine, because the evil facts which it refuses positively to account for are a genuine portion of reality; and they may after all be the best key to life's significance, and possibly the only openers of our eyes to the deepest levels of truth.[8]

Perhaps the most important reason, however, why 'count your blessings' doesn't do the whole job with some people is that a person must 'want' to achieve the good feelings that come with counting one's blessings. If you believe that you *ought* to count your blessings, or to achieve good feeling, then you might be disposed to do so. But if you have had little experience in your lifetime with simple good feeling, this goal will not seem a reasonable or achievable one. More about this in Chapter 18 on Values Treatment.

SWEETENING THE DENOMINATOR BY LEARNING YOUR HISTORY

Learning how and why you acquired certain benchmark standards of comparison can often make it easier for you to change your denominator. This is often a matter of realizing that you did not choose the standard yourself on the basis of reasonable experience and thought, but rather the standard was thrust upon you. Then you can be responsive to Ellis's *command* (!) that you not let yourself be commanded to accept any goal or standard that others have set for you, or that you have set for yourself; this is the heart of his method for overcoming depression.

Take, for example, my mother always telling me (surely with the best of intentions) that I could do better than I had done. This caused me to feel that I had accomplished less than I *ought* to have accomplished (and less than I *had* accomplished). After I came to understand that as an adult I criticize *myself* in the same way that my mother criticized me as a child, I could then take the next step— understanding that I am not obligated to accept my mother's point of view about this; I am not required always to judge that I could do better, always to get closer to perfection. And with that discovery I learned to say to myself 'Don't criticize' every time I hear myself saying, in imitation of my mother, 'You can do better', or 'That's not up to the standard you should reach'. And with that discovery I took the first step on the road to conquering depression (though in itself this did not, and could not, cure me of depression, for my own idiosyncratic reasons; more about that later.)

The Freudian method known as psychoanalysis is essentially a technique for self-discovery, and especially for learning about one's childhood, which is assumed by Freudians to be necessary for a cure. Delving into memories of one's early years usually takes place in several hour-long weekly sessions over the course of several years. Discovery of the causes of your contemporary behavior and feelings—for example, the causes of your contemporary negative self-comparisons and depression—might be enough to cure your depression, because the necessary change in your behavior and outlook may be obvious. But more likely, the discovery is not enough, though it can be used as valuable input to careful thinking about your present and future.

In contrast cognitive-behavioral therapy does not find that examining one's childhood memories is usually crucial in overcoming depression.

The learning gained in psychoanalysis may come from dredging up forgotten or repressed memories of childhood events. This can be a sudden illumination induced by free association or related techniques. Or the learning may come from creating a new set of experiences to offset the old ones, for example, learning that one can trust a therapist and other people after coming to believe as a child that all other persons are untrustworthy, or that one is helpless to deal successfully with other people. This learning is closely related to the more recently-developed method of Interpersonal Therapy, which has had considerable success in helping depressed people. And if the focus is on learning that one is capable of dealing with other people rather than being helpless, the learning is related to Seligman's approach to depression, discussed in Chapter 17. Once more, different therapeutic strokes help different folks, but all of these approaches fit nicely into the general intellectual framework of Self-Comparisons Analysis.

Psychoanalysis intends that a patient identify, relive, and understand childhood experiences—either traumatic experiences such as losing a parent, or repeated experiences such as being criticized for not doing better in school. The aim is that the person learn that the childhood experiences were not what they are subconsciously remembered to be—that all relationships need not be the same as the person's relationships with his or her parents, and that as an adult the person need not be obedient to the dictates of his or her parents in the past. That is, like behavior-modification and cognitive therapies, psychoanalysis is supposed to be a special process of learning (and unlearning) with respect to negative self-comparisons.

With respect to traumatic childhood experiences, a person can learn to recognize the continuing influence of the childhood event, to understand its impact, and perhaps to lessen its tension by reliving it in a context where it is no longer so terrible. For example, Joan H., a woman of 35 who relived in therapy the death of her mother when she was seven, came to understand that the deprivation she felt at seven no longer applies at 35. That is, the difference between being a woman of 35 *without* a mother versus being a woman of 35 *with* a mother is much less important than the difference between having a mother versus not having a mother *at age seven*. If Joan recognizes that the traumatic loss—a huge negative self-comparison—that she experienced at seven (and still remembers vividly) no longer applies, then she can feel less sad.

Another aspect of reliving traumatic experiences is that a person can finally get the facts straight, and hence get rid of damaging misconceptions. For example, many children whose parents (or siblings) die in childhood actually feel responsible for the event, believing that the death happened through the child's neglect or misbehavior. Joan was such a person. As an adult, she can finally realize that her mother's heart attack did not occur because Joan was being too noisy, and hence she can now shed that horrible guilty self-comparison, and with it the attendant sadness. This is really an improvement in one's numerator, the perceived facts of one's life, but I've mentioned it here for convenience.

With respect, now, to *non-traumatic* childhood experiences: understanding one's history can also have beneficial effects in reducing negative self-comparisons, as illustrated by the story about my mother and me just above. Knowledge of one's history also can help you understand why your inner logic leads you to *choose* being depressed, if this is your pattern. This observation may convince you that the benefits of self-pity in depression may not be worth the pain. Being obviously depressed may be effective for a child by inducing others to show pity and love. But exhibitions of depression by adults tend to turn away other people. The people most needing love are usually the least lovable, someone once said.

So, a device that was successful for the child, and therefore made into a habit, may be counterproductive as an adult. If the adult recognizes this change in circumstances, and correctly evaluates the cost/benefit ratio of adult depression, the adult may quit the habit. Of course the direct pleasures of self-pity may continue to outweigh the pains of depression, in which case the depression will continue to be relatively attractive. But with the recognition that depression is not a profitable tactic outwardly, the balance may tip away from choosing to be depressed.

It may also be helpful to understand destructive patterns of interpersonal relationships learned in childhood. For example, my difficulty in dealing with bosses stems from my childhood relationship with my father. I concluded that he did not have my interests at heart but rather only his own. I never felt he could be believed, or relied upon to deal honestly with me. Psychoanalysts believe that, without psychoanalytic reliving of the event it would be a waste of time in a case like mine to try to build a *habit* of dealing confidently with a boss. They believe that unless one goes back to the original problem, cleans out the Stygian stables and builds a new solid groundwork, one cannot have a psychologically-safe future. In this case a psychoanalyst would attempt to show me, by laboriously building a trustworthy relationship with me—that is, by laying a new groundwork of interpersonal experience—that all relationships need not be like the relationship I had with my father. In this way, the psychoanalytic therapy might improve my numerator, that is, my view of my possibilities.

It is as if psychoanalysts say that one can never simply replace a bad faucet successfully; the past will always ruin such simple replacements unless one replaces all the old plumbing and hence gets the past straightened out.

Psychoanalytic inspection of the past—whether by yourself, as was mostly the case with me, or with a therapist—certainly may be of value in discovering the historical sources of contemporary negative self-comparisons. But in the majority of cases professional psychoanalysis is of dubious value for treating depression:

> Most psychoanalysts will not treat patients with clearcut depression for a number of reasons. First, the energy-depletion process, however they may understand it, contributes a pathogenic factor which strongly resists psychoanalysis. Second, the frankly depressed patient usually has insufficient interest in treatment to be able to pursue the arduous regimen of psychoanalysis. Third, the frankly depressed patient is too miserable to have patience for analysis. Moreover there are far too many depressed patients to be treated by psychoanalysts, and psychoanalysis is far too costly for most individuals.[9]

In my own case, I did not want to spend the time or money to reflect at length with a therapist about my childhood relationship with my parents. Furthermore, psychoanalysis by itself does not have a very good statistical record of relieving depression, even after prolonged therapy. In contrast, cognitive therapy has been proven successful in controlled tests.

GETTING THE HABIT OF A SWEET DENOMINATOR

After you have decided to substitute a new and less demanding denominator for the harsh old one, you must build the *habit* of implementing that decision. With such a habit, your 'insight' and decision to change the denominator becomes more than just a bit of interesting self-knowledge. The principles of building such a habit are similar to those we discussed for improving your numerator.

An illustration: Basil T. is a small businessman who makes a decent living—but only a decent living. No Cadillac for him, no three-month trips down the Nile for his family, no fat portfolio of stocks and bonds. Basil used to spend most of his hours working around his store. When he wasn't working he felt sad because he wasn't getting enough done, or earning enough; he was frequently depressed. Then Basil came to understand that his sadness arose from the negative self-comparison between his actual income and what he felt he *ought* to earn. And it was easy for him to figure out why he felt he *ought* to have an upper-middle-class income, and *ought* to be able to afford luxury rather than just a decent living.

In the extended family in which Basil grew up, the only mark of success was being 'rich'. Basil long ago decided that he rejected this benchmark standard. But he kept on with his workaholic schedule, and continued to be depressed, until he built the habit that resolved the problem. He built the habit of saying to himself, 'Stop pushing, you've got enough', together with taking in a deep relaxing breath deep in his abdomen, each time he noticed himself thinking 'You aren't getting any work done'. And Basil found that he liked his new, more-relaxed way of life well enough so that it reinforced his habit and kept it going. And Basil began to enjoy his life, and afterwards he seldom let depression stay with him for more than a few hours at a time.

The key point about Basil's case is that no single anti-depression tactic by itself was enough. It was necessary that Basil a) understand the role of negative self-comparisons, and the need to reduce them; b) notice that his benchmark standard of an upper-middle class income was depressing him; c) recognize that he held that particular denominator because he carried the ideas of the particular family in which he grew up, rather than because of any objective or logical or moral basis for it; d) decide to change the denominator; and e) build a habit of pushing that benchmark standard out of his thinking as soon as it came in.

SUMMARY

One's actual state, almost no matter how bad it is in objective terms, can only cause sadness when you compare it to some benchmark hypothetical state of affairs, the denominator in your self-comparisons Mood Ratio. That is, whether a self-comparison is positive or negative depends on the benchmark standard of comparison as well as the perceived facts of your life. Many cases of depression can best be attacked by changing the benchmark state. This chapter discusses how that may be done.

People we consider 'normal' tend to adjust their denominators flexibly in such fashion that they will feel good about themselves. In contrast, depressives—people with a propensity for depression—usually have a tendency to hang onto their denominators even when afflicted by them.

You can use the following procedure to alter your denominators: 1. First, recognize the importance of the denominator in the Mood Ratio as the standard of comparison. 2. Then, accept that your denominator *can* be changed, and that *you* can change it, though of course you may decide not to do so. 3. Next, consider whether you are *willing* to change your denominator, that is, whether you are willing to exert the effort as well as give up any rewards (including the benefits of depression) that you obtain for yourself from the old denominator.

CHANGE YOUR DIMENSIONS

Consider some dimension of your life on which you frequently compare yourself negatively. Let's say that you have not found a way to improve your numerator—your perceived actual state of affairs. And you are not prepared to sweeten the denominator—the benchmark state to which you compare yourself. This leaves you with a Mood Ratio which causes you to suffer sadness and depression. The best strategy may be to replace that entire Rotten Ratio with another one—that is, to turn away from that entire dimension of comparison.

There are two related sets of tactics for changing the dimension: a) changing your priorities about the various aspects of your life, and b) focusing your attention on the good things in your life rather than the bad things. Both of these sets of tactics are staples of folk wisdom. And they both call upon our capacity to direct our attention toward some dimensions of our lives and away from others.

COUNTING YOUR BLESSINGS

The device of 'counting your blessings' can be used to change your denominator, by changing the benchmark comparison that you make, as discussed in Chapter 13. Much the same device is used to shift to a more positive dimension for self-comparison. Instead of brooding on lack of job success, you make yourself remember your family's good health. When you lose your money in the stock market, you try to keep in mind your wonderful children.

Literature and folklore are full of stories of people whose brushes with catastrophe turned their lives around by making them realize how well off they were. And others have come to the same conclusion by simply reflecting on this aspect of their lives, and they have overcome depression in that fashion. But counting your blessings is not always enough by itself, as discussed in Chapter 13 on sweetening your denominator. And a great deal of effort often is required to keep the blessings at the center of your attention—sometimes so much effort that the cost seems greater than the benefit.

Counting your blessings can be like a curse when someone *else* tells you how well off you *really* are, and that you have no cause to be depressed. Unless you are able to accept the advice to count your blessings—and usually you are not—then the suggestion that you do so simply makes you more miserable, because it seems to show how little the other person understands your situation and your feelings. The specifics of the blessings to be counted must come from you.

SHIFTING YOUR PRIORITIES

Re-arranging your priorities is a second device for changing Mood Ratio dimensions. A frequent and important example is the person whose actual occupational achievements do not measure up to the person's aspirations, yet is unwilling to scale down his or her aspirations so as to keep the denominator from dominating the numerator. The person may then prevent negative self-comparisons by focusing attention on another related ratio—perhaps the person's courage in persisting against obstacles, or the person's success in helping co-workers achieve important successes in their work.

Bert F. is a poet who has struggled for years to win readers and respect for his poetry, with only occasional small success and never a really big success. Whether it is his ideas or his unconventionally simple style that keep him from succeeding, he does not know. He continues to believe that his poetry is fine and exciting work, but the overwhelming lack of interest in his work on the part of critics finally wore him down and left him depressed. After months of deep sadness, however, he decided that he could at least give himself high marks for courage and fortitude. And now when his mind turns to the failure of his poems, he consciously directs his mind to his courage. This lifts his spirits. There are also many physically-disabled persons who struggle to learn and work against tough odds, and who keep up their spirits with much the same device.

The non-depressive healthy-minded person usually is quite flexible about choosing dimensions on which to compare himself or herself— often, more flexible than friends and associates would like. The man who doesn't support his family because he seldom has a job tells himself and his family that he is a good father because he spends so much of his time with his children. And the university professor who does no research takes pride in his teaching, and insists that teaching is more important than research for the purpose of deciding salaries; the professor who does lots of good research but teaches badly argues exactly the opposite. But depressive personalities usually do not use this escape hatch.

You can go beyond changing the dimensions you focus on, and actually shift your life goals. Instead of aiming for financial success, you may decide to concentrate on the number of people you help get a start in life. Instead of aiming for popularity, you may aim at moral purity.

This anecdote—in answer to a question put to former astronaut Edwin E. Aldrin, Jr. who suffered much mental pain—shows how a person may shift to new dimensions of life to find happiness:

> Question: "What was your most positive experience as an astro-naut, and how has it helped you in your life today?"
>
> Aldrin: "The aftermath of Apollo II made me realize that I had no idea what I was looking for in my life. It took hospitalization for psychiatric treatment and the acceptance of myself as an alcoholic to make me see that faith, hope and love for people are infinitely better goals than individual achievement."[1]

Some people, however, are not flexible in their choice of dimensions on which to compare themselves; they now cannot choose at will the best 'product line' for them to carry. For some people this is a matter of basic values: they refuse to accord importance to characteristics simply because it is psychologically convenient to do so.

In some cases people seem to get stuck with dimensions that cause them sadness because of values implanted in childhood and unexamined since then. For example, that one should get maximum formal education, or that one should not think ungodly thoughts. In some other cases, people seem to purposely focus only on dimensions which make them look bad in their self-comparisons; people who live fine lives but insist on being guilt-ridden because they think they don't do enough, say, for their aged relatives.

How can you, even if you are the type that doesn't typically change dimensions of evaluation to suit your own psychological convenience, do so anyway? One way is to force yourself to do so in the name of a higher value. This is another example of Values Treatment (see Chapter 18); this tactic cured me of my 13-year-long depression. The higher value was the welfare of my children, which I came to believe was being threatened by my continued depression. In my hierarchy of values, the welfare of my children is most important.

Another fundamental value for me, I discovered, is that a person enjoy life for the gift that I believe it to be, rather than to live as if life were no better than death. Therefore, I decided that I simply would not allow myself to make comparisons of my actual occupational achievements to the aspirations I have had for my work, or to the achievements of some others whose work has been better received than mine. I determined that whenever such comparisons came into my mind I would either turn my mind toward other comparisons, such as the wonderful health of our family relative to the bad health that luck could have given us, or to the happy home life I mostly have, or to the useful role I play in the lives of some friends and colleagues, or the peacefulness of our community—or else I would make no comparisons at all. (More about this later.)

CHANGE WHAT YOU PAY ATTENTION TO

You may wonder: Is it really possible to alter your own thinking so as to change your ratios of comparison—just by effort and will? Yes, it is. This may be easier to accept if you notice that how we feel and what we think about is influenced by what we pay attention to. And we have some choice about what we pay attention to, just as we choose one television program or another. For example, one year I had annoyed feelings toward the neighbors on our south side, while I was very fond of our neighbors on the north side. Why is it that some weeks I thought more often about the south-side neighbors than in other weeks, while not changing how much I thought about the north-side neighbors? I found I could alter this pattern by deciding to do so. And by doing so I could influence how much of the time I was angry.

Investigating your personal history for the origins of the dimensions on which you evaluate yourself can sometimes help you give up some dimensions that have held you prisoner in depression. Psychotherapy can sometimes discover these origins. And you may then be prepared to acknowledge that you need not be stuck with your old dimensions, but rather are free to choose dimensions that fit your needs for a happy life. Once having made the decision to shift to one or more new dimensions, the various devices of habit formation, as discussed in Chapter 10, help you implement your resolve to turn your back on the old dimensions, and turn your mind toward the new ones.

Overgeneralizing one or more specific dimensions of comparison to the dimension of *you as a person* is very common for depressives, and it is extraordinarily destructive. Instead of saying 'I was not able to do what was required to succeed in that job' a depressive says 'I'm worthless as a person'. Ellis and Harper emphasize this mechanism, referring to it as "rating yourself". They urge you instead to focus on the *specifics* of your performance on particular dimensions, and upon the specific implications of poor performance where it occurs, rather than generalizing to overall lack of personal worth. I'll quote one of Harper's cases at length, partly because it offers another chance to see their sort of counseling skill in action:

> Geraldine [was] a highly intelligent and efficient 33-year-old female client who came to see me (R.A.H.) about six months after she obtained a divorce. Although she had felt decidedly unhappy in her marriage to an irresponsible and dependent husband, she had gotten no happier since her divorce. Her husband had drunk to excess, run around with other women, and lost many jobs. But when she came to see me, she wondered if she had made a mistake in divorcing him. I said:
>
> "Why do you think you made a mistake by divorcing your husband?"
>
> "Because I consider divorce wrong," she replied. "I think when people get married, they should stay married."
>
> "Yet you do not belong to a religious group that takes that

position. You do not believe that heaven somehow makes and seals marriages, do you?"

"No, I don't even believe in a heaven. I just *feel* wrong about getting divorced and I blame myself for having gotten one. I have felt even more miserable since I got it than I felt when living with my husband."

"But look," I asked, "where do you think your feelings about the wrongness of divorce originated? Do you think you had them at birth? Do you think that humans have built-in feelings, like built-in taste buds, that tell them how to distinguish right from wrong? Your buds tell you what tastes salty, sweet, sour, or bitter. Do your feelings tell you what proves right or wrong?"

The young divorcee laughed. "You make it sound pretty silly. No, I don't suppose I have inborn feelings about right or wrong. I had to learn to feel as I do."

Seeing a good opening, I rushed in where less directive and less rational therapists often fear to tread. "Exactly," I said. "You had to learn to feel as you do. Like all humans, you started life with tendencies to learn, including tendencies to learn strong prejudices—such as those about divorce. And what you learned you can unlearn or modify. So even though you don't hold fundamentalist faith in the immorality of divorce, you could have easily picked up this idea—probably from your parents, school-teachers, stories, or movies. And the idea that you picked up, simply stated, says:

"Only bad people get divorces. I got a divorce. So I must qualify as a bad person. Yes, I must acknowledge my real rotten-ness! Oh, what a no-good, awful, terrible person!"

"Sounds dreadfully familiar," she said with a rather bitter laugh.

"It certainly does," I resumed. "Some such sentences as these probably started going through your mind—otherwise you would not feel as disturbed as you do. Over and over again, you have kept repeating this stuff. And then you have probably gone on to say to yourself:

"'Because I did this horrible thing of getting a divorce, I deserve *damnation* and *punishment* for my dreadful act. I deserve to feel even more miserable and unhappy than when I lived with that lousy husband of mine.'"

She ruefully smiled, "Right again!"

"So of course," I continued, "you have felt unhappy. Anyone who spends a good portion of her waking hours thinking of herself as a terrible person and how much she *deserves* misery because of her rottenness (notice, if you will, the circular thinking involved in all this)—any such person will almost certainly feel miserable. If I, for example, started telling myself right this minute that I had no value because I never learned to play the violin, to ice-skate, or to win at tiddly-winks—if I kept telling myself this kind of bosh, I could quickly make myself feel depressed.

"Then I could also tell myself, in this kind of sequence, how much I *deserved* to feel unhappy because, after all, I had my chance to learn to play the violin or championship tiddly-winks, and I had messed up these chances. And what a real worthless skunk this made me! Oh, my God, what a *real* skunk!"

My client, by this time, seemed highly amused, as I satirically kept emphasizing my doom. "I make it sound silly," I said. "But with a purpose—to show you that *you* act just as foolishly when you start giving yourself the business about your divorce."

"I begin to understand what you mean," she said. "I *do* say this kind of thing to myself. But how can I stop? Don't you see quite a difference between divorce, on the one hand, and violin-playing or tiddly-winks, on the other hand?"

"Granted. But has your getting a divorce really made you any more horrible, terrible, or worthless than my not learning to play the fiddle?"

"Well, you'll have to admit that I made a serious mistake when I married such an irresponsible person as my husband. And maybe if I had behaved more maturely and wisely myself, I could have helped him to grow up."

"O.K., agreed. You did make a mistake to marry him in the first place. And, quite probably, you did so because you behaved immaturely at the time of your marriage. All right, so you made a mistake, a neurotic mistake. But does this mean that you deserve punishment the rest of your life by having to live forever with your mistake?"

"No, I guess not. But how about a wife's responsibility to her husband? Don't you think that I should have stayed with him and tried to help him get over his severe problems?"

"A very lovely, and sometimes even practical, thought. But didn't you tell me that you tried to help him and he refused even to acknowledge that he had disturbances? And didn't you say that he strongly opposed your going for any kind of therapy during your marriage, let alone his going for help, too?"

"Yes, he did. The mere mention of the word *psychologist* or *marriage counselor* sent him into a fit of temper. He'd never think of going or even letting me go for help."

"The main thing you could have done, then, would have involved playing psychotherapist to him, and in your state, you'd hardly have proved effective at that. Why beat yourself down? You made a mistake in marrying. You did your best to do something to rectify it after marriage. You got blocked, mainly by your husband, but partly by your own feelings of severe upset, on both counts. So you finally got out of the marriage, as almost any reasonably sane person would have done. Now what crime have you committed? Why do you *insist* on blaming yourself? You think, erroneously, your unhappy situation makes you miserable. But does the situation—or what you keep telling yourself *about* this situation?"

"I begin to see your point. Although my marital situation never has felt good, you seem to say that I don't *have* to give myself such a hard time about it. Quite a point of view you have there!"

"Yes, I like it myself—and often use it in my own life. But now if we can only help you to make it *your* point of view, not because *I* hold it but because you figure out that it really will work better for you, not even a poor marriage and an as yet difficult divorce situation will faze you. In fact, if I can really help you to adopt this viewpoint, I can't imagine anything that will ever bother you too much."

"You really mean that, don't you?"

"Mean it, hell—I *believe* it!"

And so, to some extent, did this young divorcee, after another few months of rational-emotive therapy. Whereas she previously kept telling herself how far from ideally and how horribly she behaved for not achieving this ideal, she now began to substitute problem-solving, internalized sentences for her old self-beatings. In one of her last conferences with me, she said: "You know, I looked into the mirror yesterday morning and said to myself, 'Geraldine, you behave like a happy, fairly bright, increasingly mature, growingly efficient kid. I keep getting mighty fond of you.' And then I laughed with real joy."

"Fine," I said. "But don't lead yourself up the path of rating you, Geraldine, highly because you act so much better. For then you will have to rate yourself lowly, once again, if and when you act worse. Try to stick to: 'I like *behaving* so much better' rather than 'I like *me* for doing this good behavior!'"

"Yes, I see what you mean," she replied. "I feel glad you warned me about that. Rating *myself* I unfortunately do most easily. But I'll fight it!"

This client discovered that her feelings did not derive from her unsuccessful marriage or her divorce but from her evaluations of *herself* in regard to these 'failures'. When she changed the kinds of thoughts (or internalized sentences) she fed herself, her emotions changed from depression and despair to sorrow and regret—

and these *appropriate* negative feelings helped motivate her to change the conditions of her life. Not all clients, like Geraldine, see so quickly that they cause their own depressed feelings about divorce and *decide* to accept themselves. Sometimes they may require months or years of therapy before they come to this decision. But persistence, on their and their therapist's part, certainly helps!'"[2]

In summary, shifting the dimensions on which you evaluate yourself can be a potent weapon against depression. And even if it is not enough by itself, it is a valuable complement to other tactics.

PRACTICAL STEPS FOR KEEPING JOYFUL DIMENSIONS IN YOUR MIND

Now that you know *what* to do, you need to know *how to do it*. And as anyone knows who has tried to count blessings when feeling low, it is not easy to keep your mind from drifting away from a rosy dimension to a rotten dimension. Practical tips should therefore be welcome.

Let's review how the 'I never do anything right' woman in Chapter 10 changed her dimensions. Upon reflection and argument with herself, she recognized that timeliness at meetings is not the most important dimension of her life, or even an important dimension, because she almost never goes to meetings. And in general she does things well. So instead she decided to focus on the dimension of her overall work performance, for which her firm had given her special awards in two of the last three years.

Let's try another example. I frequently criticize myself for conducting my professional life very unwisely. I'll say things to myself like 'If you would only stick to one subject, and not keep moving to develop new ideas, you would increase the chances of acceptance of *some* big idea, and you'd make a bigger contribution that way.' So I write that in column 1. In column 2 I write the usual precipitating event. And in column 3 I write who I am comparing myself with, those people who do *not* leap from one subject to another.

Now I analyze the situation. I realize that there is an important benefit, too, in my not sticking to one subject. If I had stuck to one thing from the beginning, I would have stuck to one of my first two

Table 4

Uninvited thought	*Causal Event*	*Self-Comparison*
'I never do anything right.'	Late for a meeting	I do fewer things right than do most people.

subjects, neither of which was as important or interesting as several things I have worked on since then. And at least two of the subjects that I have worked on have produced positive results beyond my wildest dreams. Therefore, it makes sense for me to accept the bad with the good, and realize that my 'vice' of following after new ideas has its virtues, as the French would say, and the good outweighs the bad. It makes sense, then, not to focus on this dimension and make myself unhappy with it. Instead I might focus on the success of some of the things that I have done, or upon the fact that my family is healthy and in good shape, or that (aside from controversial political issues) the world is now in better condition than ever before in history.

Building habits and behavioral feedback patterns offers help in keeping you focused on appropriate dimensions. Imagine that a friend could read your mind, and every time you were dwelling on a rotten dimension, the friend would jab you in the ribs and say 'Change that ratio' or 'Count your blessings'. That assistance would be useful.

The trick is to act like that friend. And indeed, you *can* read your own mind. The problem is to build the habit of changing it when a

Analysis	Response	Behavior to change
Dimension: Is your timeliness at meetings an important aspect of your life?	Of course not.	Focusing on a dimension which a) you need not attribute importance to, and b) does not reflect well upon you.

rotten dimension comes into your mind. The solution is to 'chain' the change-it habit to some cue that can remind you to do so. For example, as I mentioned earlier, my stomach often gets tight when I have a neg-comp in mind. I have trained myself that as soon as I feel my stomach tighten, I force myself to smile and to breathe deeply. And when I abuse myself about something I did not do well, and say 'You silly shit', I put into action the habit I have built of adding 'Now *that's* damn ridiculous.'

Computers use a device called an 'interrupt' to break into the current program in order to change what the computer is doing. The trick is to build an interrupt into every 'program' in your mind that plays out a Rotten Ratio, and chain to the interrupt an instruction to play out a program with a Rosy Ratio.

Another example from my experience: Fact 1: Thanksgiving is the favorite holiday in my family; Rita, the kids, and I all enjoy it greatly. Fact 2: I heard a young woman remark about writing her parents at Thanksgiving because she could not get home. I immediately felt the jab of pain from a negative emotion, accompanied by the thought of a

Table 5

Uninvited thought	Causal Event	Self-Comparison
I fail to stick to one subject.	My profession ignores one of my works.	Other social scientists who concentrate on one subject and are successful.

stack of letters that I had wanted to get out at Thanksgiving but are still delayed; the matter is annoying but not the least bit serious. When I felt the sadness, I half-consciously and half-automatically examined the uninvited thought. And my analysis led to the judgment that the unsent letters are unimportant, and instead I had better turn my mind to the wonderful family Thanksgiving we just had, and the Thanksgiving I could look forward to next year.

The cause of the painful uninvited thoughts is not illogical thinking but rather a set of connections within my brain that habitually lead first to neg-comps rather than to happy thoughts. This means that someone like me must rewire these connections, that is, create a new set of habits. No single insight about the past or present can do this job. Rather, it requires sustained work. But if you at least recognize the nature of the problem, the problem is not insuperable, and you may even get satisfaction at the workmanship and imagination that you evince in your rewiring job.

The bad news is that at first you do not have a set of habits to switch you from Rotten to Rosy Ratios; if you did have them, you would not be depressed. The good news is that the more you work on these

Analysis	*Response*	*Behavior to change*
Dimension: What would have happened throughout my professional life if I had stuck to just one subject?	I would have spent my entire professional life on my first subject, which was not very exciting.	Focusing on a dimension which is not central to my overall life, even my professional life. Learn to take the bad with the good and see the virtues of my vices.

habits, and the longer you have them, the more effective they are, and the better they protect you from sadness and depression.

SUMMARY

The best anti-depression strategy may be to replace the entire Rotten Ratio with another one—that is, to turn away from that entire dimension of comparison. There are two related sets of tactics for changing the dimension: a. changing your priorities about the various aspects of your life, and b. focusing your attention on the good things in your life rather than the bad things. Both tactics call upon our capacity to direct our attention toward some dimensions of our lives and away from others.

The device of 'counting your blessings' constitutes shifting to a more positive dimension for self-comparison. Instead of brooding on lack of job success, you make yourself remember your family's good health. When you lose your money in the stock market, you try to keep in mind your wonderful children.

Re-arranging your priorities is a second device for changing Mood Ratio dimensions. A frequent and important example is the person whose actual occupational achievements do not measure up to the person's aspirations, yet is unwilling to scale down his or her aspirations so as to keep the denominator from dominating the numerator. The person may then prevent negative self-comparisons by focusing attention on another related ratio—perhaps the person's courage in persisting against obstacles, or the person's success in helping co-workers achieve important successes in their work.

Depressives tend to be less flexible than are other people in altering the dimensions on which they compare themselves. But it is possible to change your ratios of comparison by effort and will.

THE SOUND OF A
NUMERATOR CLAPPING

If you make no self-comparisons, you will feel no sadness; that's the point of this chapter in a nutshell. A recent body of research[1] confirms that this is so. There is much evidence that increased attention to yourself, in contrast to increased attention to the people, objects, and events around you, is generally associated with more signs of depressed feeling.

Some people are forever checking their Life Report to see how they rate. They want to know the score after every point in ping-pong, they examine their reflections in every mirror they pass, they know at every moment what their grades are in each course in school, and they constantly update their estimates of their bosses' opinions of them. Other people pay much less attention to their evaluations of themselves.

Evaluating yourself can give you pleasure if your actual state stands favorably with respect to your benchmark comparison state. But if you have a propensity to evaluate yourself *unfavorably*, then each such evaluation is a source of pain and sadness for you. For such people, the frequency of self-evaluation determines the amount of pain and sadness, and the depth of depression. We depressives not only have a propensity to make negative self-evaluations, but we also have a tendency to make them frequently.

Some evaluations of how you are doing are crucial in keeping you on the right course of action. If you don't check how well you are doing when you are engaged in any productive activity, you have no way of directing your actions so that they will be fruitful. 'How am I doing,

Ma?' may be a funny line at times, but getting feedback evaluation from others and from yourself is crucial in keeping you from walking onto dangerous thin ice, and it is necessary in making a living. If you have an independent income and no responsibilities to others, you can afford to enter a monastery or a private world in which you refrain from evaluations of your activities. Yet most of us—and especially depressives—can afford to *greatly reduce* the extent of self-evaluation without much (if any) loss of useful direction.

The title for this chapter comes from the Zen question, 'What is the sound of one hand clapping?' That question (like all the rest of Zen) aims at *making no self-comparisons at all,* which is the subject of this chapter. Ceasing to make comparisons is a key element in much of Western religion, too, as well as in many secular psychological approaches to mental suffering.

Jean Piaget taught us that as a baby grows from earliest infancy, it develops striving abilities in order to survive. When you strive you classify, abstract, and especially evaluate. The act of evaluating is central to all survival and achievement—the evaluation of this path rather than that one, which tactic will produce the desired result, whether a pile of blocks will hold one's weight, and so on.

The importance of the distinction between the mode of experiencing and the mode of evaluating and comparing was long ago noted by philosophers. According to John Dewey, evaluation ('criticism' is his term)

> occurs whenever a moment is devoted to looking to see what sort of value is present; whenever instead of accepting a value-object wholeheartedly, being rapt by it, we raise even a shadow of a question about its worth, or modify our sense of it by even a passing estimate of its probable future. . . . There is a constant rhythm of 'perchings and flights' (to borrow James's terms) characteristic of alternate emphasis upon the immediate and mediate, the consummatory and instrumental, phases of all conscious experience.[2]

A stimulus to action—for a baby, hunger or a painful jab of a pin; for an older child or an adult, an insult or a challenge or a neg-comp—puts you into the active survival mode. And if the stimulus is painful, the non-depressive's first reaction is take steps to get rid of the cause of the pain. If, however, it seems to you as if you cannot manage to get rid of the painful stimulus, the mood turns to anger, and then to aggression against the actual or imagined source of the pain. And if you come to think that you are helpless to escape or prevent the painful stimulus,[3] however, the rage becomes sadness.

WAYS TO AVOID MAKING COMPARISONS

Stop Thinking About Yourself

Bertrand Russell once wrote that the secret of attaining happiness and avoiding unhappiness is not to think about yourself.

> I hated life and was continually on the verge of suicide. . . . Now, on the contrary, I enjoy life . . . with every year that passes I enjoy it more. . . . (V)ery largely it is due to a diminishing preoccupation with myself.[4]

By itself, not thinking about yourself does not seem to be a clear or sensible prescription. But let us re-interpret Russell as saying that one should get into the habit of avoiding comparisons of the self with counterfactuals, which is a common form of 'thinking about oneself'.

Non-depressives usually have well-developed skills for shifting their attention away from situations that might produce unnecessary negative self-comparisons. In a report on more than three decades of life histories of a hundred Harvard students, starting before World War II, George Vaillant tells the story of a man who shifted dimensions effectively:

> A California hematologist developed a hobby of cultivating living cells in test tubes. In a recent interview, he described with special interest and animation an unusually interesting culture that he had grown from a tissue biopsy from his mother. Only toward the end of the interview did he casually reveal that his mother had died from a stroke only three weeks previously. His mention of her death was as bland as his description of the still-living tissue culture had been effectively colored. Ingeniously and unconsciously, he had used his hobby and his special skills as a physician to mitigate temporarily the pain of his loss. Although his mother was no

longer alive, by shifting his attention he was still able to care for her. There was nothing morbid in the way he told the story; and because ego mechanisms are unconscious, he had no idea of his defensive behavior. Many of the healthiest men in the Study used similar kinds of attention shifts.[5]

Research has also shown that depressives tend to have more self-evaluating and self-comparing thoughts than do non-depressives.[6] This is additional evidence that reducing the number of self-comparisons is a logical tactic against depression for depressives.

An example of how one can force oneself to avoid negative self-comparisons and thereby prevent sadness: Linus S., himself a depressive, has a son, Daniel, who worries more than do most kids about school work, though Daniel is very good in school and Linus tells Daniel not to let school performance worry him.

One night Linus asked Daniel to 'promise' not to worry about school the next day. Daniel reported it worked. Then Linus said to his son, 'I ought to try the same thing myself'. Daniel suggested that they exchange promises that each would have a happy day on the morrow. Linus thought it was a lovely idea, and agreed. And it worked, even though Linus was in the midst of a bad period at work. Since then they exchange such promises frequently, and Linus—because he feels a responsibility to keep promises to his children—works extra hard at keeping himself in a sadness-free mood, banishing negative self-comparisons whenever they come into his mind, and turning his thoughts to family, specific work problems, and nature. This is evidence of the efficacy of the tactic of avoiding negative self-comparisons. It also shows again how one's mood depends *both* upon external conditions and *also* on one's mind set.

Will Your Attention Away from the Depressing Thoughts

All of us have very considerable powers to refuse to make evaluations and self-comparisons, and to influence our moods by sheer decision and force of will, as this small anecdote shows. The Jewish Sabbath is the center of our family's life, and an oasis of delight, especially for my wife and me. Please understand that this is a purely personal matter, and has nothing to do with any supernatural belief or religious obligation, but it is nevertheless very important for us. One

Friday afternoon I was on an airplane due to make a tight connection with another plane and arrive at home before the meal that would begin the Sabbath on Friday evening. I fell asleep in my seat just before take-off, but awoke fully 45 minutes later to find the plane still on the ground. My neighbor told me that a broken seat was in the process of being fixed, and we could not leave until it would be fixed. The plane was already so late that according to the schedule I would miss my connection, and it was the last connecting flight that night. The fixing took another 20 minutes or so. I then asked the stewardess if there was anything that could be done to hold the connecting plane. She asked if there were others in the same shape, and she found eight or nine others. She then wired ahead, but told us that there was little chance that the connecting flight would wait.

As I sat in my seat, beginning to be very anxious about whether we'd make the connection, and very upset about the possibility of having to spend the Sabbath in a hotel away from my family and the bliss of the Sabbath, I could feel anger and then depression coming on. Then I thought as follows: If I stay calm and refuse to get upset, and if I miss my connection, will I lose anything by not being upset? No. If I let myself get upset and we do make the connecting flight, will I later feel that I have been foolish in allowing myself to approach the Sabbath in a turmoil? Yes. Therefore, since being anxious and upset can do no good, and might be a foolish and misplaced internal commotion, why let myself be upset?

I therefore determined not to let myself be upset. To that end I concentrated on making small talk with my neighbor and her children, breathing deeply in my belly to relax myself and make myself feel good, thinking about the lovely time I would have on the Sabbath if I did get home, and enjoying my airline meal. My anxiety broke through my pleasant calm from time to time, but when it did I firmly pushed it out of my mind and went back to breathing deeply or chatting.

And—it worked. Even more wonderful, by unusual air traveler's luck, the other plane was late anyhow, and it was held. I got home only slightly delayed, and in good time for the Sabbath meal. I was overjoyed at that good fortune, and additionally pleased that I arrived home in such calm and good cheer because I had not allowed my anxiousness to get home upset or depress me and then ruin my festive mood.

This example from Alcoholic Anonymous's 'Big Book' is instructive even though the aim was to avoid taking a drink rather than a neg-comp:

> There have . . . been numerous times when I have thought about taking a drink. Such thinking usually began with thoughts of the pleasant drinking of my youth. I learned early in my A.A. life that I could not afford to fondle such thoughts, as you might fondle a pet, because this particular pet could grow into a monster. Instead, I quickly substitute one or another vivid scene from the nightmare of my later drinking.[7]

Substitute a depressive's propensity to dwell on a neg-comp that affords the gratification of self-pity, for example, instead of the alcoholic's thought of a drink, and the anecdote provides guidance for avoiding depressing thoughts.

Change the Subject

A device that can be useful in reducing negative self-comparisons is simply changing the subject of your thinking and internal conversation—from a work failure to family, from war in Africa to a technical question, from a sick child to tennis, or whatever. Do you wonder whether you can do this? Of course you can—just as you can often (but not always) convince *someone else* to change the subject of conversation. Of course this means that you must be willing at times to turn away from subjects of interest to you when they cause you pain.

Vaillant thus typifies the behavior of the middle-aged men who had made successful psychological adaptations of their circumstances: '[I]f you cannot bear it, forget it'. And he noticed that the only two men in his study who did *not* use this or any 'neurotic' devices to avoid painful thoughts were the two men in his sample who described themselves as "chronically depressed."[8]

Young persons often believe that purposely ignoring unpleasant facts is in some way 'dishonest' and 'untruthful'. Certainly it *can* be dishonest to *deny* unpleasant facts. And sometimes it is *unwise* to *ignore* unpleasant facts if they will cause greater harm unless you deal with them. But for those facts which you cannot alter—a chronic ailment, perhaps, or a low pay level in one's chosen occupation—then there seems neither practical nor moral virtue in keeping oneself constantly aware of the fact and of the negative self-comparison it produces; to do so is simply foolhardy and counterproductive.

Think about Work Instead of about Yourself

One of the best ways of avoiding self-comparisons is by substituting *work thoughts,* which by their very nature focus you on objects of thought outside yourself, rather than on yourself and comparisons with benchmark counterfactual states. After my first year of terrible depression, my ability to dive down into work for two to four hours every morning dragged me up from permanent occupancy at the bottom of the pit, and gave me some respite from the constant pain of sadness and awareness of worthlessness. Many depressed people do not manage to work, however. This may be because they feel hopeless that the work will amount to anything. But others may not work because they are not aware of the enormous therapeutic possibilities of work.

Composer Liz Swados is another depressive who finds refuge in her work. "Even in her depression, she worked—and found salvation in work." Einstein's collaborator narrated: "On 20 December, 1936 . . . Einstein's wife Elsa died. Ashen with grief, Einstein insisted on continuing the work, saying that now he needed it more than ever. At first his attempts to concentrate were pitiful. But he had known sorrow before and had learned that work was a precious antidote. And Virginia Woolf's husband commented on his life after her death: "Work is the most efficient anodyne—[other than] death, sleep, or choloroform—for pain, whether the pain be in your great toe, your tooth, your head, or your heart."[9]

Observe that it is almost impossible to sing and be depressed at the same time. (Singing even a blues song removes the blues!) Does this mean we should sing all the time? The prescription 'sing' is not a perfect cure for depression for at least two reasons: 1. The prospective singer must be willing to give up the benefits of depression. 2. It takes the energy involved in 'will power' to force yourself to start singing when you feel sad, energy that depressed people often lack.

Helping Others Can Help You

Altruism—which implies thinking about *other* people's welfare instead of your own, and comparing *their* numerators to their denominators instead of your own—has saved many people from depression. Vaillant[10] documents how turning to altruistic activities saved several of the men in the Grant Study from adulthood hells. Perhaps this is a fair translation of what Jesus meant when he said that in order to save one's life one must lose it—that is, by giving it to others.

How may one become altruistic? All I can suggest is that you may *decide* to do so, either because you come to realize that one of your most important values is to be altruistic, or because you are so anxious to cease being depressed that you are willing to give part of your time and strength and thought to others.

Avoid Situations That Induce Negative Self-Comparisons

Staying out of situations that force negative self-comparisons upon you is a habit that can help depressives. Arnold K. is an applied scientist who has done work that is innovative but that has mostly failed to catch the interest of his profession. Every time he picked up any one of three particular technical journals he was depressed for a day or two, because the field covered by those journals proceeds with practically no reference to his work though he has researched and published a large quantity of material in that field. Then he built the habit that each time his eye or hand lights on one of those journals, he turns his eye and hand away and redirects his mind to his family, which is a source of great satisfaction to him. At first he found this hard to do, but after trying it and finding it pleasurable, it got easier and more habitual each time. (But this habit-building has the disadvantage that if he doesn't look at those three journals, he is hampered in contributing anything more to that field, or in trying to keep his past work in that field from disappearing altogether. This is a drawback of some types of habit formation and behavior modification.)

Two similar examples are given by psychoanalyst Rubin:

> I had a patient who had been through a devastating love affair and who for a long time diligently avoided films, plays and books which depicted idealized love relationships, having learned that these filled her with self-recriminations which she could not yet control. This does not constitute avoidance of reality or denial of a problem. It simply, but very importantly, provides pain-free time in which to gather strength for constructive purpose.

I remember a period of time during which I felt particularly vulnerable. I studiously avoided news programs that were especially full of horror then because they demoralized me still further. Again, this is not sticking one's head in the sand ostrichlike. It is effecting a block to self-hate, and this or any kind of block, especially of an early and even anticipatory nature, is a definite form of compassion and constructive caring for self.[11]

Rubin's method is sound, even though his arcane psychoanalytic language and concepts ("self-hate") are not necessary here.

Writing plays is, of all types of work, the one which most requires that one keep checking the effect of the work on the audience, in the course of the play's being readied for production. Yet such checking the results can bring forth negative self-comparison. Famous playwright William Gibson puts it this way:

I learned . . . that success is no good and failure is worse—an old wisdom, the work must be done for itself, which in this system is the counsel to "act, but detach from the fruits of action". That is, act without a feedback of conflict over the outcome. But of all the arts the theatre is the most public, it does not exist without an audience, and the will to success is ingrained in its practice. The wooing of the audience is half of the art.[12]

Study Your Thoughts

Examining your thoughts in an objective fashion, the way you would study someone else's thoughts if you wanted to understand them, can be another powerful device, similar to meditation which we shall talk about below. Watching one's thoughts tends to objectify the process and reduce the sadness attached to the thoughts (if they are negative self-comparisons.)

Prayer

Still another device useful to some people is praying, or a prayerful attitude, which may or may not involve belief in a deity. These passages by a Christian minister are illuminating:

When we are melancholy, it is impossible for us to evaluate correctly our personal contributions to our loved ones, our work or to society at large. When we learn to anticipate a bad mood and to accept it philosophically when it comes, when during the period of depression we are wise enough to suspend judgment as to the worth of our achievements, we have made sincere practical advance in managing our troublesome moods.

It helps to speed the waiting process when we force ourselves to *assume a fresh viewpoint*. This entails shutting the door of our minds to hopeless and despairing thoughts and deliberately to appropriate a confident, cheerful attitude. This is an extremely difficult assignment for the person who allows himself to be carried away by his depressed moods, but through discipline of emotions and patient practice it can be accomplished. By an act of will it becomes possible to turn our minds away from gloom and to center them elsewhere . . .

Another method involves the *practical use of affirmation and prayer*. If our prayers have seemed ineffectual in combating our low moods, perhaps we have allowed them to become sporadic or stereotyped and should give them a fresh cutting edge. On awakening in the morning, for example, in the first moments of consciousness, we can begin the day with an affirmation of confidence and hope. Although this may seem trivial, in reality it helps set the emotional tone for the entire day. We may find it helpful to repeat a sentence from the Psalms, such as, "This is the day which the Lord hath made; we will rejoice and be glad in it", or a line from the Doxology, "Praise God, from whom all blessings flow", or words from a favorite hymn—"Spirit of God, descend upon my heart". . . .

The habit of starting the day with an affirmation of trust and cheer will tend to lift our spiritual horizons and to turn our thoughts outward, away from the chasm of dejection and toward the Source of power.[13]

Creating the Proper Habits

Once again, Self-Comparisons Analysis directs us to a useful tactic in fighting depression—in this case, reducing negative self-comparisons by avoiding any self-comparisons. Yet the willingness to exert the effort, and the implementation of the decision to exert the effort with habit formation, are also crucial. This adds up, then, to the following prescription: When you recognize a negative self-comparison entering your thoughts, tell yourself to direct your thoughts toward a work project or an altruistic activity—*and do it*.

Habit-formation may be more effective in suppressing comparisons than one thinks at first. Drawing upon my own experience, now: Even after I banished my daytime depression I often woke early in the morning—at 4:00 or 5:00 or 6:00 a.m.—and would lie half-asleep and half-awake with thoughts of past failures and future difficulties. The evil genius of the depression seemed to be that even if I could fight it when awake, I had no defense against it seizing me when unconscious with sleep. And I was convinced that habit-building tricks therefore could not help, because such tricks require consciousness and 'will'.

To my delight, I was wrong. It began when one of my children told me of his device to avoid bad dreams: Before falling asleep give yourself a pleasant subject to think about, such as a beaver or a swallow (this son was interested in animals). I took the suggestion, and it helped, though my subject is a family pleasure rather than an animal.

Additionally, I have now found that the habits I developed during the day began to work when half-asleep, too, shoving away intruding ugly comparisons even when half-asleep.

By now, though depressing thoughts still break into my sleep occasionally, my habits are almost always powerful enough to protect my tranquillity and allow me to return to sleep.

MILKING JOY FROM PAST AND FUTURE

Having pleasure, and feeling good because of it, is partly a matter of the events that occur to you. But even more important is whether you keep the thoughts of pleasant events in your mind long before and long after they occur, or whether you turn your mind to other things except when experiencing the event. Having thoughts of pleasant events in your mind affects your depression in two different ways, both very important. 1. As with meditation, work, and exercise, thinking about happy events substitutes for the negative self-comparisons that cause you to be depressed. 2. Even more important, perhaps, is that having pleasure in fact and thought—in memory and in expectation, as well as in actual experience—is a terrific reason to stay alive, and to believe that life is good. As Dostoyevsky remarked, one really good memory will go a long way—if you make good use of it.

It is a characteristic of depressives that their thoughts dwell on self-comparisons and do *not* dwell upon memories of past pleasures and expectations of future pleasures. But this is a tendency that can be changed if you decide to do it, if you 'allow' yourself to do it, and if you practice it. Oil-company junior executive Rollie G. always had his mind working on 'productive' thoughts about his job—whom he had to instruct to do what, what he had to remember to check before sending out the products, the job evaluation forms he had to fill out for his assistant, and so on. He felt that he 'ought' to be 'taking advantage' of spare moments to get more done, and he constantly did so—except when negative self-evaluations flooded his mood and made him sad, and that was often. Then he came to realize that there is no necessity to make a maximum production machine out of himself. And he trained himself to spend five minutes or a quarter of an hour alone or with his wife, reminiscing about the lovely times he had had with his children, and about such upcoming events as the children's confirmations, the good meals that they had had, and about trips past and future. These pleasurable thoughts pushed out negative self-comparisons, and gave him the real stuff of life to lean upon and to make life worthwhile.

How can you get yourself to spend more time remembering and expecting those happy events that are in *everyone's* life? By working at it, and teaching yourself the habit of doing so, that's how. Train yourself so that when you start to ruminate over your failings, shift your thoughts to the happy times, and stay in those happy times for a few minutes, before moving on to other thoughts.

MEDITATION

A comparison is the basic element in any evaluation or judgment. And comparing is a process of developing and using abstract concepts to deal with the sensations that your mind receives from inside and outside your body. In contrast, the various forms of meditation, and of Eastern religious practices generally, are devices to orient you *away* from abstraction, judgment, comparison, and evaluation, and toward the 'primitive' sensations themselves. The other side of the coin is that meditation points you *toward* the judgment-free perceptions of the sensory world, and perhaps toward cosmic imaginations that often arise from the elementary experience in meditation.

As the greatest interpreter of Buddhism to Westerners put it, not just meditation but Buddhism in its entirety "is a method . . . for the correction of our perceptions and for the transformation of consciousness" rather than a theology.[14] The purpose and effects of Buddhism and Hinduism, in which meditation is the key spiritual element, are more like Western psychotherapy than like Western religion. And indeed, meditation can remove sadness and depression, at least temporarily.[15]

By "meditation" I mean to include all the sorts of meditation described by Buddhist and Hindu writers as well as by such popularizers as the Maharishi of Transcendental Meditation. More specifically, I include both the sort of meditation in which one shuts out all outside stimuli, and the sort of meditation in which one lets all stimuli in. For more details about the nature of meditation, see such writers as Humphreys, Wood, Suzuki, or a delightful narrative account by Gibson. In the 1970s there also was a rash of discussion of meditation by psychologists, such as Naranjo and Ornstein, and Benson. (See reference list at end of book.)

Getting rid of suffering by one's own mental efforts in meditation is an idea found in the Western tradition, also. The psychologist James quotes with approval this statement by the essayist Carlyle:

> Once more, then, our self-feeling is in our power. As Carlyle says: "Make thy claim of wages a zero, then hast thou the world under thy feet. Well did the wisest of our time write, it is only with *renunciation* that life, properly speaking, can be said to begin."[16]

Western religious mystics in the Christian, Jewish, and Muslim traditions also have practiced meditation; among the most famous are Meister Eckhart, the Cabbalists, and Sufis, respectively.

It is of fundamental importance to understand that the nature of meditation is *not mysterious scientifically,* though one's thoughts in meditation may (or may not) be mystical and full of awe at the mysteries of life and the universe. Rather it is a process of concentration and controlled imagination.

The Technique of Meditation

Scientific writings on meditation have performed a considerable service in removing the mumbojumbo and metaphysical clap-trap from it.[17] Benson and Klipper have invented the felicitous and non-mysterious label, 'Relaxation response' for the processes that occur in meditation, and they have boiled down the necessary conditions and instructions for meditation as follows:

HOW TO BRING FORTH THE RELAXATION RESPONSE

1. A QUIET ENVIRONMENT

Ideally, you should choose a quiet, calm environment with as few distractions as possible. A quiet room is suitable, as is a place of worship. The quiet environment contributes to the effectiveness of the repeated word or phrase by making it easier to eliminate distracting thoughts.

2. A MENTAL DEVICE

To shift the mind from logical, externally oriented thoughts, there should be a constant stimulus: a sound, word, or phrase repeated silently or aloud; or fixed gazing at an object. Since one of the major difficulties in the elicitation of the Relaxation Response is 'mind wandering', the repetition of the word or phrase is a way to help break the train of distracting thoughts. Your eyes are usually closed if you are using a repeated sound or word; of course, your eyes are open if you are gazing. Attention to the normal rhythm of breathing is also useful and enhances the repetition of the sound or the word.

3. A PASSIVE ATTITUDE

When distracting thoughts occur, they are to be disregarded and attention redirected to the repetition or gazing; *you should not worry about how well you are performing the technique,* because this may well prevent the Relaxation Response from occurring. Adopt a 'let it happen' attitude. The *passive attitude is perhaps the most important element in eliciting the Relaxation Response. Distracting thoughts will occur. Do not worry about them. When these thoughts do present themselves and you become aware of them, simply return to the repetition of the mental device. These other thoughts do not mean you are performing the technique incorrectly. They are to be expected.*

4. A COMFORTABLE POSITION

A comfortable posture is important so that there is no undue muscular tension. Some methods call for a sitting position. A few practitioners use the cross-legged 'lotus' position of the Yogi. If you are lying down, there is a tendency to fall asleep. As we have noted previously, the various postures of kneeling, swaying, or sitting in a cross-legged position are believed to have evolved to prevent falling asleep. You should be comfortable and relaxed. . . .

1. Sit quietly in a comfortable position.
2. Close your eyes.
3. Deeply relax all your muscles, beginning at your feet and progressing up to your face. Keep them relaxed.
4. Breathe through your nose. Become aware of your breathing. As you breathe out, say the word, 'ONE', silently to yourself. For example, breathe IN . . . OUT. 'ONE'; IN . . . OUT, 'ONE'; etc. Breathe easily and naturally.
5. Continue for 10 to 20 minutes. You may open your eyes to check the time, but do not use an alarm. When you finish, sit quietly for several minutes, at first with your eyes closed and later with your eyes opened. Do not stand up for a few minutes.
6. Do not worry about whether you are successful in achieving a deep level of relaxation. Maintain a passive attitude and permit relaxation to occur at its own pace. When distracting thoughts occur, try to ignore them by not dwelling upon them and return to repeating 'ONE'. With practice, the response should come with little effort. Practice the technique once or twice daily, but not within two hours after any meal, since the digestive processes seem to interfere with the elicitation of the Relaxation Response.[18]

Practicing the technique of meditation need not be limited to sitting positions during fixed periods of the day. One may breathe deeply, focus the mind, and relax oneself whenever one feels stress— say, just before an athletic contest, as many athletes do—or when one recognizes the onset of a negative self-comparison. When, while walking the dog or driving to work or trying to sleep, a negative self-comparison comes into your mind—'what an immoral louse I am', or 'I just can't do anything right'—then you may turn off the comparing mode and turn on the experiencing mode as follows: Breathe in with your diaphragm so that your midsection inflates deeply and slowly, and then deflate slowly; then continue to repeat the cycle. At the same time focus your attention on your breathing, or on a leaf, or on some other unemotional stimulus, perhaps saying to yourself,

'Don't criticize' or 'I don't need to compare'. Soon you may find yourself smiling—just as I now am smiling as I am breathing in accord with the instructions I've just written. (It is difficult to believe how powerful and exciting such breathing is until you have taught yourself to do it. I hope someday to write a humorous piece entitled 'Confessions of a sensual breather'.)

It is helpful to know what *not* to expect of meditation. One will not quickly (if ever) learn to produce a state of mind in which thought seems to stop, and in which perception focuses down to a single unchanging point for prolonged lengths of time. If you try for that and fail to accomplish it, meditation may thereby be discredited with you. This is what I call the shattered-window fallacy, that as soon as a stray thought crosses the mind the meditation is 'broken'. Not at all true! Even the most experienced meditators find errant and unwanted thoughts breaking in from time to time. One must learn how to deal with these thoughts in such manner that they do not disturb the meditation; gently inspecting them, and then putting them aside and perhaps saying to yourself 'I'll deal with that later,' is one effective way.

Another misconception about meditation is that the meditator should fall into a trance. Not so. As a famous Chinese Buddhist put it:

> There is . . . a class of foolish people who sit quietly and try to keep their minds blank; they refrain from thinking of anything and then call themselves 'great'. Concerning this heretical view, I have no patience to speak. . . . When we use the mind we can consider everything;"[19]

What Meditation Does

Exactly what happens to a person while meditating is beyond general description, and varies from person to person. We can say, however, that in meditation of all sorts one does not think in normal everyday ways. Perhaps the basic difference is that one ceases to make comparisons between one's actual and benchmark-hypothetical situations. In this manner, the source of sadness is removed during meditation. Another difference is that one ceases to strive but relaxes instead, which leads to pleasant physical sensations incompatible with sadness. Furthermore, meditation often leads to a radically altered perspective, for example a cosmic rather than an individual perspective. Within such a cosmic perspective the contemporary events which are the grist for the mill of self-comparisons appear insignificant and unworthy of attention; this works against making negative self-comparisons.

The mechanism that leads to the state of meditation is a shift from the active flight-or-fight survival mode of thought in which one classifies and evaluates and makes comparisons, to the passive experiential state in which one simply takes in sensory experiences without classifying or evaluating or comparing them. In the striving mode one abstracts a limited set of elements from the sensory input, using various already-established intellectual patterns; these abstracted inputs are the materials which one compares, and which may lead to negative self-comparisons. In contrast, in meditation one makes oneself aware either of all stimuli or of just a single element. The latter is the 'one-pointed mind' of Zen in which, even outside of meditation proper, the person is aware—but fully aware—of the sensory experience, and is not 'intellectualizing'. When I eat I eat, and when I sit I just sit, Zen Buddhists say.

That is, when one meditates, one's mind and body are mostly *off duty;* they no longer are serving as watchers and laborers in keeping one alive in a biological and social sense; rather, one's body and mind relax as they surrender these tasks. The same *kind* of effects, though much milder in intensity, occur when a worker relaxes on a coffee break, or when a student leaves off reading a hard text and dreamily looks out the window, or when in the woods one's attention is absorbed by nature. Religious services often produce the same sorts of feelings with prayers, music, and beauty of setting; they take one out of the world of striving and surviving, into the world of sensing and absorbing. Sabbath observers put themselves 'off duty' for an entire day (at least those religious groups for whom the Sabbath is not a stern ascetic day).

Sometimes people worry that ceasing to make comparisons implies quietism and leaving ordinary life. Indeed, some depressives avoid the pain of neg-comps by giving up their fundamental goals, which leads them into apathy. But this is an unlikely occurrence in the present context of discussion.

During periods of relaxation from striving—whether very deeply with meditation, or less deeply in religious services or absorption in nature—the force that makes for sadness and depression is absent: One does not make comparisons—and especially negative self-comparisons—when one is in an experiential mode rather than in a survival mode.

Even non-theistic people sometimes arrive at the thought of God when meditating, because their experience transcends everyday concepts. For example, for me the knowledge that in meditation I can relax into the cessation of mental pain and the existence of physical pleasure is so wonderful, and the state itself is so awesome, that sometimes I refer to this inner refuge as 'God', though I am quite without belief in the usual Judaic-Christian concept of an active God. (More about the word 'God' below.)

Meditation also has links to the making of art. In creative moments the painter or composer or poet tends to suspend willful direction of the mind, letting thoughts drift as if they have lives of their own. But the artist continues to maintain a general supervisory control over the thoughts—like the director of a play who is out of sight in the wings, but who is nevertheless keeping a watchful eye on the stage. The artist's trick is to exert that supervisory control without worrying about it, to be thinking freely without *striving* for that freedom. In the most successful moments the artist often feels as if the work gets done by itself, without effort by the artist—just as a skilled athlete sometimes comes to feel that the game is played effortlessly, without any feeling of 'trying' to play well. Athletes call this feeling 'being in the zone'. This is commonly experienced as a moment of pure joy.

There is an apparent logical contradiction between the artist letting the mind be totally free, and supervising the mind at the same time. This pair of apparent opposites is "equivalent to the Buddha's enjoining his disciples to stop desiring, which would of course put them in a state of desiring not to desire."[20] But 'freedom' and 'desire' are complex multi-layered words, and in fact there need be no psychological contradiction in these matters.

There is a crucial difference between on the one hand, meditation, and on the other hand, habit-formation and count-your-blessings exercises to combat depression, though they may seem similar in some respects. Meditation seems to *produce increased energy* in some people, whereas counting your blessings and such habit-formation devices as behavior-modification therapy seem to *use up* energy in the exertion of 'will power' to alter one's behavior. When meditating, you husband energy because you are not 'trying' to do anything. It is a state in which you feel no 'ought'; you purposely 'let it all hang out' (really, hang *in*). This unusual cessation of activity for all your striving and physical mental faculties produces a sense of deep restedness afterward.

The Limitations of Meditation

If meditation can have such anti-depressive effects, and if—as seems to be the case—almost everyone can learn to meditate, why is meditation not the perfect cure for depression? For some people, lengthy meditation may in fact be an excellent therapy. But most people cannot leave the workday world and remain in the world of meditation. Even if one can financially afford to do so, many people feel an urgent need to work for its own sake, as a contribution to society or because their abilities cry out to be used. Another reason that people will not choose to forego involvement in the workaday world is that they hope for joys as well as pain, and full-scale Buddhist-type meditation implies putting aside the craving for joys and the joys themselves.

Zen prescribes that you should do your best at whatever you do, but you should not feel sad when you fail to succeed. This is marvelous advice, but it is a prescription for walking a tightwire so thin and so high that few of us can balance ourselves on it. To strive to do well requires evaluation of how you are doing. But not being sad requires *not* evaluating how you are doing. So unless you are capable of extraordinary skill in compartmentalizing your thoughts, this prescription is not a *perfect* cure for most of us—though trying to take the prescription will certainly help all of us somewhat.

Another way through the horns of this dilemma is to restrict your evaluation to your *act,* and refrain from allowing the evaluation of the *act* to become a judgment of *yourself as a person.* It is certainly possible to judge that a tennis stroke was hit badly without judging the hitter to be a bad person or even a bad tennis player. This separation of the evaluation of the act from evaluation of the actor is exceedingly valuable mental hygiene for everyone, at all times. And it reconciles Zen doctrine and practice with active participation in the everyday world.

Happiness and unhappiness are not simple mutually-exclusive opposites as light and dark are. Attaining happiness and getting rid of unhappiness are related but not identical goals. Watts wrote that "happiness is associated with relaxation . . . the essential principle (in achieving happiness) is one of relaxation."[21] That is not correct, I believe. It is indeed true that relaxation induced by meditation or other devices can replace sadness with a feeling of inner peace. But for most people—especially in their younger years—'happiness' means *excited* pleasant feelings—work achievement, sexual success and sexual experience, falling in love, bearing children, athletic or political victories. Peaceful relaxation is not an acceptable substitute for these aspirations in the minds of most people, especially in the first half of one's life.

Though meditation may not be a total cure, a depressed person can be cheered considerably by receiving relief in meditation from time to time, and from knowing that such relief is possible without braving the dangers.

SUMMARY

If you make no self-comparisons, you will feel no sadness.

If you have a propensity to evaluate yourself *unfavorably,* then each such evaluation is a source of pain and sadness for you. For such people, the frequency of self-evaluation determines the amount of pain and sadness, and the depth of depression. We depressives not only have a propensity to make negative self-evaluations, but we also have a tendency to make them frequently.

Reducing the number of neg-comps is a powerful and effective way of fighting sadness and depression. There are many ways of reducing self-evaluations and self-comparisons including focusing on work, engaging in altruistic activities, meditating, praying, and simply shifting one's attention to other subjects. And you can form effective habits of shifting your thoughts in such fashion. All of us have very considerable powers to refuse to make evaluations and self-comparisons and to influence our moods by sheer decision and force of will.

Some evaluations of how you are doing are crucial in keeping you on the right course of action. If you don't check how well you are doing when you are engaged in any productive activity, you have no way of directing your actions so that they will be fruitful. But much of our self-evaluation is not needed for survival.

Once again, Self-Comparisons Analysis directs us to a useful tactic in fighting depression—in this case, reducing negative self-comparisons by avoiding any self-comparisons. Yet the willingness to exert the effort, and the implementation of the decision to exert the effort with habit formation, are also crucial. This adds up, then, to the following prescription: When you recognize a negative self-comparison entering your thoughts, tell yourself to direct your thoughts toward a work project or an altruistic activity—*and do it.*

RELIGIOUS CONVERSION CAN CURE DEPRESSION

So far we have talked about rational, planned-out tactics for battling against your depression. But some people's depressions—especially deep depressions—disappear suddenly and miraculously, without systematic battles and often with great drama. Such cures fit into the broad framework of Self-Comparisons Analysis.

The most dramatic cures are religious conversions, especially those of Christians and most especially of Protestants. The cases of John Bunyan, and of the Quaker founder, George Fox, are famous because they described their salvations in autobiographies.

William James analyzed and described this phenomenon brilliantly. The process of religious conversion for a depressive appears to happen as follows: The person suffers and suffers and suffers some more, from a sense of unworthiness or sin or alcoholism or worldly failure. All the while the person strives with all his might to overcome the failures and the feeling of unworthiness, but with no success. Then finally the person gives up, because he or she comes to believe that the struggle cannot be won; emotional exhaustion accompanies the giving up. (James emphasizes the exhaustion.) Then after the person surrenders hope and struggle, there suddenly occurs a process of relaxation and inner peace.

I felt this happen once, six months after depression hit me, a time when I was in constant and total despair. My wife and I went to the country to visit friends for a weekend, the first time we had been away since the crisis had begun, and we slept outside on the ground. When I woke in the morning I saw a shiny leaf and I heard a bird trill, the first time in half a year I had taken pleasure in a simple work of nature or humankind. I felt a radiant, delicious inner peace. Closest to this feeling in a more common context is the peace and gratitude one feels upon receiving news that a much-feared tragedy has not come to pass. One also feels a similar, though less intense, relaxation when one meditates after having been tense. For intellectual and other reasons, however, I was not a candidate for a religious conversion. Perhaps for that reason, after a matter of hours, I was back in despair. Yet I had at least experienced the feeling of redemption.

As I understand it, a person who believes in the existence of an active personal God identifies the extraordinary experience of inner peace with the manifestation of God in the person's life and body. The feeling is 'heavenly', and it seems reasonable to a believer that only God could create this amazing reversal of emotional fortune. Here are a few examples culled from the extraordinary collection by James, many of them taken in turn from Leuba. Here is the case of an alcoholic:

> One Tuesday evening I sat in a saloon in Harlem, a homeless, friendless, dying drunkard. I had pawned or sold everything that would bring a drink. I could not sleep unless I was dead drunk. I had not eaten for days, and for four nights preceding I had suffered with delirium tremens, or the horrors, from midnight till morning. I had often said, 'I will never be a tramp. I will never be cornered, for when that time comes, if ever it comes, I will find a home in the bottom of the river'. But the Lord so ordered it that when that time did come I was not able to walk one quarter of the way to the river. As I sat there thinking, I seemed to feel some great and mighty presence. I did not know then what it was. I did learn afterwards that it was Jesus, the sinner's friend. I walked up to the bar and pounded it with my fist till I made the glasses rattle. Those who stood by drinking looked on with scornful curiosity. I said I would never take another drink, if I died on the street, and really I felt as though that would happen before morning. Something said, 'If you want to keep this promise, go and have yourself locked up'. I went to the nearest stationhouse and had myself locked up.
>
> I was placed in a narrow cell, and it seemed as though all the demons that could find room came in that place with me. This was not all the company I had either. No, praise the Lord; that dear Spirit that came to me in the saloon was present, and said, Pray. I did pray, and though I did not feel any great help, I kept on praying. As soon as I was able to leave my cell I was taken to the police court and remanded back to the cell. I was finally released,

and found my way to my brother's house, where every care was given me. While lying in bed the admonishing Spirit never left me, and when I arose the following Sabbath morning I felt that day would decide my fate, and toward evening it came into my head to go to Jerry M'Auley's Mission. I went. The house was packed, and with great difficulty I made my way to the space near the platform. There I saw the apostle to the drunkard and the outcast—that man of God, Jerry M'Auley. He rose, and amid deep silence told his experience. There was a sincerity about this man that carried conviction with it, and I found myself saying, 'I wonder if God can save *me?*' I listened to the testimony of twenty-five or thirty persons, every one of whom had been saved from rum, and I made up my mind that I would be saved or die right there. When the invitation was given, I knelt down with a crowd of drunkards. Jerry made the first prayer. Then Mrs. M'Auley prayed fervently for us. Oh, what a conflict was going on for my poor soul! A blessed whisper said, 'Come'; the devil said, 'Be careful'. I halted but a moment, and then, with a breaking heart, I said, 'Dear Jesus, can you help me?' Never with mortal tongue can I describe that moment. Although up to that moment my soul had been filled with indescribable gloom, I felt the glorious brightness of the noonday sun shine into my heart. I felt I was a free man. Oh, the precious feeling of safety, of freedom, of resting on Jesus! I felt that Christ with all his brightness and power had come into my life; that, indeed, old things had passed away and all things had become new.

From that moment till now I have never wanted a drink of whiskey, and I have never seen money enough to make me take one. I promised God that night that if he would take away the appetite for strong drink, I would work for him all my life. He has done his part, and I have been trying to do mine.[1]

Next is "the case of our friend Henry Alline . . . his report of the 26th of March, 1775, on which his poor divided mind became unified for good".

As I was about sunset wandering in the fields lamenting my miserable lost and undone condition, and almost ready to sink under my burden, I thought I was in such a miserable case as never any man was before. I returned to the house, and when I got to the door, just as I was stepping off the threshold, the following impressions came into my mind like a powerful but small still voice. You have been seeking, praying, reforming, laboring, reading, hearing, and meditating, and what have you done by it towards your salvation? Are you any nearer to conversion now than when you first began? Are you any more prepared for heaven, or fitter to appear before the impartial bar of God, than when you first began to seek?

It brought such conviction on me that I was obliged to say that I did not think I was one step nearer than at first, but as much condemned, as much exposed, and as miserable as before. I cried out within myself, O Lord God, I am lost, and if thou, O Lord, doest not find out some new way, I know nothing of, I shall never be saved, for the ways and methods I have prescribed to myself have all failed me, and I am willing they should fail. O Lord, have mercy! O Lord, have mercy!

These discoveries continued until I went into the house and sat down. After I sat down, being all in confusion, like a drowning man that was just giving up to sink, and almost in an agony, I turned very suddenly round in my chair, and seeing part of an old Bible lying in one of the chairs, I caught hold of it in great haste; and opening it without any premeditation, cast my eyes on the 38th Psalm, which was the first time I ever saw the word of God: it took hold of me with such power that it seemed to go through my whole soul, so that it seemed as if God was praying in, with, and for me. About this time my father called the family to attend prayers; I attended, but paid no regard to what he said in his prayer, but continued praying in those words of the Psalm. O, help me, help me! cried I, thou Redeemer of souls, and save me, or I am gone forever; thou canst this night, if thou pleasest, with one drop of thy blood atone for my sins, and appease the wrath of an angry God. At that instant of time when I gave all up to him to do with me as he pleased, and was willing that God should rule over me at his pleasure, redeeming love broke into my soul with repeated scriptures, with such power that my whole soul seemed to be melted down with love; the burden of guilt and condemnation was gone, darkness was expelled, my heart humbled and filled with gratitude, and my whole soul, that was a few minutes ago groaning under mountains of death, and crying to an unknown God for help, was now filled with immortal love, soaring on the wings of faith, freed from the chains of death and darkness, and crying out, My Lord and my God; thou art my rock and my fortress, my shield and my high tower, my life, my joy, my present and my everlasting portion. Looking up, I thought I saw that same light [he had on more than one previous occasion seen subjectively a bright blaze of light], though it appeared different, and as soon as I saw it, the design was opened to me, according to his promise, and I was obliged to cry out: Enough, enough, O blessed God! The work of conversion, the change, and the manifestations of it are no more disputable than that light which I see, or anything that ever I saw.

In the midst of all my joys, in less than half an hour after my soul was set at liberty, the Lord discovered to me my labor in the ministry and call to preach the gospel. I cried out, Amen, Lord, I'll go; send me, send me. I spent the greatest part of the night in ecstacies of joy, praising and adoring the Ancient of Days for his free and unbounded grace. After I had been so long in this transport and heavenly frame that my nature seemed to require sleep, I thought to close my eyes for a few moments; then the devil stepped in, and told me that if I went to sleep, I should lose it all, and when I should awake in the morning I would find it to be nothing but a fancy and delusion. I immediately cried out, O Lord God, if I am deceived, undeceive me.

I then closed my eyes for a few minutes, and seemed to be refreshed with sleep, and when I awoke, the first inquiry was, Where is my God? And in an instant of time, my soul seemed awake in and with God, and surrounded by the arms of everlasting love. About sunrise I arose with joy to relate to my parents what God had done for my soul, and declared to them the miracle of God's unbounded grace. I took a Bible to show them the words that were impressed by God on my soul the evening before; but when I came to open the Bible, it appeared all new to me.

I so longed to be useful in the cause of Christ, in preaching the gospel, that it seemed as if I could not rest any longer, but go I must and tell the wonders of redeeming love. I lost all taste for carnal pleasures, and carnal company, and was enabled to forsake them.[2]

THE NATURE OF THE CONVERSION PROCESS

Alcoholics Anonymous insists that having a belief in a 'higher power' is *necessary* for its program to work. "If, when you honestly want to, you find you cannot quit entirely, or if when drinking, you have little control over the amount you take . . . you may be suffering from an illness which only a spiritual experience will conquer."[3] I have no data on the extent to which this is true, and the extent to which alcoholism is similar to depression in this respect. But in light of the vast experience of A.A., their opinion at least merits consideration. (It should be noted that in A.A., the 'ideas' (their word) of faith, God, and spiritual experience are interpreted very broadly, seemingly to include almost everything beyond the mundane that elicits awe and wonder and mystery. Indeed, "belief in the A.A. group" to which one belongs apparently is a common form of such faith and is accepted by the group as sufficient, minimal though it be.[4]

All this has a physiological and psychological connection to the forces at work in meditation. A major difference, however, is that meditation is a voluntarily induced state that one reaches most easily with various learned techniques of breathing, concentration, body position, chanting, and rhythmic movements, whereas religious conversion is more likely to be spontaneous.

Some Christian ministers and religious communities try to foster conversions by inculcating the belief in its possibility, and by providing the conditions of personal acceptance that make it more attractive.

> General Booth, the founder of the Salvation Army, considers that the first vital step in saving outcasts consists in making them feel that some decent human being cares enough for them to take an interest in the question whether they are to rise or sink.[5]

And a person may increase the likelihood of conversion or salvation from depression by participating in such religious groups. But more than that the individual cannot do, except perhaps to try 'surrendering' his or her striving so as to be open to the conversion experience.

Though religious conversion differs from other modes of fighting depression because one usually cannot induce a religious conversion by one's own will and efforts, one may make the process more likely to happen by steeping oneself in the religion of conversion, by reading and discussing, and by hoping that one will be saved by religious experience; these are the key tactics of Alcoholics Anonymous (which also relies on mutual support, and group discussion which point out distorted thinking processes). Yet the process of conversion can occur only when one is *not* trying to be converted, or trying to do anything else. Conversion is one of those many processes—like remembering a forgotten word, or a man having an erection—where trying to produce the event only prevents its occurrence.[6]

After the conversion itself the person may continue to be 'God-intoxicated', in religious terms. I take this phrase to mean that the person continues to hold the conversion experience and the idea of God in the conscious mind much of the time. The person perceives what seems to be the evidence of God in all aspects of the world about her. And almost anything—even, for example, the ugly bleeping sound of a warning device telling of a hole in the road as one walks by the way—can be heard as a reminder of God's presence in the world. In this manner, conversion can maintain a continuing barrier against negative self-comparisons and the consequent depression.

SUMMARY

Some people's depressions—especially deep depressions—disappear suddenly and miraculously, without systematic battles and often with great drama. Religious conversions are of this nature, but the phenomenon can occur without the intervention of theistic concepts, as Alcoholics Anonymous has proven.

There is an important similarity between religious conversion and meditation. The state of exhaustion that occurs prior to the radical religious conversions of some very depressed persons is, like meditation, a state of sudden relaxation from striving. It is a time when the person no longer has strength to strive, fight, or even flee, but rather simply falls into exhaustion. At such moments the mental processes of classification, evaluation, and comparison that lead to sadness for the depressive person cease to operate, and the person gets relief—which is then attributed to God, and a religious conversion takes place.

WAYS TO STOP FEELING HELPLESS AND HOPELESS

Self-comparisons constitute the choke point for depressing thoughts. They are the final common path through which all depressing forces exert their influence. And if the person feels helpless to improve her situation, the sense of helplessness combines with the negative self-comparisons to cause sadness and depression rather than a state of mobilized activity or an angry mood; this description has been repeated many times earlier in this book because it is the core mechanism of depression. This short chapter briefly discusses the sense of helplessness, and how to fight it.[1]

GETTING HOPE BACK

Negative self-comparisons (neg-comps) by themselves do not necessarily make you sad. Instead, you may get angry, or you may mobilize yourself to change your state of affairs. But a helpless, hopeless attitude *along with* neg-comps leads to sadness and depression. This has even been shown in experiments with rats.[2] Rats which have experienced unavoidable electric shocks later behave with less fight, and more depression, with respect to electric shocks that they *can* avoid than do rats that did not previously experience unavoidable shocks. The rats which experienced unavoidable shocks also show chemical changes associated with depression similar to humans. It behooves us, then, to consider how one can mitigate the helpless feeling.

People as well as rats learn general attitudes about their capacity to act effectively, which then affect their outlook on specific situations.

When I was an infant, my parents put me into a large box-like structure hung outside a second-floor window, well-checked by an architect friend for safety. In accord with the theory of the times, they taught me independence by refusing to accede to my cries when I sought attention and company. Throughout my life, I have had a predisposition not to ask others for help such as advice, and support within institutions, because I assumed that help would not be forthcoming. It is entirely possible that my attitude of not expecting help from people, stems from my experiences outside the window as a child, probably accompanied by a general attitude on the part of my parents of making me go it alone. On the other hand, I have always had the feeling that I could master my physical and mental circumstances with study, hard work, and patience so as to make my living situation comfortable and convenient, and my intellectual problems superable, and to make do with my own company. Perhaps in such fashion lifelong attitudes are acquired with respect to capability and helplessness. (But perhaps this is simply coincidence. Scientific studies of such historical processes apparently do not exist.)

One obvious tactic is to realize that you are *not* helpless and you *can* change your actual state of affairs so that the comparison will be less negative. Sometimes this requires gradual relearning through a graded series of tasks which show you that you can be successful, eventually leading to success in tasks that at the beginning seemed overwhelmingly difficult to you. This is the rationale of many behavioral programs that teach people to overcome their fears of going out in public, of heights, of various social situations, and so on.

Indeed, the rats mentioned above which first learned to be helpless when given inescapable shocks afterwards were taught by experimenters to learn that they could escape the later shocks, and they thereby showed diminished chemical changes associated with depression. The underlying assumption of 'learned helplessness' is that if a depressive learns to feel more capable and less helpless, she will be less prone to sadness and depression, because her neg-comps will then be accompanied by purposeful activity to change them.

It is not always clear just *how* capable people *ought* to feel. Sometimes vacationers are told that they are capable of swimming across a body of water which they are not capable of swimming, and hence they drown. Sometimes students are told they are capable of mastering programs which are too much for them, and hence they fail painfully. People's situations are not always like the situations of the laboratory rats which have been taught to act as if they are helpless when in fact they are able to escape from the shocks they receive.

External conditions may dictate that the individual is indeed helpless to improve a particular neg-comp. A 55-year-old tennis player cannot realistically hope to improve his speed afoot to again beat the younger partner who has just begun to beat him.

Exhaustion and ill health also restrict a person's possibilities for improving one's situation. It is thoroughly reasonable that lack of energy and sad feelings often keep company.

Relearning That You are Not Helpless

Often, however, people feel helpless because they have 'learned' to think that they are helpless in circumstances which another person would feel capable of changing in order to improve the neg-comp. Whereas a 'normal' person might decide to change her work-habits so as to remove the cause of a boss's criticism, a depressive might think that she is helpless to alter the boss's judgment.

Sometimes you can change your state of belief about what you can do so, in order to feel less helpless. Athletic coaches often encourage players and persuade them that they can attain goals that they believe are beyond them, and thereby enable them to attain performances they otherwise would not reach. Toward the end of every marathon, there are bystanders who shout 'You can do it' as flagging runners stagger toward the finish, and these shouts may help them along.

The underlying idea is that our judgments are affected by the opinions of others as well as by the experiences that we bring to the judgment; if the others' opinion is that we 'can do it', we are more likely to believe that we can, and hence feel less helpless. Teachers in all fields employ to good effect the arts of encouragement and reassurance.

It is important to keep in mind that the very fact of being depressed biases our judgments of our capabilities in a negative direction, just as the other polar mood—mania—makes us feel capable of doing anything, including many things that we should not do.

Practice is Important

Another way to increase your sense of mastery and decrease your sense of being helpless is by a graded series of practice exercises which demonstrate that you can indeed do more than you think you can. This is dramatically evident in the physical therapy of persons who have been injured or otherwise suffered diminished physical capacity. Taking one step, then two steps, then four steps, and so on, builds both physical capacity and belief. The same is true of learning to overcome phobias. The person who is afraid of heights can first practice on small hillocks, then hills, then low buildings, and continuing into higher places. This sort of practice is a key staple tactic of behavioral psychotherapy in fighting fears.

Taking a gradual view of improvement is important in occupational and educational matters, too. I once knew a gifted student of mathematics who had dropped out of school several times because he could not stand the pressure. Then each time he would return, vow to make up for all his past defaults, and proceed to work 16 hours a day—until he again cracked up, at which point he became depressed. With each crackup he felt more helpless to get back on the track and mold his life into sound order. It would have been much better if he had studied part-time for a while, first just one course while working, then two courses, then perhaps three courses on a 'full-time basis', and so on, to build his confidence and a record of success.

It is important to arrange the practices in such fashion that they do not arouse the very sense of helplessness that is being attacked. For example, the instruction 'Bend down and touch your toes' only discourages a person who cannot now do it. But the instruction 'Bend downwards as far as you comfortably can' does not set up an unattainable goal but rather an attainable one.

A Counselor Can Help

A counselor can go beyond simply stating an opinion about our abilities, and can engage in argument with us about our capacities. And a counselor can show us how we are biased in our negative opinions about our own capabilities. The counselor can even get us going on the process of successfully learning from experience that we can do more than we had thought we could. But much more than that another person cannot do for us, and indeed, much more than that one cannot do for oneself. This is not to diminish the importance of the process, but rather to suggest how little there is to say about the process of coming to feel less helpless.

Judging from animal experiments,[3] it is probably possible to reduce the sense of helplessness in humans with the use of chemicals. And this can constitute a basis for drug treatment of depression; the drugs reduce the helpless feeling, which in turn reduces the sadness, and also perhaps enables the person to learn to overcome obstacles which lead to unlearning the sense of helplessness. Assessing the usefulness of this approach is part of the overall assessment of drug therapy discussed in the Appendix to Chapter 4.

The building of trust in a therapeutic relationship may also have a beneficial effect on the numerator of the Mood Ratio. Believing that you are helpless is equivalent to believing that nothing you do can improve your actual situation. When you distrust the reliability and goodwill of the world around you, you are more likely to feel helpless and hence depressed. So improvement of the ability to trust—to have hope that the world will respond positively toward your initiatives—can work against depression. And this can sometimes be learned in a patient-therapist relationship.

A Success Story

Here is the story of a woman journalist, Nancy Chevalier, who learned that she was not helpless to control her depression, and has actually done it:

> After my long ordeal, I came to realize that all the doctors and pills and therapies psychiatry had to offer would never be enough. Somehow, I would have to build up my own resistance to this horrible mental illness. I, myself, would have to develop some control over it.
>
> In addition to taking the medication, I began to walk an hour every day, to do every volunteer job I could find and to take up creative writing and yoga. I listened to music—all kinds of music at all hours of the day and night. Charlie Byrd, Vivaldi, Johann Strauss, Stan Getz—all played a role in my self-styled therapy.
>
> Although I had never been a good dancer, I began to twirl

around the living room, fantasizing I was in Vienna in a gorgeous ballgown, waltzing the night away.

In my fantasy, I imagined that there was a mangy black dog on my shoulders, but I waltzed so fast that he finally couldn't hang on any longer, so he fell to the floor and ran off. And I just kept on dancing the whole night through.

The visualization was so powerful that I literally felt myself to be there in Vienna, in that ballroom. No one could be depressed in that ballroom. I would not be depressed; I would be well and happy. I told myself this over and over again while listening to the music. After several weeks, the depression lifted and I was well once more . . .

For over three years now, I have managed to keep my illness at arm's length by taking my medication and using these various techniques.

Two years ago, while vacationing with my husband on the Hawaiian island of Kauai, severe depression struck once again. But I made up my mind to try to control it. Although barely functioning, I drove 30 miles to the nearest drugstore, where I located some dusty tapes of Strauss waltzes, which I then played day and night. At first, I could only move one finger slowly to the music, but I kept on playing the tapes over and over. I told myself that I would not be depressed in Hawaii, I would be joyful in Vienna. The music and visualization worked and the depression disappeared in a few weeks.

That mangy black dog is still there; he didn't die and I know it. I can sometimes feel him lurking around. But as he approaches me and begins to pounce, I take out my medication, my writing notebook and my waltz tapes and I scare him off. It's all I can do, but I do it so faithfully and fiercely that I like to believe that I've gotten rid of him forever. And maybe, just maybe, I have. (Chevalier 1990, 12–14)

My own is another story of learning that I could control the depression—though at first only one day a week—and then successfully doing so for more than 17 years now without relapse, after 13 years of depression. (See the Introduction and Epilogue for more details.)

SUMMARY

Self-comparisons are the final common path through which all depressing forces exert their influence. And if the person feels helpless to improve her situation, the sense of helplessness combines with the negative self-comparisons to cause sadness; this is the core mechanism of depression. A helpless, hopeless attitude along with neg-comps leads to sadness and depression.

Often people feel helpless because they have 'learned' to think that they are helpless in circumstances which another person would feel capable of changing in order to improve the neg-comp.

One obvious tactic is to realize that you are *not* helpless and you *can* change your actual state of affairs so that the comparison will be less negative. Sometimes this requires gradual relearning through a graded series of tasks which show you that you can be successful, eventually leading to success in tasks that at the beginning seemed overwhelmingly difficult to you.

Sometimes you can change your state of belief about what you can do so, in order to feel less helpless.

Another way to increase your sense of mastery and decrease your sense of being helpless is by a graded series of practice exercises which demonstrate that you can indeed do more than you think you can. It is important to arrange the practices in such fashion that they do not arouse the very sense of helplessness that is being attacked.

POSTSCRIPT: ON INCREASING THE AMOUNT OF PLEASURES

All of this book focuses on the down side—pain and negative self-comparisons. But the up side—pleasure—enters into depression, too. Still, the book has not previously considered it, nor have I seen it discussed systematically by other writers in the psychological literature on depression. It would seem that the pleasure aspect of life needs attention, too. (Here I may be influenced by my years doing economics. Economists always want to see both the demand and the supply sides of any question.)

It is reasonable—and anecdotal accounts seem to bear this out—that one's mood, and one's desire to continue living, are affected by the quantity of pleasurable experiences one has, and not only the quantity of pain. If so, it makes sense to increase the quantity of pleasure in the depressed person's life.

So one wonders: What do we know—if anything—about how to increase a person's drive to obtain pleasurable experiences, and the person's capacity to find them?

Here we must distinguish various kinds of wants and satisfactions. And especially must we distinguish between the satisfactions from work and the satisfactions from non-work pleasures.

Work is a crucial element in fighting depression, of course. One of its benefits is that (by definition) it is the opposite of being helpless, and hence must reduce felt helplessness. Creating also is intrinsically satisfying, I would guess. But at the end of work one is often fatigued from the effort which work demands and expends, and fatigue increases the propensity for sadness and depression. Also, unsatisfactory work—always possible in any enterprise—can be depressing.

Non-work pleasures differ from work in that they do not cause fatigue (except for sports, which causes bodily rather than mental fatigue, and hence is not depressing). And non-work pleasures never cause the feeling of failure because (again by definition) one is not attempting to accomplish an objective. (The best discussion of the differences between work pleasures and non-work pleasures is found in Jewish religious discussions of the Sabbath.)

So it is non-work pleasures that the depressed person needs more of. But how to induce them? This is a subject which needs research. In the meantime, I can only recommend that on your own behalf, or on behalf of the depressed person whose welfare you are concerned about, you try whatever devices you can dream up to increase the amount of experiences that the depressed person can find pleasurable—a walk in the sunshine, a funny movie, making love, a tasty soup, whatever.

One thing more: Understand that it is *legitimate* to enjoy pleasures. Sometimes depressed people feel guilty about enjoying themselves. One of the few categorical assertions I make in the book is this: You are *entitled* to enjoy yourself. Indeed, you should feel that you *ought* to enjoy yourself. This is as much part of your cure as any medicine. So do it.

VALUES THERAPY: A NEW SYSTEMATIC APPROACH FOR TOUGH CASES

Values Therapy suits some tough cases of depression, where the cause of the depression is not obvious and easily altered. It may be especially suitable for a person who has suffered a severe shortage of parental love as a child, or experienced over-long grief following loss of a loved one as an adult.

Values Therapy is a more radical departure from conventional modes of fighting depression than are the tactics discussed earlier. Other writers have mentioned and used some of its elements in an ad hoc fashion, and have emphasized that depression is often a philosophical problem (for example Erich Fromm, Carl Jung, and Viktor Frankl). Values Therapy is quite new, however, in offering a *systematic* method of drawing upon a person's fundamental values so as to conquer depression.

Values Therapy is especially appropriate when a person complains that life has lost its meaning—the most philosophical of depressions. You may wish to re-read Tolstoy's vivid description of this state in Chapter 6, as well as pages 38 to 39.

THE NATURE OF VALUES THERAPY

The central element of Values Therapy is searching within yourself for a latent value or belief which conflicts with being depressed. Bringing such a value to the fore then causes you to modify or constrain or oppose the belief (or value) that leads to the negative self-comparisons. Russell describes his passage from a sad childhood to happy maturity in this fashion:

> Now, on the contrary, I enjoy life; I might almost say that with every year that passes I enjoy it more. *This is due partly to having discovered what were the things that I most desired, and having gradually acquired many of these things.* Partly it is due to having successfully dismissed certain objects of desire—such as the acquisition of indubitable knowledge about something or other—as essentially unattainable.[1]

This is quite different from trying to argue away the sadness-causing way of thinking, which is the main approach of cognitive therapy.

The discovered value may be (as it was for me) the value that says *directly* that life should be happy rather than sad. Or it may be a value that leads *indirectly* to a reduction in sadness, such as the value that one's children should have a life-loving parent to imitate.

The discovered value may be that you are unwilling to subject people you love to the grief of having you respond to your depression by killing yourself, as was the case with this young woman:

> My mother died seven years ago by her own hand . . .
> I can't imagine what [my father] must have felt when he found her. I *can* imagine how my mother must have felt as she descended the stairs to the garage for the last time . . .
> I know. I've been there. I tried suicide several times in my life when I was in my early 20s and was quite serious at least twice . . . Besides actually attempting suicide, I've wanted, wished and even prayed to die more times than I can count.
> Well, I'm 32 now and I'm still alive. I'm even married and have moved from a secretarial position into entry-level management . . . I'm alive because of my mother's death. She taught me that in spite of my illness I had to live. Suicide just isn't worth it.
> I saw the torment my mother's death caused others: my father, my brother, her neighbors and friends. When I saw their overwhelming grief, I knew I could never do the same thing she had

done—force other people to take on the burden of pain I'd leave
behind if I died by my own hand.[2]

The discovered value may lead you to accept yourself for what you
and your limitations are, and to go on to other aspects of your life. A
person with an emotionally-scarred childhood, or a polio patient
confined to a wheelchair, may finally look facts in the face, cease railing
at and struggling against their fates, and decide not to let those
handicaps dominate their lives but rather to pay attention to what they
can contribute to others with a joyful spirit. Or they may devote
themselves to being better parents by being happy instead of sad.

A FIVE-STEP PROCESS OF VALUE TRANSFORMATION

Values Therapy need not always proceed systematically. But a
systematic procedure may be helpful to some, at least to make clear
which operations are important in Values Therapy. This is the outline
of such a systematic procedure:

Step 1: Ask yourself what you want in life—both your most
important desires as well as your routine desires. Write down the
answers. The list may be long, and it is likely to include very disparate
items ranging from peace in the world, to professional success, to a new
car every other year, to your oldest daughter being more polite to her
grandmother.

Step 2: Rank these desires corresponding to their importance *to
you*. One method is to put numbers on each want, running from '1'
(all-important) to '5' (not very important).

Step 3: Ask yourself whether any *really* important wants have been
left off your list. Good health for yourself and your family? The present
and future happiness of your children or spouse? The feeling that you
are living an honest life? Remember to include matters that might
seem important when looking back on your life at age 70 that might
not come to mind now, such as spending plenty of time with your
children, or having the reputation as a person who is helpful to others.[3]

Step 4: Look for the conflicts in your list of wants. Check if
conflicts are resolved in a manner that contradicts the indications of

importance that you accord to the various elements. For example, you may put health for yourself in the top rank, and professional success in the second rank, but you may nevertheless be working so hard for professional success that you are doing serious harm to your health, with depression as a result.

In my case, the future and present happiness of my children is at the top of the list, and I believe that the chance that children will be happy in the future is much better if their parents are not depressed as the children are growing up. Close to the top for me, but *not* at the top, is success in my work as measured by its impact upon the society. Yet I had invested so much of myself in my work, and with such results, that my thoughts about my work depressed me. It therefore became clear to me that if I am to live in accordance with my stated values and priorities, I must treat my work in some fashion that it does not depress me, for the sake of my children even if for no other reason.

In my discussions with others about their depressions, we usually discover a conflict between a top-level value which demands that the person not be depressed, and one or more lower-level values that are involved in depression. The goal that life is a gift to be cherished and enjoyed is a frequent top-level value of this sort (though, unlike such writers as Abraham Maslow, Fromm, Ellis, and others, I do not consider this to be an instinct or a self-evident truth. More about this later.)

Step 5: Take steps to resolve the conflicts between higher-order and lower-order values in such manner that higher-order values requiring you not to be depressed are put in control. If you recognize that you are working so hard that you are injuring your health and additionally depressing yourself, and that health is more important than the fruits of the extra work, you will be more likely to face up to a decision to work less, and to avoid being depressed; a wise general physician may put the matter to you in exactly this fashion. In my case I had to recognize that I owe it to my children to somehow keep my work-life from depressing me.

Many sorts of devices may be employed once you address yourself to a task such as this one. One such device is to make and enforce a less-demanding work schedule. Another device is to prepare and follow an agenda for future projects that promises a fair measure of success in completion and in reception. Another device is to refuse to allow negative self-comparisons concerned with work to remain in the mind, either by pushing them out with brute force of will, or by training yourself to switch them off with behavior-modification techniques, or by meditation techniques, or whatever.

MAPPING OUT YOUR WANTS

Your wants, goals, values, beliefs, preferences, or desires by any other name are a most complex subject for anyone. Counselors often ask people, 'What do you *really* want?' This question tends to confuse and mislead the person of whom it is asked. The question suggests that a. there is *one* most-important want that b. the person can discover if she will only be sufficiently honest and sincere, the word 'really' suggesting such honesty and truth. In fact there usually are *several* important wants, and no amount of 'sincere' searching can determine which one is 'really' most important.

The key point here is that we must aim at learning the *structure of our many wants,* rather than fruitlessly chasing after just one most-important want.

We must also recognize that our wants cannot easily be sorted out. Consider this curiousity: No matter how depressed a person is, he usually would not say that he would prefer to change places with other individuals who are not depressed, even super-happy or super-successful people. Why? Is there some deep confusion here about the meaning of 'I' in the sentence 'I would like to change places with X'? What can one make of this? Does it show some greater self-affection than we attribute to depression sufferers? Or is it simply the impossibility or meaninglessness of 'changing places'? Would memories remain with the person after the change? Is there just a problem of misfitting, as a beggar would not prefer the clothes of a rich man if the clothes are a grossly bad fit to the beggar? I do not urge you to break your head on this curious question, but only to recognize that the structure of wants is more complex than a shopping list.

Behavior-modification therapy can offer help in Values Therapy by building the habit of interposing the discovered value in front of the depression-causing value whenever you feel sad.

The result of the values-discovery process may be that a person becomes 'twice born', as in the cases described by William James. Clearly this is radical therapy, like surgery that implants a second heart in a person to aid the leaky and failing original heart.

What about Innate Wants?

There is a school of thought—two prominent representatives of which are Maslow[4] and Selye[5]—who believe that the most important and basic values are biologically inherent in the human animal. This implies that there are inherent goals which are the same for all people. For this school of thought the explanation of depression and other ills is that "life must be allowed to run its natural course toward the fulfillment of its innate potential."[6] Or in Frankl's words, "I think the meaning of our existence is not invented by ourselves, but rather detected."[7] For Selye, one's innate potential is a capacity to do productive work with a feeling of success. For Maslow[8] the potential is for 'self-actualization', which is basically the state of freedom to experience one's life fully and enjoyably.

I think the better view is that though one's values and aims are inevitably influenced by the physical make-up of *Homo sapiens* and the social conditions of human society, there is a wide range of possible basic values. And I think one will do better in discovering what one's own values are, and what they ought to be, by looking into oneself, rather than by looking at human experience in general and then deducing what one's basic values 'really' are or ought to be.

The very fact that different observers such as Maslow and Selye point to different basic 'innate' values should warn us of the difficulty or impossibility of making such deductions soundly. And if a person exhibits basic values that do not jibe with Maslow's self-actualization— for example, if a person sacrifices family for religion or country, and is never sorry afterward—Maslow simply assumes that this is not healthy and that the person will inevitably have to pay a price later on. But that kind of reasoning only proves what one wishes to prove. I prefer to accept the simple evidence of my eyes that people differ greatly in their values. I believe that neither I nor anyone else can determine which values are 'inherent' and hence 'healthy', and which are not.

I recommend, therefore, that you look into yourself—but with diligence and with the urge to find some truth—to determine what are your basic values and priorities. This is quite consistent with believing that a more fundamental source of one's values is outside oneself, of religious or natural or cultural origin.

THE VALUE OF DOING GOOD FOR OTHERS

Saying that a person should look into herself or himself for one's basic values does *not* imply that the basic values are, or ought to be, those that refer only to the individual or the family. With the possible exception of Maslow, all the philosophical-psychological writers— whether or not they believe in 'inherent' values, and whether they are religious or secular—make clear that a person's best chance to shake off depression and instead lead a satisfying life is to seek life meaning in contributing to others. As Frankl puts it:

> We have to beware of the tendency to deal with values in terms of the mere self-expression of man himself. For *logos,* or 'meaning', is not only an emergence from existence itself but rather something confronting existence. If the meaning that is waiting to be fulfilled by man were really nothing but a mere expression of self, or no more than a projection of his wishful thinking, it would immediately lose its demanding and challenging character, it could no longer call man forth or summon him . . .
>
> I wish to stress that the true meaning of life is to be found in the world rather than within man or his own *psyche,* as though it were a closed system. By the same token, the real aim of human existence cannot be found in what is called self-actualization. Human existence is essentially self-transcendence rather than self-actualization. Self-actualization is not a possible aim at all, for the simple reason that the more a man would strive for it, the more he would miss it. For only to the extent to which man commits himself to the fulfillment of his life's meaning, to this extent he also actualizes himself. In other words, self-actualization cannot be attained if it is made an end in itself, but only as a side effect of self-transcendence.[9]

Oscar Wilde descended into the depths of despair when he was sent to jail for perjury, sex offenses, and complicity in England's underworld. His story of how he came "out of the depths" (as he titled his essay in Latin) reveals how his salvation lay in re-ordering his priorities:

> I have lain in prison for nearly two years. Out of my nature has come wild despair; an abandonment to grief that was piteous even

to look at; terrible and impotent rage; bitterness and scorn; anguish that wept aloud; misery that could find no voice; sorrow that was dumb. I have passed through every possible mood of suffering. Better than Wordsworth himself I know what Wordsworth meant when he said, "Suffering is permanent, obscure, and dark, and has the nature of infinity". But while there were times when I rejoiced in the idea that my sufferings were to be endless, I could not bear them to be without meaning. Now I find hidden somewhere away in my nature something that tells me that nothing in the whole world is meaningless, and suffering least of all. That something hidden away in my nature, like a treasure in a field, is Humility.

It is the last thing left in me, and the best: the ultimate discovery at which I have arrived, the starting-point for a fresh development. It has come to me right out of myself, so I know that it has come at the proper time. It could not have come before, nor later. Had any one told me of it, I would have rejected it. Had it been brought to me, I would have refused it. As I found it, I want to keep it. I must do so. It is the one thing that has in it the elements of life, of a new life, a Vita Nuova for me. Of all things it is the strangest; one cannot give it away and another may not give it to one. One cannot acquire it except by surrendering everything that one has. It is only when one has lost all things, that one knows that one possesses it.

Now I have realized that it is in me, I see quite clearly what I ought to do; in fact, must do. And when I use such a phrase as that, I need not say that I am not alluding to any external sanction or command. I admit none. I am far more of an individualist than I ever was. Nothing seems to me of the smallest value except what one gets out of oneself. My nature is seeking a fresh mode of self-realization. That is all I am concerned with. And the first thing that I have got to do is to free myself from any possible bitterness of feeling against the world.

Morality does not help me. I am a born antinomian. I am one of those who are made for exceptions, not for laws. But while I see that there is nothing wrong in what one does, I see that there is something wrong in what one becomes. It is well to have learned that . . .

The fact of my having been a common prisoner of a common jail I must frankly accept, and, curious as it may seem, one of the things I shall have to teach myself is not to be ashamed of it. I must accept it as a punishment, and if one is ashamed of having been punished, one might just as well never have been punished at all. Of course there are many things of which I was convicted that I have not done, but then there are many things of which I was convicted that I had done, and a still greater number of things in my life for which I was never indicted at all. And as the gods are strange, and punish us for what is good and humane in us as much as for what is evil and perverse, I must accept the fact that one is punished for the good as well as for the evil that one does. I have no doubt that it is quite right one should be. It helps one, or should help one, to realize both, and not to be too conceited about either. And if I then am not ashamed of my punishment, as I hope not to be, I shall be able to think, and walk, and live with freedom.[10]

Wilde's story reveals that very different values are fundamental for different people. Wilde found that for him the most basic value was the "ultimate realization of the artistic life [which] is simply self-development."[11]

VALUES AND RELIGION

Values Therapy frequently has connections with religion. This is sometimes problematic from the standpoint of communication, because even the word 'religion' alienates many people. Religious experience has a very specific God-orientation for some people, whereas for others it is any experience of the awesome mysteries of life and the universe.

Suggesting as I will that religious values and spiritual (though not supernatural) experience may be the solution for some people may alienate those who are militantly anti-religion. On the other hand, suggesting as I will that rejecting the concept of a historical father-like God may help for others may alienate those who have a traditional Judeo-Christian belief in an active God. But so be it.

(Alcoholics Anonymous seems to have little trouble with this problem, as mentioned earlier. Its minimum requirement—that members have faith that there is some power greater than the individual—seems to be widely acceptable because almost anyone can accept the idea that the 'greater' power may simply be the strength and energy of 'the group'. So perhaps the problem is not grave.)

A religious value, or a value for being a religious person, can be the discovered value in Values Therapy. For a person who discovers the value of being a Christian, the discovery implies believing that God forgives you for all your sins, and you must hand over to God responsibility for both your decisions and your actions. If this is the case with you, as long as you live in such manner as you believe a Christian ought to live, any negative comparison between what you are and what you ought to be is inappropriate. In other words, even if you have low status in the daily world, or if you have been a sinner, you may still feel worthy if you believe as a Christian.

Christianity says that if you love Jesus, Jesus will love you in return—no matter how low you are; this is crucial for the Christian depressive. It means that if one accepts Christian values, one is bound to feel loved in return. This operates to diminish the force of negative self-comparisons, both by making one feel less bad because all are equal in Jesus, and because the feeling of love tends to diminish any sadness.

Believing that Jesus suffered for you—and hence that you should not suffer—keeps some people out of the clutches of depression. In this way Christianity offers unusual succor to those afflicted by sadness.

For a Jew, a religious value that works against depression is the Jewish commitment to cherish life. A traditional Jew accepts as a religious duty that one must enjoy her or his life, both materially and spiritually. Of course, 'cherishing' life does not mean just 'fun'; rather it means being constantly aware that life is good and all-important. A Jew is not permitted by religious dictates to be inordinately sad; for example, one is not allowed to mourn more than 30 days, and to do so is to sin.

One must be careful, of course, that the religious 'requirement' of enjoying life does not turn into just another 'must' that you fail to achieve and therefore leads to additional negative self-comparisons. If you tie yourself into this sort of a knot, then you obviously are better off without this religious committment. But this is not a black mark against such a religious idea; no set of guidelines for living is without its own dangers, just as the kitchen knife that is so useful for cutting food can be the instrument of a self-inflicted injury, accidental or intentional.

In the Epilogue, I describe at length how Values Therapy saved me from depression. The highlights relevant to this particular section are as follows: I first learned to keep depression at bay on the Sabbath, following the Jewish injunction that one must not be sad on the Sabbath. Then I recognized that a more general Jewish value demands that one must not throw away the largest part of one's life in sadness. Then, and perhaps most important, I faced up to the conflict between my depression and my children's future happiness. These discoveries cracked my depression and permitted me to enter into a period (lasting until now) when I am basically undepressed and even happy (sometimes *very* happy), though I must continue to fight against depression on a day-to-day basis.

It is interesting that Tolstoy invented for himself (though he ostensibly took the value from Catholicism) a value which resolved his depression and which is like the Jewish value concerning life. Tolstoy concluded that life itself is its own meaning for the peasant, whom he proceeded to try to imitate:

> The life of the whole labouring people, the whole of mankind who produce life, appeared to me in its true significance. I understood that *that* is life itself, and that the meaning given to that life is true: and I accepted it . . . a bird is so made that it must fly, collect food, and build a nest, and when I see that a bird does this, I have pleasure in its joy . . . The meaning of human life lies in supporting it . . .[12]

(If one realizes that the question 'What is the meaning of life?' is probably semantically meaningless, one can be free to find other values and philosophical constructions.)

Another Jewish value is that a person must respect oneself. For example, a great Talmudic sage asserted: "Be not wicked in thine own esteem."[13] And a recent scholar amplified this as follows:

> *Be not wicked in thine own esteem.*
> This saying preaches the duty of self-respect. Do not think yourself so abandoned that it is useless for you to make "an appeal for mercy and grace" before God. "Regard not thyself as wholly wicked, since by so doing thou givest up hope of repentance" (Maimonides). Communities, like individuals, are under the obligation not to be wicked in their own esteem. Achad Ha-am wrote: "Nothing is more dangerous for a nation or for an individual than to plead guilty to imaginary sins. Where the sin is real—by honest endeavour the sinner can purify himself. But when a man has been persuaded to suspect himself unjustly—what *can* he do? Our greatest need is emancipation from self-contempt, from this idea that we are really worse than all the world. Otherwise, we may in course of time become in reality what we now imagine ourselves to be."[14]

SOME EXAMPLES OF VALUES THERAPY

Frankl provides interesting examples of how depression can be relieved by a procedure like Values Therapy:

> Once, an elderly general practitioner consulted me because of his severe depression. He could not overcome the loss of his wife who had died two years before and whom he had loved above all else. Now how could I help him? What should I tell him? Well, I refrained from telling him anything, but instead confronted him with the question, "What would have happened, Doctor, if you had died first, and your wife would have had to survive you?" "Oh," he said, "for her this would have been terrible; how she would have suffered!" Whereupon I replied, "You see, Doctor, such a suffering has been spared her, and it is you who have spared her this suffering, but now, you have to pay for it by surviving and mourning her." He said no word but shook my hand and calmly left my office. Suffering ceases to be suffering in some way at the moment it finds a meaning, such as the meaning of a sacrifice.[15]

Frankl says that "in logotherapy [his name for a process like Values Therapy] the patient is actually confronted with and reoriented toward the meaning of his life . . . The logotherapist's role consists in widening and broadening the visual field of the patient so that the whole spectrum of meaning and values becomes conscious and visible to him."[16]

Frankl calls his method 'paradoxical intention'. His procedure can be understood in terms of altering negative self-comparisons. As noted in Chapter 10, Frankl asks the patient to imagine that his *actual* state of affairs is different than what it is. For example[17] he asks the man whose wife has died to imagine that the man himself had died first and that the wife is suffering from losing him. Then he leads the person to compare the actual with that imagined state, and to see that the actual state is *preferable* to the imagined state on the basis of some deeper value—in this case, the man's value that his wife not suffer from losing him. This produces a positive self-comparison in place of the former negative self-comparison, and hence removes sadness and depression.

Values Therapy may be thought of as a systematic and understandable form of what used to be called 'changing one's philosophy of life'. It operates directly on the person's view of the world and himself.

Based on his personal experience, Bertrand Russell urged us not to underestimate the curative power of such philosophical thinking. "My purpose is to suggest a cure for the ordinary day-to-day unhappiness from which most people in civilized countries suffer . . . I believe this unhappiness to be very largely due to mistaken views of the world, mistaken ethics . . ."[18]

Many psychologists—particularly those with psychoanalytic training—will question whether such 'deep' problems as depression can be solved with such 'superficial' treatments. But Values Therapy is not superficial—indeed, just the opposite. Of course it is not a perfect therapy, even for those whose depression is not well-handled with other therapeutic approaches. In some cases it may be that the struggle to make one value dominate another requires too much energy of a person, and perhaps a complete psychoanalytic cleansing would bring the person to easier ground (though psychoanalysis's track record with depression is poor). In other cases, the person may lack the powers of reasoning to carry out Values Therapy, at least by himself. Or, a person may have a strong motivation to stay miserable. Lastly, a person's hunger for love and approval may be unslakable.

THE ROLE FOR A COUNSELOR

A counselor can certainly help many people in their struggles to get their values in order and hence overcome depression. The counselor's role here is that of good teacher, clarifying your thoughts for you, helping you concentrate on the task, pushing you to stay at it rather than running away from the hard work. For some people who lack the discipline and mental clarity to do their own Values Therapy, a counselor may be indispensable. For others, however, a counselor may be unnecessary or even a distraction, especially if you cannot find a counselor who will help you do what needs to be done for *you*. Too many therapists insist on doing what they are accustomed to doing, or cannot work within your value structure but insist on inserting their own values into the process.

MAKING IT HAPPEN

Is Values Therapy an easy and comfortable cure for depression? Usually it is not, just as all other anti-depression tactics require effort and stamina. At the beginning, Values Therapy requires considerable mental hard work and discipline, even with the help of a counselor, in constructing an honest and inclusive graded list of your desires in life. After you have decided which are your most fundamental values, you must remind yourself of those values when you start to make negative self-comparisons and get depressed. But it takes effort and dedication to *keep* reminding yourself of those values—just as it takes effort to remind *another person* of important matters when they are being forgotten.

So staying undepressed with Values Therapy is not perfectly easy. But did you really expect otherwise? As the lady said, I never promised you a rose garden. You'll have to judge for yourself whether this is too high a price to pay for being free of depression.

The list of steps given above for Values Therapy may seem pedestrian (a modest play on words, for which I trust you will forgive me) because it is stated in simple, operational terms. You may also assume that this procedure is standard and well-known. In fact, Values Therapy as embodied in these operational steps is quite new. And I hope that you will consider the procedure seriously if other procedures have not managed to overcome your depression. I also hope that theoreticians and empirical workers in psychology will recognize the newness of this approach and will consider it with some gravity, even though it is not simply an extension of the approaches they are accustomed to.

POSTSCRIPT: VALUES TREATMENT AS UPSIDE-DOWN SPECTACLES

Depressives see the world differently than do non-depressives. Where others see a glass as half-full, depressives see the glass as half-empty. Hence depressives need devices to turn many of their perceptions upside down. Values Therapy often can provide the impetus for the reversal of viewpoint.

A person's capacity to alter his or her perspective of the world by effort and practice is astonishing. An interesting example comes from a long-ago experiment in which subjects were given 'upside-down' eyeglasses that inverted everything seen; what is normally seen below appeared above, and *vice versa*. Within a period of weeks the subjects had grown so accustomed to the glasses that they responded quite normally to visual cues. Depressives need to put on psychological spectacles which turn their comparisons upside down, make them perceive the glass as half full rather than half empty, and invert a 'failure' into a 'challenge'.

Values Therapy radically alters one's life perspective. Humor, too, changes one's perspective, and a little humor about one's depression can help you. Not the black humor of 'I wasn't cut out to be a human being', but rather amusement at how one twists reality to give oneself a ridiculously bad shake. For example, at 9:30 a.m. today, I've now been at my desk for one and a quarter hours, working on notes for this book, a bit of stuff for class, some filing, and so forth. But then I notice I haven't *written* anything yet. I haven't done something both creative and solid, haven't created any pages yet. So I tell myself that I can't let myself have breakfast yet, because I don't deserve it, as if all the other things I have done have not been useful work. When I catch myself in this kind of willfully rotten interpretation of reality, I'm amused, and it relaxes me.

Another example: As I was looking for the elevator on the sixth floor of an apartment house while I was depressed, I saw a sign on the wall that said, "Incinerator—Trash and Garbage". I immediately said to myself, "Ah, *that's* the way I should go down." This amused me and reminded me how silly was my lack of self-esteem that led me to have such thoughts.

In the case above of the man whose wife had died, we saw an example of how Frankl's paradoxical intention turns the world upside down. Here is another example of his upside-down technique:

> W. S., aged 35, developed the phobia that he would die of a heart attack, particularly after intercourse, as well as a phobic fear of not being able to go to sleep. When Dr. Gerz asked the patient in his office to "try as hard as possible" to "make his heart beat fast and die of a heart attack" right on the spot", he laughed and replied: "Doc, I'm trying hard, but I can't do it." Following my technique,

Dr. Gerz instructed him "to go ahead and try to die from a heart attack" each time his anticipatory anxiety troubled him. When the patient began laughing about his neurotic symptoms, humor entered in and helped him to put distance between himself and his neurosis. He left the office relieved, with instructions to "die at least three times a day of a heart attack"; and instead of "trying hard to go to sleep", he should "try to remain awake". This patient was seen three days later—symptom-free. He had succeeded in using paradoxical intention effectively.[19]

Ellis stresses the importance of humor in getting you to see how ridiculous are many of our 'oughts' and 'musts'. He has written funny songs for the depressive to sing to help change your mood.

Still another example of how turning your picture of the world upside-down can help you: A good rule for depressives much of the time is the opposite of the Hillel-Jesus Golden Rule. The 'Sunshine Rule for Depressives' is: 'Do unto yourself as you would do unto others'.

To illustrate the Sunshine Rule: Let's say that good and wise friends point out to you your better traits and successes, and encourage you even to the extent of giving you the benefit of the doubt when the facts are not clear. But enemies do the opposite. Depressives dwell on their own shortcomings, as does an enemy. The Sunshine Rule implies that one has a moral obligation to act as a friend to yourself.

SUMMARY

Values Treatment is an extraordinary new (though very old) cure for depression. When a person's negative self-comparisons—no matter what their original cause—are expressed as shortfalls between the person's circumstances and her most fundamental beliefs (values) about what a person should be and do, Values Treatment can build on other values to defeat the depression. The method is to find within yourself other fundamental beliefs and values that call for a person not to suffer but rather to live happily and joyfully, for the sake of God or for the sake of man or woman—oneself, family, or others. If you believe in the superordinate value of a belief which conflicts with being depressed, that belief can induce you to enjoy and cherish life rather than to be sad and depressed.

VALUES THERAPY AND RELIGIOUS DESPAIR

A person with a traditional Western belief in God sometimes loses that belief because the world of events does not square with the traditional belief in God the Father who rewards good and punishes evil. This is the story of Job—why is the good man Job so afflicted? The other side of the coin is found in Psalm 73, where the psalmist inveighs that the wicked flourish. The Nazi Holocaust affected many survivors in this fashion. Such tragedies can shake a traditional Western religious belief to the extent that it cannot be repaired with simple arguments that evil and good get their just rewards in the long run or in heaven.[1] Values Therapy may be the *only* cure in such a situation.

A related cause of depression that requires Values Therapy is 'loss of meaning', as discussed in the previous chapter. Often this occurs when a person implicitly has a view of the world derived from the Greco-Christian concept of a world ordered by God or nature to 'serve' humankind. If for scientific or theological reasons a person comes to doubt this purposive view of the world, life may 'lose its meaning', as it did for Tolstoy. Today this is commonly called 'existential despair'.

A person's psychological structure and personal history interact with the event that leads to loss of meaning, both in explaining its occurrence and in influencing the severity of the depression that results. But Values Therapy focuses on the beliefs themselves rather than on the precipitating event.

There are two approaches to the good-and-evil crisis—spiritual and secular. The secular approach also is often appropriate for a loss-of-meaning crisis.

Buber's Cure for Religious Despair

Misfortune to good people, and the triumph of evil, causes bitterness and then religious despair to some religious people. This is the theme of Job and of Psalm 73, and it is a subject with which Western religious thinkers have struggled.[2] The traditional believer experiences a loss of faith in the concept of God the Father who wisely rules the world rewarding good and punishing evil. A requirement of an appropriate reply to this enigma is that it remove this suffering.

Buber's answer to the contrast and conflict "between the horrible enigma of the happiness of the wicked and [the] suffering" of the author of Psalm 73 is that the sufferer must become "pure in heart".

> The man who is pure in heart, I said, experiences that God is good to him. He does not experience it as a consequence of the purification of his heart, but because only as one who is pure in heart is he able to come to the sanctuaries. This does not mean the Temple precincts in Jerusalem, but the sphere of God's holiness, the holy mysteries of God. Only to him who draws near to these is the true meaning of the conflict revealed.[3]

But what does Buber mean by 'purification'? Laymen—and even other theologians, I suppose—have difficulty in understanding theological writings because they are couched in special theological language and concepts. Hence we often conclude—perhaps correctly—that theological writing is gibberish. But elucidation of theological writings can sometimes reveal great truths, though perhaps stated only obliquely. I believe this to be the case with Buber's interpretation of Psalm 73.

'Purification' clearly does not mean 'moral purification' to Buber. He tells us that the Psalmist found that "to wash his hands in innocence" did not purify his heart.

As I understand Buber, to purify one's heart is to turn inward and to seek inner peace. This inner peace Buber identifies with and labels 'God', though it could just as well be called 'Feeling X' or 'Experience X'. And the *quest* for inner peace will almost inevitably produce inner peace. "To seek God is to have found him", in the words of one sage. Or in Buber's words, "The man who struggles for God is near Him even when he imagines that he is driven far from God."[4]

How may one achieve the purification of inner peace? For Buber, prayer certainly was an important element, 'prayer' here meaning the reading or saying or thinking expressions of such sentiments as awe at life and the universe, and gratitude for them, though of course there are also many other sorts of prayer. For some other people, however, a similar inner peace and purification can be achieved by systematic breathing and relaxation, concentration exercises, immersion in nature, meditation, or other procedures. A *combination* of these methods —all of which are related psychologically and physiologically—can be particularly efficacious.

But why 'purification'? It is common to identify experiences of awe and wonder and inner peace with the term 'God', and hence Feeling X has a connection to God. But how does 'purification' fit in?

The answer lies in the commonly-observed fact that, in addition to inner peace, along with Feeling X comes joy and a sense of awe at life and the universe. Even more, Feeling X tends to produce a cosmic sense of kinship with all people and all nature, which dissolves anger, envy, and greed. For this the term 'purification of the heart' certainly fits.

The sequence, then, is not from purity to Experience X, but rather from the search for Experience X, to achieving Experience X, to purity of the heart. This process can remove the depression following loss of faith that an active God intervenes in the world to punish evil and reward virtue.

Only some fabled yogis can achieve Feeling X permanently. And few of us would want to.[5] But Buber stresses that, for the Psalmist, God says, "I am continually with thee". (Christians would say that grace is always being offered.) This means that the *possibility* of Feeling X is always there, to be achieved whenever a person diligently seeks after it, whenever a person directs and molds the mind in these ways that conduce to inner peace.

One may choose to think of the occurrence of Feeling X as purely natural, a product of one's mind (self-control and imagination) and of body (effects of breathing and posture on the nervous system). Or one may believe that a transcendent non-natural force, commonly called God, is responsible. But if one chooses the latter course, the God concept is not a God involved with the course of human affairs or reward and punishment, but rather a God of the creation of inner peace and purification of the heart, concerning which "there is nothing left of Heaven."[6]

Not all people can or are willing to follow Buber's way. It requires that a person not automatically reject such a spiritual way. It also requires that the person have a modicum of natural capacity for spiritual experience, just as enjoying music requires some natural capacity (though perhaps all persons are so endowed). For those who cannot follow Buber's way there is at least one other way, completely secular. This way also is appropriate for a loss-of-meaning crisis.

A Secular Response to Religious Despair

The secular way is to inquire into what a person considers important—which might be non-violence, happiness for one's children, a beautiful environment, or one's nation's success. Upon inquiry, most people will agree that they have a 'taste' for their own values and believe these values to be important without having to justify them from a religious or world view.

Values Therapy then asks the person simply to treat as important the values he says he believes are important—to recognize that he is *asserting* and *affirming* that there is meaning in these values and their associated situations. Bertrand Russell commented that no philosopher is in doubt about objective reality when holding a crying baby in the middle of the night. Similarly, secular Values Therapy asks a person to acknowledge that which is implicit in his values and behavior, to wit, that the person does find meaning in various aspects of life even while the person is ostensibly in doubt about meaning in general. This contradiction sometimes leads a person to abandon the general question about whether life has meaning, on the grounds that the question is a meaningless linguistic expression in the person's mind, and itself the source of the unnecessary and avoidable depression. (For others, of course, statements about the meaning of life can be unconfused and meaningful.)

SUMMARY

Sometimes a person with a traditional Western belief in God loses that belief because events in the world do not square with the traditional belief in God the Father who rewards good and punishes evil. A related cause of depression is 'loss of meaning' about one's life. There are two approaches to such crises—spiritual and secular. The chapter discusses both these approaches that are so intertwined with a person's most fundamental beliefs.

PART FOUR

Some Final Matters

SUMMING UP

The aim of this book is to better understand and cure depression—people's generally, and yours in particular. The core of depression is prolonged sadness plus a sense of worthlessness, in the context of an attitude of helplessness. To understand depression we must therefore understand how sadness is caused, and why it is prolonged in some people.

The most important idea in the book—the key difference between modern scientifically-successful cognitive therapy and the older psychoanalysis which was never able to prove success in curing depression—is that you have the power to alter your mood by changing your current patterns of thought. The current patterns of thought are largely under your conscious control, and are not dictated irrevocably by your childhood or your genes.

More specifically, your feelings are determined by your Mood Ratio, the comparison between what you think is your present state of affairs, and a counterfactual (hypothetical) benchmark state of affairs. You feel pain when a negative comparison—a Rotten Ratio—is in your mind. And when a negative comparison is combined with a sense of helplessness you feel sadness. If this occurs habitually, you will experience depression. The concept of Mood Ratio and the accompanying Self-Comparisons Analysis constitute the key new theoretical and practical element presented in this book. This structure integrates and reconciles the apparently-conflicting central ideas of the main writers within the field of cognitive therapy.

The 'numerator' in your Mood Ratio is what you believe your actual state of affairs to be at present. If you misconceive your actual situation to be worse than it really is, you expose yourself to a painful Rotten Ratio.

The hypothetical benchmark-state 'denominator' in your Mood Ratio may be, for example, circumstances you were formerly accustomed to but have now lost, or a situation you once expected or hoped for but that has not occurred, or a state of affairs you believe you ought to achieve but have not achieved.

Actual present conditions do not explain well why some people get sad (depressed) for a long period of time while others do not. A variety of factors may be at work, singly or together, to produce a propensity for depression in an individual. These influences may usefully be thought of as existing in the present, though their causes are in the past: an example is poor methods of interpreting reality. Other influences must be seen in the context of the past, such as the death of a parent or severe parental punishment for not being sufficiently successful or dutiful. Different factors combined in a variety of ways cause depression in different individuals.

Though understanding the historical roots of one's depression may be illuminating, the main work of combatting depression deals with the contemporary thinking processes. You must reform the ways that you think so as to control the self-comparisons that you make.

Antidepressant medications have an important part in helping some depressed people banish the pain of depression. But true cure calls for psychotherapy, by yourself or with the assistance of a therapist. A wise therapist can help you, but it is not easy to find a therapist who will be good for you, and an unwise therapist can make depression worse.

The fight against depression best begins by learning *which* negative self-comparisons the sufferer habitually makes. This is done by noticing and recording the self-comparisons that you make when you are depressed.

The next step is to determine *why* the person is making those particular negative self-comparisons; this requires an understanding of the psychological structure that is related to such negative self-comparisons. You should also ask yourself why you feel *helpless* to change your circumstances or the goals that you set, and why you feel that you *must* make the particular self-comparisons that you do make. It is possible to get rid of the sadness-causing negative self-comparisons even without understanding why you make them, but the understanding often is valuable. The causation of depression is not simple.

Understanding it helps point you toward successful tactics for combatting the depression.

Then you should formulate a strategy for attacking the depression. Improving the numerator in the Mood Ratio, by improving the accuracy with which you assess the actual state of your life, is often the best place to begin. If this tactic does not suffice, you may next attempt to change the denominator, the benchmark state against which you compare your actual state of affairs. If this still does not suffice, you may consider changing the dimensions on which you commonly compare yourself, away from dimensions on which you compare negatively and toward those on which you compare positively. Still a further step is to reduce the number of self-comparisons and self-evaluations you make, by immersing yourself in work or altruism, or by recourse to meditation or related devices. A combination of several intervention devices, including an effort to reduce the feeling of being helpless, may be best.

A new (though very old) cure for some is Values Treatment. When a person's negative self-comparisons—no matter what their original cause—are expressed as shortfalls between the person's circumstances and her most fundamental beliefs (values) about what a person should be and do, Values Treatment can build on other values to defeat the depression. The method is to find within yourself other fundamental beliefs and values that call for a person not to suffer but rather to live happily and joyfully. If you believe in the superordinate value of a belief which conflicts with being depressed, that belief can induce you to enjoy and cherish life rather than to be sad and depressed.

Practical exercises are important, especially recording your negative self-comparisons followed by analyzing and demolishing them. And don't forget to plan and carry out lots of pleasurable experiences, an important part of therapy for depression.

IN A NUTSHELL

Understand the key role of negative self-comparisons. Then study how you developed the propensity to construe your numerator or your denominator in such a manner that the self-comparisons are negative, and why you make self-comparisons as frequently as you do. Then decide what changes in your thinking you intend to make. Then develop the habit of thinking in these new ways which will reduce or eliminate your depression.

These are the possible tactics: 1. Improve the numerator in your Mood Ratio, by getting rid of misconceptions about yourself, or by learning that your capacities to influence events in a desirable direction are greater than you thought. 2. Alter your denominator to make it less formidable, by changing the benchmarks against which you compare your actual state of affairs. 3. Change the dimensions on which you habitually compare yourself. 4. Retrain yourself so you seem to yourself more competent and less helpless. 5. Reduce the number of comparisons you make each day, by immersing yourself in work or altruistic activity, or by recourse to meditation or related devices. 6. Examine your basic values to learn what is important to you that may influence your wanting to be depressed or wanting not to be depressed.

Others soon find their way back to joyful and productive life, and chances are you will, too. I wish you the best of luck.

EPILOGUE: MY MISERY, MY CURE, AND MY JOY

'Physician, heal thyself!' At the least, the doctor should be sure that the cure works on himself or herself before prescribing it to others. I have healed myself. That's why I tell you my personal story here.

I'll begin by telling you how my life seemed to me in March, 1975, when I was living for a year in Jerusalem. The first-draft notes for this description were written while I was still depressed, based on what I said to a family physician in December, 1974. The purpose of the writing was to serve as the basis for consulting one or more famous psychotherapists by mail—that's how desperate for help I had become —before finally concluding that my depression was incurable. Shortly after I made these first notes I went through the process of thought that removed my depression immediately, the first time I had been free of depression in 13 years.

As of December, 1974, my external situation was the best it had been in 13 years. I had just finished what I hoped would be an important book, and I had no troubles with health, family, money, or other material matters. Nevertheless, there was no day that I wanted to see. Each morning when I awoke, my only pleasant expectations were taking a nap early in the evening, and then (after more work) finishing the day gasping with relief like an exhausted swimmer reaching shore, then having a drink and going to sleep. Looking ahead to each day I had no sense of accomplishment in advance, only the expectation that I might finish a little bit more of what I considered to be my duty.

Death was not unattractive. I felt that I had to stay alive for my children's sake, at least for the next ten years until the children would be grown, simply because children need a father in the house to constitute a complete family. At many, many moments, especially in the morning when waking, or when walking back home after taking the children to school, I wondered whether I would be able to get through that ten years, whether I would have strength enough to fight back the pain and fears rather than to simply end it all. Those next ten years seemed very long, especially in the light of the past 13 years that I had spent depressed. I thought that after that next ten years I would be free to choose to do what I wanted with my life, to end it if I then wished, because once my children would be 16 or 17 years old they would be sufficiently formed so that whether I would be alive or not would not make much difference in their development.

To repeat, as I thought about the day ahead I saw nothing pleasurable. When I had talked to a psychologist a few times about a year and a half earlier he had asked me which things I truly enjoy in this world. I told him that the list was short: sex, tennis and other sports, poker, and at some happy times in my past when I had been working on new ideas which I thought might result in some impact on the society, the work was really fun, too.

I remember as early as 1954, when I was in the Navy, noticing that I get pleasure from very few things. At sea one Saturday or Sunday, sitting on the ship's fantail, I asked myself what I really enjoyed. I knew that I did not get much pleasure out of what gives most people the most pleasure—just sitting around talking about the events of the day, and about the doings of themselves and other people around them. The only conversations I really looked forward to with pleasure were those concerning some common project in which I was engaged with the other person. But now (as of 1975) I had even lost the pleasure of such joint-work conversations.

My depression had its proximate cause in an event in 1962. I was then a businessman running my own new small business, and I did something that was morally wrong—not a big thing, but enough to throw me into the blackest depths of despair for more than a year, and then into an ongoing grey depression thereafter.

Of course, the long-run causes of the depression—and in every way I fit the textbook description of a depressive personality—were more basic. I lacked a basic sense of self-worth. I did not esteem myself highly, as do so many people whose 'objective' accomplishments might be considered small compared to mine. My work did not, and still does not, fill me with a sense of what a fine fellow I am. For most people in the university occupation I'm in, a tenth of the books and articles that I've written would enable them to feel that they had done a lifetime's worth of scholarly work, enough to enable them to claim with a straight face the highest rewards a university can offer. But for me it all seemed hollow. I asked myself (and continue to ask myself) what real impact upon the society my work has had. When I can't point to some substantial change, I feel that the work is all waste. And in truth, up to 1975 a fair amount of my work had not been received well or much esteemed, and this had given me a sense of futility toward those of my writings that were about to appear, or those which I considered writing in the future. (To get ahead of the story, starting in 1980 some of my work brought me wide recognition. From time to time I believe that I affect some people's thinking and perhaps public policy. This was delightful at its height for a few years, and gave me much pleasure. It still gives me much pleasure even though the effect has paled, and brought considerable negative reaction with it. But the change this has brought about in my daily feeling about my life is small compared to the change brought about by my recovery from depression in 1975.)

To give you an idea of how my depression swallowed me up: The day in 1962 when the U.S. confronted the U.S.S.R. over the Cuban missiles is indelibly imprinted on the mind of almost everyone who was then an adult. But I was so deep in the pit of depression that even though I was then living in New York City—where people seemed particularly frantic about the situation—I was almost unaware of the world crisis, and I was little affected by it.

People who have never been severely depressed sometimes pooh-pooh the pain the depressed person suffers. But experienced psychiatrists know better:

> The emotional pain experienced by a depressed person can easily rival the physical pain suffered by a cancer victim. The suffering of a depressed person is difficult for his healthy colleague to appreciate. Sometimes the complaints of the depressed seem absurd and childish. You may wonder whether the patient is behaving much like the 'Princess and the Pea'—over-reacting to subjective feelings which could not possibly be so terrible as the patient describes them.
>
> I doubt that depressed patients are playing games with their friends and physicians.[1]

The following comparisons may make depression more vivid and understandable to the non-depressive. In 1972 I had a major surgical operation, a spinal fusion, serious enough to keep me on my back almost constantly for two months. The day of the *operation* was worse for me than most of my depressed days, made so by the fear that the operation might be disastrously botched and leave me permanently disabled. But though I was full of pain and discomfort, the first day *after* each operation (when I already knew that there had been no disaster) was easier to get through than were the run-of-the-mill days of my first couple of years of black depression, and was about the same as the average days in my later depression years.

Another example: A day in which a wisdom tooth was pulled had about the same pain content for me as a day in my later 'grey depression' years. The nice side of an operation or of a tooth-pulling is that when you are already safe, though in pain and confined to bed or crutches for months, you know the pain will end. But my depression went on for month after month and year after year, and I became convinced that it would *not* ever end. That was the worst of all.

Here is another comparison: If I were presented with the choice, I'd choose to spend three to five years of that period in prison rather than live the 13 years in the depressed state I passed them in. I've not been a prisoner, so I can't know what it is like, but I do know the years of depression and I believe that I'd make such a deal.

I refused to let myself do the pleasurable things that my wife wisely suggested I do—go to the movies, take a walk on a sunny day, and so on—because I thought that I ought to suffer. I was superstitiously operating on the nutty presumption that if I punished myself enough, no one else would punish me for my misdeed. And later on I refused to do these casual pleasurable things because I thought that I would be kidding myself by doing them, covering up the symptoms of my depression and therefore preventing a real cure—more bad depressive-type thinking.

During my first year of depression there was one good day. My wife and I went to visit overnight at a country shack with friends. In the morning when we woke in sleeping bags I heard a bird and saw the trees against the sky, and I felt exquisite joy of relief—the relief that one feels at the finish of a long exhausting ordeal of physical or mental work when you can at last rest, lightened of your burden. I thought, maybe it is over. But after a matter of hours I was again full of fear and dread and hopelessness and self-loathing. And even an hour of such relief did not return for perhaps another full year. (The next good moment was the night our first child was born, about three years after the depression began. Incidentally, I will seldom mention my good wife because it is not possible to do justice to one's spouse in an account such as this one.)

Though the pain grew less acute with time, and my outlook came to seem only a constant grey rather than totally black, after six to eight years of it I became more and more convinced that I would never escape. Such prolonged depression is medically unusual, and physicians can honestly reassure patients that they may expect relief within weeks or months, or a year or so at most, though the depression may return. But that was not the case with me.

For a while I dreamed about entering a monastery, perhaps a silent monastery, where there would be no burdens or expectations. But I knew that I could not run away until the children would be grown. The prospect of hanging on for that long period of future depression depressed me more.

Upon awakening every single morning for all those years my first thought was, 'All those hours! How am I going to get through them?' That was the worst moment of the day, before I could get my fear and sadness under conscious control. The best moments of the day were crawling into bed finally to go to sleep, at night or for a nap in the late afternoon.

You may doubt that I was really depressed for so long or that my depression was deep. How could anyone be continually depressed for 13 years? In fact, there *were* hours when I was not depressed. Those were the hours when I was deep enough in my work and in creative thinking that I forgot about my depression. These hours happened almost every morning, once I had gotten myself started on the day, provided that the work I was doing was reasonably creative rather than just such routine work as editing or proofreading—and providing, also, that I was not overly pessimistic about the probable reception of that particular piece of work. This meant that for probably half the days during the year I had a couple of hours in the morning, and perhaps an hour late in the evening after I had a drink, when I was not consciously sad.

Only work helped. For a long time my wife thought that she could distract me with movies and other entertainment, but it never worked. In the midst of the movie I'd be thinking how worthless a person I am, and about the failures of all my efforts. But in the midst of work—and especially when I would have a beautiful hard problem to think through, or a new idea would come to me—my depression would ease. Thank goodness for the work.

You may wonder, as I did: If the sadness and self-loathing hurt so much, why didn't I resort to liquor and tranquilizers (the new drugs were not then available) to cut the pain? I didn't do so, even during the worst half-year or year at the beginning, for two reasons: First, I felt that I had no 'right' to use artificial gimmicks to escape from the pain because I felt it was my own fault. Second, I was afraid that tranquilizers or other drugs would interfere with the one part of me that I continued to respect, my ability to have ideas and think clearly. Without explicitly recognizing it, I acted as if the only possible avenue of escape for me, in the short run and the long run, was to be able to think well enough to involve myself in some work for a while every day, and maybe eventually to do enough useful work to bring about self-respect. Booze or pills could ruin that avenue of hope, I thought.

All those years I concealed my depression so that no one except my wife knew about it. I was afraid to seem vulnerable. And I saw no benefits in revealing my depression. When occasionally I hinted about it to my friends, they did not seem to respond, perhaps because I did not make clear how badly off I really was.

In December, 1974, I told the family physician that I had reduced my possibilities of happiness to "two hopes and a flower". One of the hopes was a book which I hoped would make an important contribution to people's thinking and perhaps to some government policies. I worried that the book was not written in a sufficiently attractive manner to make any impact, but it was one of my hopes anyway. The second of my hopes was that some time in the future I'd write a book about how to think, how to use one's head, how to use one's mental resources, in such a way as to make the best use of them. I hoped that that book would put together a lot of what I've done and what I know into a new and useful form. (As of 1993, I have finished a second draft of that book.)

The flower was a flower that I often looked at while I was

meditating. In that meditation I could let everything go and feel that there is absolutely no 'ought' of obligation upon me—no 'ought' to continue meditating, no 'ought' to stop meditating, no 'ought' to think about this or to think about that, no 'ought' to telephone or not to telephone, to work or not to work. The flower was for that moment an enormous relief from 'ought', the flower that demanded nothing yet offered great beauty in quiet and peace.

About 1971, give or take a year, I decided that I wanted to be happy. I had figured out that one cause of my depression was my self-punishment for what I felt were my bad deeds, in the superstitious belief that if I punished *myself* this might ward off *other people's* punishment. And I then concluded that I no longer felt the need to be unhappy as a way of punishing myself. So, the first thing that happened in this sequence of events was that *I decided explicitly that I wanted to be happy.*

Starting perhaps 1972, I tried a variety of devices to break through my depression and give me happiness. I tried Zen-type concentration on the moment to prevent my thoughts from slipping to anxious memories of the past or anxious fears about the future. I tried think-happy exercises. I tried breathing exercises, separately and also together with concentration exercises. I started a list of 'good things that I can say about myself' in those moments when I felt low and worthless and devoid of self-esteem, to pep myself up. (Unfortunately, I only managed to get two things down on the list: a. My children love me. b. All students who have done theses with me respect me, and many continue our relationship. Not a very long list, and I never managed to use it successfully. None of these schemes helped for more than half a day or a day.)

Starting in the summer or fall of 1973, a revolution lasting one day each week came into my life. An Orthodox Jewish friend of mine told me that it is one of the basic precepts of the Jewish Sabbath that one is not allowed to think about anything that will make him or her sad or anxious during that day. This struck me as an extraordinarily good idea, and I tried to obey that rule. I tried to obey it not because of a sense of religious dictate, but rather because it seemed to me a wonderful psychological insight. So on the Sabbath I have tried to act in ways that would keep me thinking in a friendly and happy manner, ways such as not allowing myself to work in any way, not think about work-connected things, and not letting myself be angry with the children or other people no matter what the provocation.

On this one day a week—and *only* on this one day of the week—I found I could usually fend off depression and be content and even joyful, though on the other six days of the week my mood ranged from grey to black. More specifically, on the Sabbath if my thoughts tended to drift toward things which were unhappy, I tried to act like a mental street-sweeper, using my broom to gently deflect my mind or sweep away the unpleasant thoughts, and to nudge myself back to a pleasant-er frame of mind. The fact of knowing that there was one day in which I would do no work probably was itself very important in alleviating my depression, because an important factor in my depression has been my belief that my hours and days should be devoted entirely to work and to the duty of work. (It's worth noting that I've often had to *struggle* to keep myself from being depressed on the Sabbath, and sometimes the effort of the struggle seemed so great that it just wasn't worth it to keep struggling, but rather seemed easier just to give myself over to the depression.)

After that I'm not sure exactly in which order things happened. Starting September, 1974, the work-load felt lighter than for many years. (Of course my work-load is largely self-imposed, but deadlines felt less pressing.) Starting in 1972, I began no new works, and instead tried to finish up all the things which were in my pipeline so as to get my desk clear. And starting in September, 1974, the various books and articles and research that I had in process were, one by one, getting done. From time to time, of course, I was jerked up short by a new set of proofs or a new deadline for something that I had set in motion a long time before. But for the first time in a very long time there were at least some interludes during which I felt unrushed and free. I also had the feeling that I really was approaching that nirvana when I really would be very free, and able to feel a sense of relaxation. But still I was depressed—sad, and full of self-loathing.

Starting about the middle of December, 1974, I had a special feeling of nearing completion, and I felt that in many ways it was the best period that I had had for the past 13 years. Because I had no troubles with health, family, or money, nothing pressed on me from outside my own psychology. That certainly did not mean that I was happy or undepressed. Rather, it meant that I was sufficiently undepressed that I was willing to spend some time on myself and my depression.

I therefore determined that if I was *ever* going to rid myself of depression, then was the time to do it. I had the time and energy. And I was in a cosmopolitan city (Jerusalem) which I thought (wrongly) was likely to have more possibilities of help than my small home city in the U.S. I decided to look for someone who might have the wisdom to help me. I thought to consult some eminent psychologists in person, and others by mail. And at the same time I went to a family physician to ask him to refer me to someone—physician, psychologist, religious wise man, or whatever—who might help. All this should illustrate how desperate I was to get rid of my depression. I figured that it was my last chance—now or never: If it didn't work then, I'd give up hope of ever succeeding. I felt like a man in a movie hanging by his fingertips to the edge of the cliff, figuring he has strength enough for just one more try to pull himself up and over to safety—but the fingers are slipping . . . his strength is waning . . . you get the picture.

The family physician suggested a psychologist, but one visit convinced us both that—good as he probably is—that he was not the right man for my problem. He in turn suggested a psychoanalyst. But the psychoanalyst suggested a long course of therapy which exhausted me just thinking about it; I didn't believe it would succeed, and it didn't seem worth spending the energy or money to try.

Then in March, 1975, about four weeks before writing the first draft of this account, I felt that my current work was really complete. I had no work lying on my desk, all my manuscripts had been sent to publishers—simply nothing pressing. And I decided that now I owed it to myself to try to spend some of my 'good time'—that is, the time when my mind is fresh and creative in the morning—thinking about myself and my problem of depression in an attempt to see if I could think my way out of it.

I went to the library and took out a bag of books on the subject. I began to read, think, make notes. The book which made the greatest impression upon me was Aaron Beck's *Depression.* The main message I got was that one can alter one's thinking by consciously working at it, in contrast to the passive Freudian view with its focus on the 'unconscious'. I still didn't have much hope that I could work my way out of depression, because many times I had tried without success to understand it and deal with it. But this time I decided to devote my full energies to the subject when I was fresh, rather than thinking about it only at those times when I was exhausted. And armed with that key message of Beck's cognitive therapy, I at least had *some* hope.

Perhaps the first big step was my concentrating on the idea—which I had understood for a long time but had simply taken for granted—that I'm never satisfied with myself or what I do; I never allow myself to be satisfied. I have also known the cause for a long time: With all good intentions, and though we were (until her death in 1986) quite fond of another even if not very close, my mother (with the best of intentions) never seemed satisfied with me as a child (though perhaps she really was). No matter how well I did something, she always urged that I could do better.

Then this startling insight came to me: Why should I still pay attention to my mother's stricture? Why should I continue dissatisfied with myself just because my mother had built that habit of dissatisfaction into me? I suddenly realized that I was under no obligation to share my mother's views, and I could simply tell myself 'Don't criticize' whenever I begin to compare my performance to the level of greater achievement and perfection urged by my mother. And with this insight I suddenly felt free of my mother's dissatisfaction for the first time in my life. I felt free to do what I wanted with my day and my life. That was a very exhilarating moment, a feeling of relief and freedom which continues until this moment, and which I hope will continue for the rest of my life.

This discovery that I am not *obligated* to follow my mother's orders is exactly the idea that I later discovered is the central substantive idea in Albert Ellis's version of cognitive therapy. But though this discovery helped a great deal, by itself it was not enough. It removed some of the knives I felt sticking into me, but it did not yet make the world look bright. Perhaps the depression persisted because I felt I was not succeeding in making a real contribution with my research and writings, or perhaps it was because of other underlying connections between my childhood and my present self-comparisons and mood which I do not understand. Whatever the reason, the structure of my thinking was not giving me a happy life-loving life, despite my discovery that I need not keep criticizing myself for lapses from perfection.

Then came another revelation: I remembered how my depression lifted on one day each week, on the Sabbath. And I also remembered that just as Judaism imposes an obligation not to be anxious or sad on the Sabbath, Judaism also imposes an obligation upon the individual to enjoy his or her life. Judaism enjoins you not to waste your life in unhappiness or to make your life a burden, but rather to make of it the greatest possible value. (I am here using the concept of obligation in a rather vague and unspecified fashion. I am not using the concept in the way that a traditional religious person would use it—that is, as a duty imposed upon a person by the traditional concept of God. Nevertheless, I did feel some kind of a vow in which there is a compact, an obligation which goes a little bit beyond me and me.)

After it occurred to me that I have a Jewish obligation not to be unhappy, it occurred to me that I also have an obligation to my children not to be unhappy, but rather to be happy, in order to serve as a proper model to them. Children may imitate happiness or unhappiness just as they imitate other aspects of their parents. I think that by pretending not to be depressed I had avoided giving them a model of unhappiness. (This is the one part of our relationship in which I have falsified and play-acted, rather than being openly and truthfully myself.) As they would have gotten older they would, however, have seen through this play-acting.

And like the happy ending of a fairy tale I promptly became undepressed and have (mostly) stayed undepressed. It was a matter of pitting one value against another. On the one side was the value of trying with all my strength, and damn the personal consequences, to create something of social value. On the other side was the value that I derived from Judaism: life is the highest value, and all have an obligation to cherish life in others and in oneself; to allow oneself to be depressed is a violation of this religious injunction. (I also got some help from the sage Hillel's injunction. "One may not neglect the work, but one is not required to finish it, either.")

Those, then, were the main events in my passage from black despair, then to constant grey depression, then to my present state of non-depression and happiness.

Now a few words about how my anti-depression tactics work out in practice. I have instructed myself, and have pretty much got into the habit, that whenever I say to myself 'You're an idiot' because I forgot something or don't do something right or do something sloppily, I then say to myself, 'Don't criticize'. After I start to browbeat myself because I didn't prepare a class well enough, or I was late for an appointment with a student, or I was impatient with one of my children, I say to myself, 'Lay off. Don't criticize'. And after I say this it's like feeling the yank of a reminder rope. I then feel my mood change. I smile, my stomach relaxes, and I feel a sense of relief run all through me. I also try the same kind of plan with my wife, whom I also criticize too much, and mostly for no good reason. When I start to criticize her about something—the way she cuts the bread, puts too much water on to boil, or pushes the children to get to school on time—I again say to myself 'Don't criticize'.

Since the start of my new life, there have been several family problems or work failures which previously would have deepened my depression from grey to black for a week or more. Now, instead of these events throwing me into deep and continuing depression, as would have happened before, each of them has caused me some pain for perhaps a day. Then after doing something active to deal with the event—such as trying to improve the situation, or writing a letter blowing my top at the responsible person (usually not mailed)—I have been able to forget the matter, and to leave behind the pain caused by it. That is, I'm now able to get over these unpleasantnesses fairly easily. And taken together, this means that I enjoy most of my days. When I wake up—which has always been the hardest time for me, as for many depressives—I'm able to draw a mental picture of the oncoming day which seems reasonably free of events that I'd have to criticize myself for, such as not working hard enough. I look forward to days mostly of freedom and tolerable pressures and burdens. I can tell myself that if I really don't want to do all the things that are more-or-less scheduled for that day, I have the right not to do a fair number of them. In that way I can prevent much of the dread I used to have when looking forward to duty-filled days with no sense of coming pleasure.

That ends the description of my life written just before and soon after my release from depression. Here are a few reports on my progress later on, as they were written at the time:

March 26, 1976

It is almost a year from the time my new life began. Inscribing the date makes me think with pleasure that tomorrow is my youngest son's birthday, and that gives me a joyful apprehension of life such as I never had before April of 1975. I am able to smile, close my eyes, feel melting tears and inner pleasure when I think—as I did just now—of one of the children's birthdays.

I am, by now, less often ecstatic with my new joy of living than I was at the beginning of this new life. Partly that may be due to getting used to my new life without depression, and accepting it as permanent. It may also be partly because I'm no longer in Jerusalem. But still I have these ecstatically-joyful skipping-and-leaping feelings probably more often than most people who have never been severely depressed for a long time. One has to have experienced pain for a long time to be able to be wildly joyful just from noticing the absence of pain.

January 16, 1977

Soon it will be two years since I decided to get rid of depression, and did so. There still is a constant running skirmish between me and the wolf that I know still waits for me outside the door. But aside from a two-week period that followed an accumulation of professional problems, when my spirits were sufficiently low that I worried I was relapsing into permanent depression, I have been undepressed. Life is worth living, for my own sake as well as for my family's sake. That's a lot.

June 18, 1978

No news is often good news. I've hit some bumps in the past three years, but I've recovered each time. Now I think of myself as like a buoyant swimmer. A wave can force me below the surface, but my specific gravity is less than that of water, and eventually I'll float back up after each ducking.

I remember the years when, except for stretches during hours when I was writing, not 15 minutes of a day would pass without my reminding myself how worthless I am—how useless, unsuccessful, ridiculous, presumptuous, incompetent, immoral, I am in my work, family life and community life. I used to make an excellent argument for my worthlessness, drawing on a wide variety of evidence, and constructing a watertight case.

One important reason that I castigated myself so often and so well was that I believed that I *ought* to keep telling myself how worthless I am. That is, I made sure that I escaped no punishment for my many sins. I functioned as an ever-diligent avenging angel. Then I would finish off the job by being depressed because I felt so depressed in response to all these reminders of my worthlessness. (Being depressed because of being depressed is a common routine with depressives.)

The only force inside me that opposed the gloom was my sense of the ridiculousness of it all—the vision of myself as avenging angel, perhaps, or the jest of carrying the process to absurdity with jokes like titles for an autobiography, 'Ten Thousand Leagues Up the Creek Without an Ego'. That humor did help a bit, though, by giving me some perspective on how silly it was for me to take myself and my worthlessness so seriously.

Now that I am undepressed I still acknowledge myself to be less than a success with respect to the goals I struggle to attain. But now I only infrequently tell myself how worthless and failing I am. I can sometimes go through an entire day with only occasional rememberances of my worthlessness. I avoid these thoughts by banishing them at first appearance with repression, humor, and misdirection (depression-fighting devices described earlier) and by reminding myself that my family is well, I am suffering no pain, and the world is mostly at peace. I also try to keep in mind that I'm not a bad father, in my family's eyes as in my own.

One important reason that I now act as I do is that I now believe that I *ought not to let myself* dwell on my being of little worth, and that I ought not to be depressed by it. And that 'ought' comes from the Values Therapy that was an essential part of my salvation.

October 18, 1981

I have hit the jackpot. The world has now made it easy for me to remain undepressed. I no longer must deflect my mind from my professional difficulties in order to stay happy, but instead I can now dwell on my worldly 'success' and take pleasure from it.

It is important for both you and me to remember that before my ship came in I had many days in the past few years when I said to myself that I could be no happier. I remember a Thursday in the Spring of 1980 when I was walking to my office and I thought: The trees are lovely. The sun feels good on my back. Wife and children are physically and mentally well. I feel no pain. I have a good job and no money worries. I see peaceful activities on the campus around me. I'd be a fool not to be happy. And I *am* happy, as happy as one could be. In fact, this is the best day of my life. (On other days since 1975 I had also said to myself, this is the best day of my life, or the best Sabbath of my life. But there is no contradiction among such superlatives.)

Then starting June, 1980, many good things happened to me professionally. It started with a controversial article that immediately became very well-known, and led to many invitations to speak and write; that represented a chance for me to reach a wide audience with a set of ideas that had previously fallen mostly on deaf ears, or more precisely, on no ears. Each new writing expanded my possibilities and invitations even more. Then a book on these ideas came out in August, 1981, and immediately was taken up by magazines, newspapers, radio and television. Journalists call me frequently for my views on happenings in this field. My work has come to be seen as legitimate though controversial. My friends joke that I'm a celebrity. Who wouldn't find this easy to take?

But my happiness is not based on this 'success'. I was undepressed before it happened, and I'm rather confident I'll be undepressed after all this blows over. Being happy because of what is happening outside you is too shaky a basis for happiness. I want the joy and serenity that comes from within me, even despite adversity. And it is that joy and serenity that the methods of this book brought to me—and perhaps will bring you, too. With all my heart I hope that you, too, will soon reflect on some days as being the best days of your life, and that the other days will be without pain. Please struggle to reach that peaceful shore, for your own sake and for me.

October 12, 1988

In 1981 I *thought* I had hit the jackpot. And in perhaps the most important respect this was so: My main professional work had a large effect in changing the thinking of both academic researchers and the lay public. But for a variety of reasons, some of which I understand and some of which I do not understand, my profession did not take me to its bosom on this account, or make the way easier for my subsequent professional work; access to the non-technical public did become easier, however.

The organizations that oppose my viewpoint continue to dominate public thinking, though the scientific basis for their arguments has been eroded. I have had to conclude that though I may have made a dent in the armor of the opposing viewpoint, and perhaps provided some ammunition for others engaged on the same side of the struggle as I am, the opposing viewpoint will continue to roll on inexorably, though perhaps with a bit less exuberance and carelessness than in the past.

These outcomes have pained and frustrated me. And I have had to keep my pain and frustration to myself lest my unbuttoned words and acts seem 'unprofessional' and therefore work against me. (Indeed, I am being quite careful in these very words on the subject.)

The pain and frustration have taken me to the brink of depression many times during the years since about 1983 or so. But the methods for fighting depression described in this book—and especially my basic values about human life as described in Chapter 18, even though it is no longer necessary for my grown-up children's sake that I remain undepressed—have pulled me back from the brink again and again. That is a lot to be thankful for, and perhaps as much as a human being can expect. As to the future—I must wait and see. Will continued unsuccessful struggle make me feel so helpless that I will feel driven from the field, and therefore escape from the negative self-comparisons into either cheerful or apathetic resignation? Will I re-interpret what has happened as success rather than failure, as acceptance rather than rejection, and therefore have positive self-comparisons with respect to this work?

I end 1988's report with an open question: If I had continued to experience complete lack of success with my main work, rather than the breakthrough that occurred around 1980, could I have continued to maintain my underlying cheerfulness, or would the quagmire of rejection have sucked me inexorably into depression? Perhaps I could have escaped by giving up that line of work entirely, but that would have meant giving up some of my most cherished ideals, and it is not at all sure that I could have produced more positive results in any related field of work that I enjoyed and respected.

I began this epilogue by saying that I healed myself. But healing is seldom perfect, and health is never forever. I hope that you can do even better than I have done. It will make me happy if you do.

January 1, 1993

I continue to be very lucky. My family and I are all healthy, and all of us are engaged in productive work that we enjoy. Humanity is in better condition than ever before. This book is being published. I hope that it will put and keep a smile on your face, and a laugh in your voice and heart. Good luck!

APPENDIX A

BACKGROUND INFORMATION FOR RESEARCHERS AND PRACTITIONERS

The book uses 'you' language to address the depression sufferer. And some general readers will find interesting the information in the appendixes. But the book also is aimed at psychotherapeutic professionals, both researchers and practitioners, with an additional message: it contains a new theoretical understanding of depression, which implies new ways of confronting depression.

The fundamental idea of modern psychological therapy for depression is that individuals can change their thinking processes in ways that will eliminate the patterns which cause the depression. The layperson may consider this to be plain common sense. But when seen in light of the older Freudian view, this commonsense foundation is revolutionary. And though the fundamental assumption is 'only' common sense, the scientific structure constructed upon it is not at all obvious. Building upon this foundation, various researchers have focused on different aspects of the thinking processes which are commonly faulty among depressives. And they have shown how altering the defective thinking can improve people's moods.

This book develops a broader framework that encompasses all the major insights of earlier writers. Within that framework, it focuses on the key cognitive channel—self-comparisons—through which all the other influences flow. Philosophers have understood for centuries that the comparisons one makes affect one's feelings. But this element has not previously been explored or integrated into scientific understanding of the thinking of depressives, or exploited as the central pressure-point for therapy. Instead, the concept 'negative thoughts' has been used.

Appendix B continues the theoretical discussion with an analysis of how this approach to depression fits with, and broadly encompasses, the other modern cognitive psychological approaches to depression. The remainder of this Appendix A adds some theoretical underpinning to discussions in early chapters. It also briefly discusses how this approach, along with cognitive therapy in general, has been moving toward the use of concepts found in philosophy and the social sciences, some by borrowing but even more by independent invention. In this way, cognitive therapy moves toward what may eventually be the first application of integrated social science.

In brief, Self-Comparisons Analysis does the following: 1. It presents a theoretical framework which identifies and focuses on the common pathway through which all depression-causing lines of thought must pass. This framework combines and integrates other valid approaches, subsuming all of them as valuable but partial. All of the many variations of depressions that modern psychiatry now recognizes as heterogeneous but related forms of the same illness can be subsumed under the theory except those that have a purely biological origin, if there are such. 2. It sharpens each of the other viewpoints by converting the rather vague notion of 'negative thinking'[1] to a precise formulation of a self-comparison and a negative Mood Ratio with two specific parts—an assumed actual state of affairs and a hypothetical benchmark state of affairs. This idea opens up a wide variety of novel interventions. 3. It offers a new line of attack upon stubborn depressions, called here Values Treatment, which leads the patient to make a committed choice to give up depression in order to attain more important deeply-held values.

ON THE THEORY OF DEPRESSION AND ITS TREATMENT

Beck has properly claimed as an advantage of his Cognitive Therapy that "the therapy is largely dictated by the theory" rather than being simply ad hoc (1976, 123, 312). Beck also notes that

---

[1]In the appendixes, notes are at the bottom of the page and the references are named in the text, because of the likelihood that professional readers will want to see them.

The American Psychiatric Association's publication *Depression and Its Treatment* by John H. Greist and James W. Jefferson (Washington, D.C.: American Psychiatric Press, 1984) may be taken as canonical: "Depressed *thinking* often takes the form of *negative thoughts* about one's self, the present and the future" (page 2, italics in original).

"Currently, there is no generally accepted theory within the cognitive-clinical perspective." This book offers a more comprehensive theory of depression than do the others, and includes the others as elements in it. Furthermore, the therapeutic approaches suggested here are dictated even more clearly by the more specific theory given here, and more possibilities are suggested by it, than any of the previous approaches alone.

Each of the contemporary "schools", as Beck (dustjacket of Klerman et al. 1986) and Klerman et al. (1986, 5) call them, addresses one particular part of the depression system and, therefore, depending upon the "theoretical orientation and training of the psychotherapist, a variety of responses and recommendations would be likely . . . there is no consensus as to how best [to] regard the causes, prevention, and treatment of mental illnesses" (Klerman et al. 1986, 4,5). Any 'school' is therefore likely to achieve best results with people whose depression derives most sharply from the point in the cognitive system that that school focuses upon, but less well with people whose problem is mainly at some other point in the system. (Of course the depression sufferer may have a defective mechanism that spreads into several aspects of the system, and therefore therapy at any one point can benefit the system as a whole, but that is beside the point here).

Self-Comparisons Analysis provides an expanded theoretical understanding of depression which encompasses and integrates the elements pinpointed and explored by these writers and others. This means that instead of the field being seen as a conflict of 'schools', each of the 'schools' has a distinctive method that fits the needs of different sorts of sufferers from depression. The overall framework of Self-Comparisons Analysis helps weight the values of each of these methods for a particular person. Though the various methods may be serviceable substitutes for each other at times, to a considerable extent they are *not* simply competitive alternatives for the same situations, and Self-Comparisons Analysis helps one choose. This should be of particular benefit to the physician or other professional who must make the crucial decision of referring a patient to one or another specialist for depression treatment. Heretofore, the choice had to be made mainly on *competing* merits, and in practice the choice probably is made mainly on the basis of which 'school' the referring professional is most familiar with, which has led to considerable frustration with the field voiced by recent writers (for instance Papalos and Papalos 1987).

There are hazards in offering a theory which claims to comprehend and integrate others. Psychotherapists, just like professionals in others fields, have "intense loyalties to the schools they espouse" (Wender and Klein 1981, 264). And contending schools in any field are greatly attached to their controversies; to offer to remove the cause of the controversy is to be in the position of a cop in a household dispute. The one matter that contending parties always can agree upon is that an outsider has nothing to contribute. Nevertheless, I step in where angels professionally trained in particular 'schools' of clinical therapy would be prudent enough not to tread. And not being the member of any 'school' confers an advantage: Lack of socialization into, and absence of professional connection with, any particular school of therapy promotes breadth of thought and synthetic theory.

If you work at enough different tasks you sometimes experience the eerie and then exciting sensation that you have met the same idea before in another context. And so it is with many of the ideas in cognitive therapy, especially the types of thinking characteristic of depressed persons. The distortions of thought common to depressives are much the same, though with different names, as the obstacles to sound scientific knowledge faced by researchers, the logical fallacies that have been pointed out by philosophers through the ages, the devices used by propagandists to influence audiences, the causes of bias in estimates of probabilities, and many of the sources of faulty decision-making in business and other organizations. Once you recognize the similarity in these conceptual schemes, each one illuminates the others, and the overall scheme gains in generality.

Indeed, cognitive therapy has been moving toward greater use of concepts found in philosophy and other social sciences, some by borrowing but even more by independent invention. The analysis of logical and linguistic fallacies is a prime example of the bridge with philosophy. The utilization of the theory of information processing by Bowlby (1980) is another connection. Still another example is the employment (see Burns 1980, 150; Beck 1987, 31) of such ideas from managerial economics as cost-benefit analysis, and supply of resources, and even the term 'economy' with respect to the thinking mechanism.

And the time is ripe for cognitive therapy to link up with decision theory, as studied in economics, psychology, political science and other fields.[2] Cognitive therapy may eventually be the first truly integrated social science.[3]

Another aspect of cognitive therapy that one meets in other contexts: The dialogues between therapist and patient that Ellis and Beck and their colleagues conduct are identical in form to the Socratic form of dialogue used especially in law schools and also elsewhere in education. The back-and-forth between student and teacher is an attempt on the part of the teacher to have the student practice clearer thinking about the subject at hand, just as is the back-and-forth between therapist and patient.

SOME ADDITIONAL THEORETICAL UNDERPINNING

Self-comparison is the link between cognition and emotion—that is, between what you think and what you feel. This traditional joke

---

[2]An interesting connection is the 'prospect theory' of Kahnemann and Twersky 1979. They find that people's evaluations of uncertain alternatives are best described as *relative rather than absolute,* in contrast to the assumption of expected-utility theory; this they explain in terms of perception theory, which fits in with the discussion of comparisons in Chapter 3. Furthermore, they find that the common reference point is to the present state of affairs. This comparison scheme would seem to have appropriate properties for maximization of one's psychic well-being, in accord with discussion in this book of the appropriate choice of a benchmark-comparison state for a Rosy Mood Ratio, whereas expected-utility theory assumes that people will maximize their *monetary wealth* without reference to any particular state of affairs. In turn, the analysis given in this book should illuminate prospect theory by explaining *why* the prospect-theory form of utility function is held by people, and it suggests that the individual's utility function should be related to the individual's score on a depression inventory. And philosophers, psychologists, and economists have joined in exploring the logic and action of such mental mechanisms as "multiple selves", which fits with the practice of cognitive therapeutic techniques.

[3]My work in related cognitive fields—economics, research methods, philosophy, and decision-making has dealt with a wider range of concepts than are traditionally available in clinical psychology. My experience with cognitive psychology and this set of subjects goes back to my undergraduate thesis on concept formation in 1952–53, and has continued with books and articles on each of these subjects mentioned above plus some others; each part of this experience has contributed to the conceptual scheme presented here. There are other remarks on this topic in Chapter 1.

highlights the nature of the mechanism: A salesman is a person with a shine on his shoes, a smile on his face, and a lousy territory. So imagine yourself a saleswoman with a lousy territory.

You might first think: I'm more entitled to that territory than Charley is. You then feel anger, perhaps toward the boss who favored Charley. If your anger focuses instead on the person who has the other territory, the pattern is called envy.

But you might also think: I can, and will, work hard and sell so much that the boss will give me a better territory. In that state of mind you simply feel a mobilization of your personal resources toward attaining the object of the comparison.

Or instead you might think: There is no way that I can ever do anything that will get me a better territory, because Charley and other people sell better than I do. Or you think that lousy territories are always given to women. If so, you feel sad and worthless, the pattern of depression, because you have no hope of improving your situation.

Or you may think: I only have this lousy territory another week, after which I move to a terrific territory. Now you are shifting the comparison in your mind from a. your versus another's territory, to b. your territory now versus your territory next week. The latter comparison is not consistent with depression.

Or still another possible line of thought: No one else could put up with such a lousy territory and still make any sales at all. Now you are shifting from a. the comparison of territories, to b. the comparison of your strength with that of other people. Now you feel pride, and not depression.

Cognitive therapy dovetails with the recent broad movement toward regarding individuals as responsible for themselves rather than as being automatons of social forces. For example, this anti-authoritarian pro-freedom trend in thought appears in criminology's shift away from social causation in its view of how to reform criminals, and in economics's evidence that private property rights better motivate individuals to produce than do collective incentives. Whereas in traditional Freudian therapy the analyst is a father figure who always knows best, in cognitive therapy—especially when carried out by oneself without a therapist—the individual determines his or her own fate in cognitive-behavioral therapy.

SOME OTHER TECHNICAL ISSUES THAT SELF-COMPARISONS ANALYSIS ILLUMINATES

1. An earlier section in this appendix discusses how the concept of negative self-comparisons pulls together into a single coherent theory not only depression but also paranoia, schizophrenia, normal responses to neg-comps, angry responses to neg-comps, dread, anxiety, mania, phobias, apathy, and other troubling mental states. Recently, perhaps largely as a result of DSM-III (APA 1980) and DSM-III-R (APA 1987), the relationships of the various ailments—anxiety with depression, schizophrenia with depression, and so on—has generated considerable interest among students of the field. The ability of Self-Comparisons Analysis to relate all these mental states should make the theory more attractive to students of depression. And the distinction this theory makes between depression and anxiety fits with the recent findings of Steer et al. 1986 that depression patients show more 'sadness' on the Beck Depression Inventory than do anxiety patients, and that this characteristic and loss of libido are the *only* discriminating characteristics. The loss of libido fits with the part of Self-Comparisons Analysis that makes the presence of helplessness—that is, felt incapacity—the causal difference between the two ailments.

2. No distinctions have been made here among endogenous, reactive, neurotic, psychotic, and other types of depression. This jibes with recent writings in the field (such as DSM-III, and see the review by Klerman 1988), and also with findings that these various supposed classes "are indistinguishable on the basis of cognitive symptomatology" (Eaves and Rush 1984, cited by Beck 1987.) But the reason for the lack of distinction is more fundamentally theoretical: All varieties of depression share the basic element of Self-Comparisons Analysis—the common pathway of negative self-comparisons in combination with a sense of helplessness. This element both distinguishes depression from other syndromes and constitutes the key and choke point at which to begin helping the patient change his or her thinking so as to overcome depression.

3. The connection between cognitive therapy, with its emphasis on thought processes, and therapies of emotional release ranging from some aspects of psychoanalysis (including 'transference') to 'primal

scream', merits some discussion. There is no doubt that some people have obtained relief from depression from these experiences, both in and out of psychological treatment. Alcoholics Anonymous is replete with reports of such experiences. William James, in *Varieties of Religious Experience,* makes a great deal of such "second births". In my own case, one quiet Saturday soon after I started to read and think hard about my depression, I decided not to go to the beach with my family and friends, and stayed alone in the quiet apartment. I felt an unusual lack of pressure to do anything, a freedom to do and be whatever I desired. After wandering around aimlessly for a bit, I lay on the bed face down and began to cry. I was racked with sobs for a while, and then cried more quietly. And after I stopped I felt wonderful, full of peace in a way that I had not felt for a long time. And a series of thoughts began which led me to sense that my depression would soon be finished. Perhaps most important was the idea that I was not *obligated* to hold myself to the standards that I had attempted to meet in my work, and I was not *required* to compare myself with the elevated goals that had previously been before me. (The discovery of my value for my children not having a depressed father would come soon.)

The nature of this sort of process—which evokes such terms as 'release' or 'letting go' or 'surrender to God'—may hinge on the very sort of sense of 'permission' that Ellis makes so much of. The person finds that she or he is free from the musts and oughts that had made the person feel enslaved. There is truly a 'release' from this emotional bondage to a particular set of benchmark-state denominators that cause a constant Rotten Mood Ratio. So here, then, is a plausible connection between emotional release and cognitive therapy, though there undoubtedly are other connections as well.

4. There is a long tradition in psychology—of which Freud was perhaps the leading practitioner—of using clinical psychological theories to explain non-clinical phenomena of particular interest to the writer. I, too, shall briefly indulge in this entertainment in the next few sections.

It seems to me that there are related non-therapeutic phenomena that Self-Comparisons Analysis illuminates particularly well. One such is the apparently-increasing secular trend in depression, wherein increased suicide accompanies increased income,[4] but the short-term reverse of that relationship over the business cycle where decreased suicide accompanies increased income.[5] In the short run, people's denominators (their income) expectations do not change much, and therefore when lower income occurs they compare it unfavorably with their former income. But over the long run, expectations change along with the change in income, and as comparisons are rooted less in such unarbitrary physical matters as a full belly, and more in such arbitrary non-physical matters as social standards. No more than a sketch of the analysis can be given in this short space, but perhaps this paragraph will at least be suggestive.

5. The apparently-unrelated phenomenon of special-interest-lobby doomsaying rhetoric points up the generality of this conceptual scheme beyond individual therapy. Consider as an example the devices used by those who wish to prove that the United States must protect its oil industry. To that end they attempt to cause depressing thoughts with a gloomy assessment of the situation. They distort the actual facts in the *numerator* of the Mood Ratio by claiming that there is an increasing shortage of oil, though the key fact is that the availability of oil as measured by the key indicator of its price has been falling in the long run and also in the short run; they also point to declining production capacity in the U.S., but omit mention of increasing production capacity elsewhere in the world which can provide for U.S. consumption. They present a frightening *denominator* for comparison, a prospect of running out of gasoline and electricity, and the absence of an idyllic world in which people would no longer have to apply effort and resources to obtain energy supplies. They focus attention only on the *dimension* of oil, without mention of substitute possibilities such as coal, nuclear power, hydropower, and solar energy, or they pooh-pooh them. They also do not mention that in each successive decade energy is a relatively less important part of the economy by all economic measures. And they threaten us with the inevitability of the decline of the U.S. industry, making us feel *helpless* to improve our situation by developing other alternatives. The entire mechanism of neg-comps-cum-helplessness is exploited to produce depressing thoughts, which

---

[4]See Klerman et. al., 1985, for birth-cohort trends, and Klerman, 1986 for a survey of the evidence. Seligman (1988) offers a wide-ranging impressionistic discussion with which the analysis sketched here may be compared.
data

[5]For evidence on this, see Barnes and Simon 1968.

presents the palliative of government subsidies and protection for the U.S. oil industry as the only apparent alternative. This is a case study in propaganda technique. The entire world-view schema that underlies doomsaying rhetoric (see Simon 1981) is similar to the negative bias of depressives to which Beck (1987) also has applied the term 'schema'.

6. A classic case of unsound thinking with respect to money and business concerns the phenomenon of sunk cost. The amount that a person has paid to acquire a good—whether it be a house or a stock or a patent—has no proper place in the decision about whether to sell it, or at which price it should be sold; 'sunk costs are sunk' and should be disregarded. But many people feel unable to disregard the sunk cost, especially when the sale might be below the purchase price because it would then apparently represent a 'loss'—the same word which has been so salient in the depression literature. The problem is the negative comparison between the actual sale price and the benchmark price; the resulting sale would be painful and 'depressing', and therefore is often not made even though foregoing the sale is money-losing and bad business. (This phenomenon is related to the discussion of prospect theory above.)

7. Political scientists theorize that social disturbances occur, not in stable periods of bad times, but after a period of improvement and then cessation of improvement. The period of improvement raises the benchmark denominator of what people expect, and their actual state of affairs seems to fall short of that. This will evoke active efforts to win change if people feel potent, or anger if their efforts are thwarted. If they come to feel helpless, people lapse into depression and lack of activity, or finally into apathy.

APPENDIX B

RELATIONSHIP OF SELF-COMPARISONS ANALYSIS TO OTHER THEORY

Professional readers, both researchers and practicing therapists, will wish to compare the theory and methods offered here—which I call Self-Comparisons Analysis—with the cognitive therapies of Beck and of Ellis, behavioral therapy, the Interpersonal Therapy of Klerman and Weissman, Seligman's prescriptions about the sense of helplessness, and other views of depression. They will want to know what is new about the ideas and practices presented here. This Postscript responds to that question, and takes up some other matters of interest to the professional reader.

Before discussing differences, however, I would like to emphasize the key element in common: From Beck and Ellis I gained the central insight that particular modes of 'cognitive' thinking cause people to be depressed. This implies the cardinal therapeutic principle that people can change their modes of thinking by a combination of learning and will-power in such fashion as to overcome depression. For this I am indebted to them not only intellectually but also for my own welfare. And now to the differences and novelties.

This book offers a more comprehensive theory of depression than has been offered heretofore, a theory which includes the others as elements in it. The therapeutic approaches suggested here are dictated even more clearly by the specificity of the theory given here, and more possibilities are suggested by it, than any of the previous approaches alone. Even folk wisdom nicely takes its place within Self-Comparisons Analysis, as for example the dimension-shifting common sense of counting your blessings, living one day at a time, and devoting yourself to helping others rather than rehearsing your own woes.

SOME SPECIFIC DIFFERENCES

This section barely dips into the vast literature on depression; a thorough review would not be appropriate here, and the works mentioned below contain comprehensive review. I have merely selected some major themes for discussion.

In reading the following discussion of differences between Self-Comparisons Analysis and other approaches, please notice this in particular: Beck focuses on distortion of the actual-state *numerator,* and loss is his central analytical concept. Ellis focuses on absolutizing the benchmark-state *denominator,* using ought's and must's as his central analytical concept. Self-Comparisons Analysis embraces both of these approaches by pointing out that either the numerator or the denominator can be the root of a Rotten Mood Ratio, and the comparison of the two (in the context of belief that one is helpless to make changes) causes sadness and depression. Hence, Self-Comparisons Analysis reconciles and integrates Beck's and Ellis's approaches, and at the same time the self-comparisons construct points to many additional points of therapeutic intervention in the depression system.

Aaron Beck's Cognitive Therapy

Beck's original version of Cognitive Therapy has the sufferer "Start by Building Self-Esteem" (title of Chapter 4 of Burns 1980). Excellent advice, but not very systematic. Neither 'self-esteem' nor 'negative thought' is a precise theoretical term. Focusing on your negative self-comparisons is a better method—clearcut and systematic —for achieving the aim Beck sets. But there are also other paths to overcoming depression that are part of the overall approach given here.

Beck et al. focus on the depressive's actual state of affairs, and her distorted perceptions of that actual state. Self-Comparisons Analysis agrees that such distortions—which lead to negative self-comparisons and a rotten Mood Ratio—are (together with a sense of helplessness) a frequent cause of sadness and depression. But Beck et al.'s exclusive focus on distortion keeps them from seeing the deductively-consistent inner logic of many depressives, and accepting as valid such issues as which goals should be chosen.[1] It has also distracted their attention from the role of helplessness in disabling the purposive activities which sufferers might otherwise undertake to change the actual state and thereby avoid the negative self-comparisons.

Beck's view of depression as "paradoxical" (1967, 3; 1987, 28) is not helpful, I believe. Underlying this view is a comparison of the depressed person to a perfectly-logical individual with full information about the present and future of the person's external and mental situation—like the model of the perfectly-rational consumer in economics. A better model for therapeutic purposes is an individual with limited analytic capacity, only partial information, and a set of conflicting desires. Given these inescapable constraints, it is inevitable that the person's mental behavior will not take full advantage of all opportunities for personal welfare, and will proceed in a manner which is quite dysfunctional with respect to some goals. With this view of the individual, we may try to help the individual reach a higher level of satisficing (Herbert Simon's concept) as judged by the individual, but recognizing that this is done by means of trade-offs as well as improvements in thinking processes. Seen this way, there are no paradoxes.

Burns nicely summarizes Beck's approach (which he espouses) as follows: "The first principle of cognitive therapy is that *all* your moods are created by your 'cognitions'" (1980, 11). Well said (though a bit over-stated; anger at being hit by a stray snowball is something other than cognitive). Self-Comparisons Analysis makes this proposition more specific: Moods are caused by a particular type of cognition, self-comparisons, in conjunction with such general attitudes as (for example, in the case of depression) feeling helpless.

Burns says "The second principle is that when you are feeling depressed, your thoughts are dominated by a pervasive negativity" (12). Self-Comparisons Analysis also makes this proposition more specific: it replaces 'negativity' with negative *self-comparisons*, in conjunction with feeling helpless.

According to Burns, "The third principle is . . . that the negative thoughts . . . nearly *always* contain gross distortions" (12, italics in

---

[1]In some later work, such as Beck et al. 1979, 35, they widen the concept to "patients' misinterpretations, self-defeating behavior, and dysfunctional attitudes". But the latter new elements border on the tautologous, being approximately equal to "thoughts that cause depression", and hence contain no guidance to their nature and treatment.

original). Below I argue at some length that depressed thinking is *not* always best characterized as distorted.

Another difference between Beck's and my point of view is that he makes the concept of loss central to his theory of depression. It is true, as he says, that "many life situations can be interpreted as a loss" (1976, 58), and that loss and negative self-comparisons often can be logically translated one into the other without too much conceptual strain. But many sadness-causing situations must be bent and massaged in order to be interpreted as losses; consider, for example, the tennis player who again and again seeks matches with better players and then is pained at the outcome. It seems to me that most situations can be interpreted more naturally and more fruitfully as negative self-comparisons. Furthermore, this concept points more clearly to a variety of ways that one's thinking can change to overcome depression than does the more limited concept of loss.

It is also relevant that the concept of comparison is fundamental in perception and in the production of new thoughts. It therefore is more likely to link up logically with other branches of theory (see the discussion below of decision-making theory) than is a less basic concept. Hence this more basic concept would seem preferable on the grounds of potential fruitfulness.

Albert Ellis's Rational-Emotive Therapy

Ellis operates primarily upon the benchmark state, urging that the depressive not consider goals and 'ought' states as strongly binding 'musts'. He teaches people not to 'musturbate'—that is, to free themselves of unnecessary musts and oughts. Again this is fine advice which helps a depressive adjust his or her benchmark state, and the person's relationship to it, in such fashion that one makes fewer and less-painful negative self-comparisons. Coming to recognize that I did not have to accept the particular goals and standards that I had previously accepted was the first of the key events in my own victory over depression. But as with Beck's (and below, Seligman's) therapeutic advice, Ellis's focuses on only one aspect of the depression structure. As a system, therefore, his doctrine restricts the options available to the therapist and patient, omitting some other avenues which may be just what a particular person needs.

Interpersonal Therapy

Klerman, Weissman, et al. focus on the neg-comps that flow from interactions between the depressive and others as a result of conflict and criticism. There can be no doubt that bad relationships with other people damage a person's actual interpersonal situation and exacerbate other difficulties in the person's life. And it is therefore undeniable that teaching a person better ways of relating to others will improve their real situation and therefore their state of mind. But the fact that people living alone often suffer depression makes clear that not *all* depression flows from interpersonal relationships, and therefore to focus *only* on interpersonal relationships to the exclusion of other cognitive and behavioral elements is too limited.

Learned Helplessness

Seligman focuses on ways to reduce the helplessness that almost all depression sufferers report, an element which combines with neg-comps to produce sadness. And he expresses what other writers say less explicitly about their own core ideas, that the theoretical element he concentrates on is the main issue in depression. Talking about the many kinds of depression classified by another writer, he says: "I will suggest that, at the core, there is something unitary that all these depressions share" (1975, 78).

I agree that the sense of helplessness is centrally involved in all depressions. But Seligman gives the impression that helplessness is the *only* invariable element, which I believe is not the case; negative self-comparisons are also omnipresent. His therapeutic focus on reducing the sense of helplessness points him away from adaptations of other parts of the system. (This may follow from his experimental work with animals which lack the capacity to make such adjustments in perceptions, judgments, goals, values, and so on, which are central to human depression and which people can and do alter. That is, people *disturb themselves,* as Ellis puts it, whereas animals do not.)

Self-Comparisons Analysis and the procedure it implies *include* learning not to feel helpless. But this approach focuses on the helpless attitude *in conjunction with* the neg-comps that are the direct cause of the sadness of depression, rather than *only* on the helpless attitude, as

Seligman does. Again, Self-Comparisons Analysis reconciles and integrates another important element of depression into an over-arching theory.

Other Approaches

Viktor Frankl's Logotherapy offers two modes of help. One mode is a philosophical attempt to help a person find meaning in his or her life which will give the person a reason to live, and to live with the pain of sadness and depression; this has much in common with Values Treatment as discussed in Chapter 18, and is discussed there. Another mode is the tactic Frankl calls 'paradoxical intention'. The therapist offers the patient a radically different perspective on the patient's situation, either the numerator or the denominator of the Mood Ratio, using absurdity and humor; this is discussed in Chapter 10. Frankl has successfully trained others in the use of his techniques, and he reviews studies showing success. Both patients and therapists can surely find his tools useful in a variety of contexts.

Substitutions and Combinations of Methods

Even a simple procedure like that of Coué could achieve good results with some sufferers by operating on just one aspect of the process in an uncomplicated fashion. Such a single view of a depressive's thinking is just the opposite of the complex view of the process in my explanatory diagram in Appendix C, which looks like spaghetti. But complexity offers opportunities for many kinds of interventions and adjustments that are obscured from the sufferer and from the therapist by a focus on a single procedure.

Self-Comparisons Analysis makes clear that many sorts of influences, perhaps in combination with each other, can produce persistent sadness. From this it follows that many sorts of interventions may be of help to a depression sufferer. That is, different causes—and there *are* many different causes—call for different therapeutic interventions. Furthermore, there may be several sorts of intervention that can help any particular depression.

In short, different strokes for different folks. In contrast, however, each of the various schools of psychological therapy—psychoanalytic, behavioral, religious, and so on—does its own thing no matter what the cause of the person's depression, on the implicit assumption that all depressions are caused in the same way. Furthermore, each school of thought insists that its way is the only true therapy despite the wise remark of Greist and Jefferson quoted earlier that because "depression is almost certainly caused by different factors, there is no single best treatment for depression" (1984, 72). As a practical matter, the depression sufferer faces a baffling disarray of treatments, and the choice is too often made simply on the basis of chance.

Self-Comparisons Analysis points a depression sufferer toward the most promising tactic to banish the particular person's depression. It focuses first on understanding why a person makes negative self-comparisons. Then it develops ways of preventing the neg-comps, rather than focusing on merely understanding and reliving the past, or on simply changing contemporary habits. With this understanding one can choose how best to fight the depression and achieve happiness.

SELF-COMPARISONS ANALYSIS COMPARED TO OTHER COGNITIVE THERAPY ON 'RATIONALITY'

A key difference between Self-Comparisons Analysis and both Beck's and Ellis's cognitive therapy is their belief that depression is always the result of 'disabled' or 'irrational' thinking. Self-Comparisons Analysis differs from Beck and Ellis in not considering depressive thinking as irrational by definition.

In my view, *everyone's* thinking is bent and twisted, especially in matters that affect one personally. Everyone's perception is biased in various ways; it is never unbiased, not just in psychologically-charged issues but in all kinds of cognitive thinking and judgments in business, science, politics, and everyday life. The question is not who sees the matter 'correctly' and who does not, but *in what fashion* the thinking of each person is inclined away from what might be a 'true' view.

Let's agree that unsound thinking either causes or is involved in many cases of depression, and improving one's thinking can therefore help fight against depression in those cases. But as I see it, this is not an appropriate or 'rational' treatment for *all* cases of depression.

Underlying Beck's and Ellis's therapy is the value (belief) that it is silly and childish and irrational to be depressed, that depression is proof-positive that one is not thinking rationally.

There are some people who are depressed yet who are not at all irrational in their thinking—at least not in the sense that Ellis and Harper use that term. Consider the following example of Ellis's, with special attention to the last sentence:

> . . . the case of a person who, as a child, is continually criticized by his parents, who consequently feels himself loathesome and inadequate, who refuses to take chances at trying and possibly failing at difficult tasks, and who comes to hate himself more because he knows that he is evasive and cowardly. Such a person, during his childhood, would of course be seriously neurotic. But how would it be possible for him to *sustain* his neurosis if he began to think later in life, in a truly logical manner?
>
> For if this person does begin to be consistently rational, he will quickly stop being overconcerned about what others think of him and will begin to care primarily about what *he* wants to do in life and what *he* thinks of himself. Consequently, he will stop avoiding difficult tasks and, instead of blaming himself for making mistakes, he will say to himself something like: 'Now this is not the right way to do things; let me stop and figure out a better way.' Or: 'There's no doubt that I made a mistake this time; now let me see how I can benefit from making it, so that my next performance will be improved.'
>
> This person, if he is thinking straight in the present, will not blame his defeats on external events, but will realize that he himself is causing them by his inadequate or incompetent behavior. He will not believe that it is easier to avoid than to face difficult life problems, but will see that the so-called easy way is invariably the harder and more idiotic procedure. He will not think that he needs someone greater or stronger than himself on whom to rely, but will independently buckle down to hard tasks without outside help. He will not feel, because he once defeated himself by avoiding doing things the hard way, that he must always continue to act in this self-defeating manner.
>
> How, with this kind of logical thinking, could an originally disturbed person possibly maintain and continually revivify his neurosis? He just couldn't. (Ellis 1962, 91–92)

If the person is, say, a biologist searching for an advance in treating cancer which he has not been able to find, the cause of the "defeats" is not "inadequate or incompetent behavior", to use Ellis's terms. This is not a person who "systematically misconstrues his experiences", as

Beck sees it (1977, 264). Hence, by itself no amount of 'straightening out the person's thinking' is the answer. Rather, the person must decide either a) to accept such defeats if they do occur, and change the denominator (of expected results) or the main dimension of comparison (from success-failure to courage or lack of it), or else b) change his work subject.

By assuming that the cognitions responsible for depression can always be shown to be logically or empirically incorrect—'distorted thinking' in Beck's terms, 'irrational thinking' in Ellis's—they run the risk of forcing an analysis that is appropriate for some people onto others for whom it is not appropriate, and thereby not doing well both by the cognitive point of view and some clients, too.

Ellis and Beck view the role of the therapist as helping the patient learn to think in 'more rational' or 'less distorted' ways. In my view, the proper role for the therapist is often more like that of a sports physician or trainer in those cases where the athlete desperately wishes to continue playing. The appropriate procedure then is: a) Determine the cause of the pain. b) Decide how the pain can be mitigated, and mitigate it if possible. c) If mitigating the pain requires cessation of play, then advise the patient that there is a trade-off between playing and avoiding pain. This is like the choice that a depressed person must make between continuing to work toward a valued goal where there has been little or no success so far, and only small hope of future success, as is sometimes the case with a scientist trying to persuade the world of a new theory. The therapist may offer some devices that will at least lessen the pain while playing, however, and this can be of value. It is important that the choice to play be respected and not just treated as irrational or perverse; doing the latter can worsen the person's depression.

Self-Comparisons Analysis also differs in viewing sadness as an effect of *negative self-comparisons plus a sense of helplessness* rather than simply *loss*, as does Beck; and there is a great deal of difference between the implications of these two concepts. Still another difference is the systematic step-by-step procedure suggested by Self-Comparisons Analysis, as described in earlier chapters, against which may be compared the following systematic description of Beck's procedures—(actually a description of Beck's cognitive therapy for a patient suffering from anxiety rather than depression):

The formulation of the progress of this patient can now be fitted into the therapeutic model: 1. self-observations that led directly to the ideation preceding the anxiety; 2. establishing the relation between the thoughts and anxiety attack; 3. learning to regard thoughts as hypotheses rather than facts; 4. testing the hypotheses; 5. piecing together the assumptions that underlay and generated these hypotheses; 6. demonstrating that these rules composing her belief system were incorrect. (Beck 1977, 261)

APPENDIX C

SCHEMATIC DIAGRAM OF THE CAUSATION OF DEPRESSION

Figure C1 summarizes graphically the description in Chapters 2 to 9 of the mental mechanisms that influence sadness and depression. It shows how the elements in a person's history and present conditions may combine to produce unfavorable self-comparisons, sadness, and depression. The aim of this figure is to present a unified picture of the depression mechanism and its elements.

Though Figure C1 is complex, please keep in mind that it is only a stylized and simplified view of the human condition, and the elements could be chosen, defined, and styled in many different fashions.

Appendix C
Schematic diagram of depression and its causes

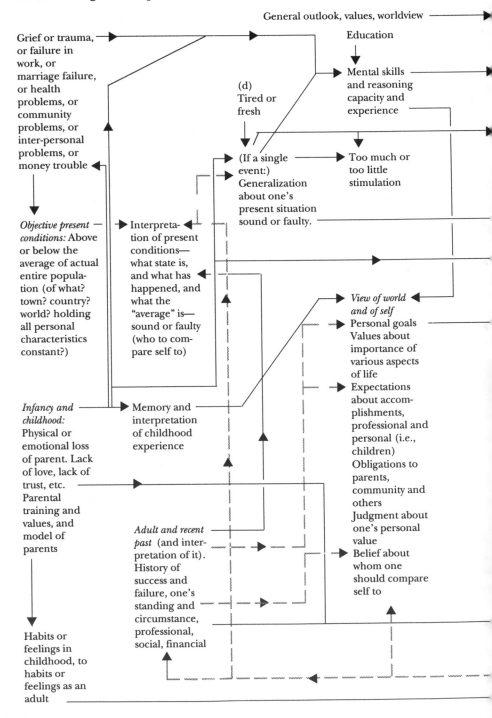

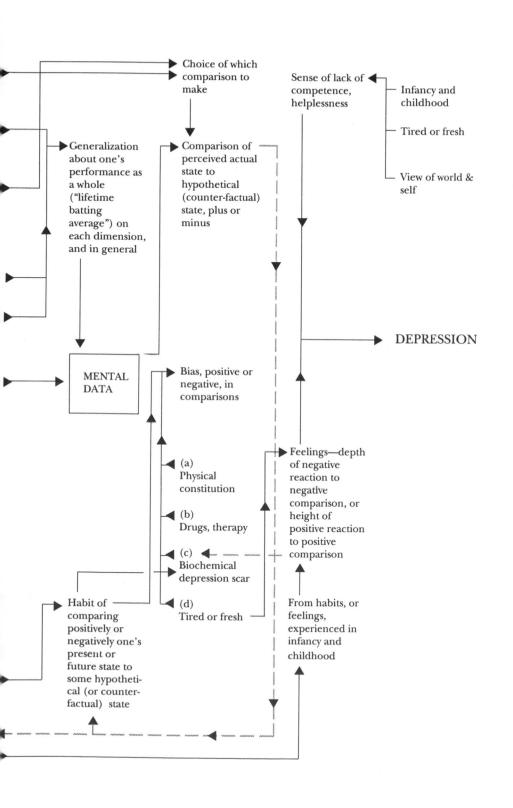

APPENDIX D

TESTS OF THE EFFICACY OF THERAPY

Unlike traditional psychoanalysis,[1] cognitive therapy has been subjected to controlled tests. Tests that compare drugs with psychotherapy, as well as tests of various forms of psychotherapy, must overcome a particularly difficult set of obstacles, such as allowing for the quality and style of the particular psychotherapist.[2] But the body of work has been sufficiently competent that we are safely able to conclude that cognitive therapy works well. Miller, Norman, and Keitner (1989) summarize as follows:

> A number of psychotherapies that can be described as cognitive-behavioral have been found to be effective treatments for depressed outpatients, producing at least as much improvement as was produced by pharmacotherapy. Combining cognitive-behavioral treatment with pharmacotherapy has been found to result in higher response rates in some studies but equivalent rates in others. (1274)

And in their own long-run follow-up study they found that "significantly higher proportions of the patients who received additional [to the standard treatment including drugs] cognitive-behavioral treatment (cognitive therapy or social skills) had responded by the end of the formal treatment period and did not relapse for the remainder of the 1-year follow-up period" (1274).

The first study seems to have been that of Ellis in 1957, which showed that his variety of cognitive therapy—Rational-Emotive Therapy—is indeed effective. Since then there have been a wide variety of studies from many different angles. Beck (1976, Chapter 12) summarized the studies of his own variety of cognitive therapy until that time; they are further reviewed in Beck et al. 1979, Chapter 18. The studies show that for unhospitalized depressed persons—both

---

[1]See Colby and Stoller 1988 for discussion of the untested and perhaps untestable status of psychoanalysis.

[2]See Elkin et al. 1988a and 1988b for a cogent discussion of these research problems.

volunteers and clinic patients—of several sorts, the groups that received cognitive therapy did better than did groups that received no therapy or only support. For hospitalized patients, cognitive therapy generally did as well or better than anti-depressant drugs, and the addition of drugs to cognitive therapy did not improve results, though Beck et al. suggest that in some cases adding drugs to cognitive therapy probably is warranted. As noted above, the long-term followup study by Miller, Norman, and Keitner (1989) showed that patients treated with cognitive-behavioral therapy in addition to drugs have fewer recurring episodes than do patients treated with drugs alone.

Interpersonal Therapy is another form of cognitive treatment that has been evaluated in controlled tests, and has been shown to be effective. Klerman et al. (1984, 18, 19; see also Klerman 1988) summarize the studies of their method.

A large-scale and well-controlled double-blind (for drugs) test was done by the National Institute of Mental Health at three separate university sites, beginning in 1980, comparing Beck's Cognitive Therapy, Interpersonal Therapy, imiprimine (a tricyclic antidepressant drug), and a placebo-plus-support-group. As of 1986, slightly more than half of the drug and psychotherapy groups had 'returned to normal' after 16 weeks, whereas only 29 percent of the placebo-support subjects had done so.[3] At the conclusion of treatment, the active psychotherapies were as successful as the drug imipramine in reducing the symptoms of depression and improving the patient's ability to function. Drug treatment produced improvement more rapidly, but the active psychotherapies caught up later. Both more-severely and less-severely depressed patients benefitted from the active psychotherapies (Elkin et al. 1986, abstract).

In addition to the outcome studies of cognitive therapy, there have been studies of the *mechanism of depression* that support the underlying theory. For example, Seligman et al. (1988) found that what has come to be called 'explanatory style'—the reasons people give for bad events that occur, and the extent to which they blame either themselves or outside forces—changes during cognitive therapy for depression in a fashion which confirms the theory; improvement in mood is accompanied by reduction of self-blame.

---

[3]Holden 1986, 723–27

TESTING SELF-COMPARISONS ANALYSIS

It should be reasonably easy and inexpensive to determine the extent to which the thought processes of depressives are indeed framed as negative self-comparisons. There exist numerous protocols of depressed patients as well as questionaire studies of samples of depressed and non-depressed persons that have been used for research on cognitive therapy: for example the studies reviewed in Peterson and Seligman 1984, and in Beck 1976, 124–28; see also Peterson, Bettes, and Seligman 1985. The content of these protocols and questionaires could be re-analyzed for the purposes at hand using standard techniques of content analysis. And questionaire studies gathering new data with instruments adapted from the existing survey instruments should be able to take advantage of the pre-existing body of research.

TESTING COMPUTER-ADMINISTERED THERAPY

Along with this book is offered the computer program *Overcoming Depression* developed by Kenneth Colby—the 'father' of computer-delivered therapy—based on the Self-Comparisons Therapy described in the book, and presented in natural-language English rather than computerese; this is the first natural-language computer program to do cognitive therapy. The findings of a study by Selmi et al. (1990) of cognitive therapy administered by computer are most relevant here. The patients suffering from mild to moderate depression who were treated with the computer program did as well as the patients who received similar cognitive therapy in person, and significantly better than control subjects.

APPENDIX E

REPLY TO JULIAN SIMON'S CRITICISMS OF RATIONAL-EMOTIVE THERAPY, BY ALBERT ELLIS

While often citing my own work on depression, Dr. Simon sometimes cavils with it, especially as presented in my book with Dr. Robert A. Harper, *A New Guide to Rational Living* (1975). I naturally disagree with his points in Appendix B, notably with his statement that "underlying cognitive therapy is the value (belief) that it is silly and childish and irrational to be depressed, that depression is proof-positive that one is not thinking rationally." No, my own rational-emotive therapy (RET) and Aaron T. Beck's cognitive therapy (CT) both hold that depression is *largely* caused by irrational thinking, but that it often has several other causes, including significant biological and environmental contributions.

Dr. Simon also holds that it is sometimes 'rational' for people to depress themselves, since they can then 'sensibly' atone for their immoral acts and can 'rationally' berate themselves for foolishly ruining their own lives. Like most writers on depression (including Beck), Simon fails to see the clearcut distinction that RET makes between sadness, sorrow, or regret, on the one hand, and depression, whining, and self-deprecation, on the other hand. RET hypothesizes that people *appropriately* or *rationally* make themselves feel sad—and sometimes *extremely* sad—when they believe, 'I really don't *like* what I've done. I strongly *prefer* to do otherwise; and I am *determined* to now do what I can do to rectify my errors, make restitution to my victims, and avoid acting badly again'. Their *wishes* and *preferences* to improve their behavior often lead to profound feelings of sadness and regret, and to their active determination to change. They then are quite *un*disturbed and *rational*.

When, however, people think *dogmatically* and *absolutistically,* they change their preferences and desires to unconditional musts, shoulds, oughts, demands, and commands. They then tell themselves, 'Because

I under all conditions at all times *must* behave well, and because I have *unforgivably* behaved badly this time, I am a *rotten, damnable person* who is completely *worthless* and who *deserves* to suffer!' With these kinds of rigid *demands,* they make themselves sad *and* depressed, regretful *and* self-denigrating—and they then almost always behave self-defeatingly and irrationally.

My main difference with Dr. Simon (and with Dr. Beck), therefore, is their failing to distinguish between sadness and depression, both of which are on different continua of feeling states, and both of which can be mild or intense. While the inappropriate feeling of depression almost always includes the appropriate feelings of sadness and regret, the latter (fortunately for the human race!) can distinctly be experienced without the former. (See, in this connection, some of my books on RET, such as *Reason and Emotion in Psychotherapy,* 1962; *Humanistic Psychotherapy,* 1973; *A Guide to Personal Happiness,* 1982; *Overcoming Resistance: Rational-Emotive Therapy With Difficult Clients,* 1985; and *How to Stubbornly Refuse to Make Yourself Miserable About Anything—Yes, Anything!,* 1988.)

I would therefore say to the readers of this book, when things go wrong with your life, and especially when you yourself mess things up, avoid depression by rigorously (not rigidly!) staying with your preferences and by stubbornly refusing to escalate them into *must*urbatory commands. Try to believe—and I mean really and strongly believe—'I would very much *like* things to go well but, but, but they never *have to! Too bad,* but never *horrible,* if they don't!' And try to consistently and powerfully believe, 'I would truly *prefer* to act competently and brilliantly, and I really *want* significant people to approve of me, but, but, but if I don't and they don't, *tough!* It's most *unfortunate* but it's never *the end of the world!'*

If you think—yes, strongly think—this way, I can't promise that you'll *never* get depressed, nor *always,* at worst, feel sad and frustrated. But you'll most probably greatly stave off your chances of experiencing depression.

REFERENCES

To the depression sufferer: The more you read about depression, the more useful ideas you will pick up. And you never know when you will stumble across an idea—which may be nothing more than everyday folk wisdom—that will explode into a breakthrough for you.

The asterisks next to books in this list mean that I recommend them—and more asterisks mean a higher recommendation. I have also added brief notes next to some key items.

To the Professional Reader: An authoritative comprehensive review by Karasu (1990a and 1990b) of the experimental and theoretical literature on depression and various therapies for it arrives at conclusions consistent with the earlier findings cited in the text, and with the theoretical ideas presented in the book. This review makes it unnecessary for the recent literature to be reviewed in great detail here. For those persons wishing a quick tutorial on the state of professional thought, I would suggest turning first to Karasu's articles, and to the collection edited by Alloy (1988).

Throughout, I have tried to refer mainly to books rather than articles so that the general reader might be able to find the referenced work in a general library. For the most recent developments in research results and depression trends, I have had to refer occasionally to the technical literature, however.

Abraham, Karl. Notes on the Psycho-Analytical Investigation and Treatment of Manic-Depressive Insanity and Allied Conditions. In Gaylin, cited below.

Alcoholics Anonymous. New York: Alcoholics Anonymous World Services, third edition, 1976.

Alloy, Lauren B. (ed.) *Cognitive Processes In Depression.* New York: The Guilford Press, 1988.

————. and Lyn Y. Abramson. Depressive Realism: Four Theoretical Perspectives. In Alloy 1988, 223–265.

American Psychiatric Association. *Diagnostic and Statistical Manual.* Washington: APA, third edition, 1980; fourth edition (DSM-IIIR), 1987.

Andreasen, Nancy C., and Ira D. Glick. Bipolar Affective Disorder and Creativity: Implications and Clinical Management. *Comprehensive Psychiatry,* Vol 29, May/June, 1988, 207–217.

Arieti, Silvano. Manic-Depressive Psychosis. In Arieti (ed.) *American Handbook of Psychiatry,* 2 vols. New York: Basic Books, 1959.

**Beck, Aaron T. *Depression: Clinical, Experimental, and Theoretical Aspects.* New York: Harper and Row, 1967. This is still one of the two most important works in the field, and the book that saved me from depression. But it is written for the professional rather than the layman.

*Beck, Aaron T. *Cognitive Therapy and the Emotional Disorders.* New York: New American Library, 1976. For the professional.

Beck, Aaron T. Cognitive Models of Depression. *Journal of Cognitive Psychotherapy,* Volume 1, Number 1, 1987, 5–37.

Beck, Aaron T., and David A. Clark. Anxiety and Depression: An Information Processing Perspective. *Anxiety Research,* Vol. 1, 1988, 23–36.

*Beck, Aaron T., A. John Rush, Brian F. Shaw, and Gary Emery. *Cognitive Therapy of Depression.* New York: Guilford, 1979. For the professional, but full of helpful tips.

Beck, Aaron T., Gary Brown, Robert A. Steer, Judy I. Eidelson, and John H. Riskind. Differentiating Anxiety and Depression: A Test of the Cognitive Content-Specificity Hypothesis. *Journal of Abnormal Psychology,* Vol. 96, No. 3, 1987, 179–183.

Behanan, Kovoor T. *Yoga: A Scientific Evaluation.* New York: Dover, 1937/1959.

Ben-David, Calev. The Philosopher's Couch. *The Jerusalem Post International Edition,* Week ending March 31, 1990, 13.

Benson, Herbert, with Miriam Z. Klipper. *The Relaxation Response.* New York: Avon Books, 1976.

Bibring, Edward. The Mechanism of Depression. In Gaylin, cited below.

Bowlby, John. *Attachment* (vol I of *Attachment and Loss*). New York: Basic Books, 1969.

Bowlby, John. *Loss: Sadness and Depression* (vol III of *Attachment and Loss*). New York: Basic Books, 1980.

Brickman, Philip, Dan Coates, and Ronnie Janoff Bulman. Lottery Winners and Accident Victims: Is Happiness Relative?, xerox, August, 1977.

Brooks, Van Wyck. *The Days of the Phoenix.* New York: Dutton, 1957. Excerpted as 'A Season In Hell', in Kaplan 1964.

Brussel, James A., and Theodore Irwin. *Understanding and Overcoming Depression.* New York: Hawthorn, 1973.

Buber, Martin. *Good and Evil.* New York: Scribner's, 1952.

***Burns, David D. *Feeling Good: The New Mood Therapy.* New York: Morrow, 1980; also in paperback. One of the two best self-help books on the subject.

Burtt, E. A. *The Teachings of the Compassionate Buddha.* New York: Mentor, 1955.

*Cammer, Leonard. *Up From Depression.* New York: Simon and Schuster, 1969, quotes from Pocket Books edn., 1971.

Campbell, Donald T., and Julian Stanley. Experimental and Quasi-Experimental Designs for Research in Teaching. In N. L. Gage (ed.) *Handbook of Research in Teaching.* Chicago: Rand McNally, 1963.

*Carnegie, Dale. *How to Stop Worrying and Start Living* (New York: Simon and Schuster, 1944.

Chevalier, Nancy Young. When Pills, Shock Therapy Failed . . . I Imagined Dancing In Vienna. *Washington Post Health,* January 16, 1990, 14.

Collingwood, Robin G. *An Autobiography.* Oxford: Oxford University Press, 1939/1970.

Conze, Edward. *Buddhism: Its Essence and Development* (New York: Cassirer, 1951; Harper Torchbook, 1959.

*Cousins, Norman. *Anatomy of an Illness as Perceived by the Patient.* New York: Bantam, 1981.

Coyne, J. C., and I. H. Gotlib The Role of Cognition in Depression: A Critical Appraisal. *Psychological Bulletin,* 94, 1983, 472–505.

Custance in Kaplan, 1964, cited below, 56–58.

Dewey, John. *Experience and Nature.* New York: Dover, 1929/1958.

Dobson, Keith S. (ed.) *Handbook of Cognitive-Behavioral Therapies.* New York: The Guilford Press, 1988.

Dominian, Jack. *Depression.* Glasgow: Collins, 1976.

Duval, S., and R. A. Wicklund. *A Theory of Objective Self-Awareness.* New York: Academic Press, 1972.

Eaves, George G. *Cognitive Patterns in Endogenous and Nonendogenous Unipolar Major Depression.* Ph.D. dissertation, The University of Texas at Dallas, 1981, Abstract.

———. and A. J. Rush. Cognitive Patterns in Symptomatic and Remitted Unipolar Major Depression. *Journal of Abnormal Psychology,* 33(1), 1984, 31–40.

Elkin, Irene, Paul A. Pilkonis, John P. Docherty, and Stuart M. Sotsky. Conceptual and Methodological Issues in Comparative Studies of Psychotherapy and Pharmacotherapy, I: Active Ingredients and Mechanisms of Change. *American Journal of Psychiatry* 145:8, August, 1988, 909–917.

Elkin, Irene, Paul A. Pilkonis, John P. Docherty, and Stuart M. Sotsky. Conceptual and Methodological Issues in Comparative Studies of Psychotherapy and Pharmacotherapy, II: Nature and Timing of Treatment Effects. *American Journal of Psychiatry,* 145:9, September, 1988, 1070–76.

———. et al. NIMH Treatment of Depression Collaborative Research Program: Initial Outcome Findings. Abstract of paper given at American Association for the Advancement of Science, May, 1986.

Ellis, Albert. Outcome of Employing Three Techniques of Psychotherapy. *Journal of Clinical Psychology,* 13, 1957, 344–350.

**———. *Reason and Emotion in Psychotherapy.* New York: Lyle Stuart, 1962. One of the two best theoretical books for the professional.

*———. The Use of Rational Humorous Songs in Psychotherapy. In W. F. Fry, Jr. and W. A. Salameh (eds.) *Handbook of Humor in Psychotherapy: Advances in the Clinical Use of Humor.* Sarasota: Professional Resource Exchange, 1987), 265–285.

———. The Impossibility of Achieving Consistently Good Mental Health. *American Psychologist,* 42, April, 1987, 364–375.

———. *How To Stubbornly Refuse to Make Yourself Miserable About Anything—Yes Anything!* Secaucus, NJ: Lyle Stuart, 1988.

***———, and Robert A. Harper. *A New Guide to Rational Living.* North Hollywood: Wilshire; revised 1977 edition. One of the two best self-help books.

**Emery, Gary, *A New Beginning.* New York: Simon and Schuster, 1981. Lots of valuable practical advice from a member of Beck's cognitive therapy 'school'.

Endler, Norman S. *Holiday of Darkness: A Psychologist's Personal Journey out of*

His Depression. New York: Wiley, 1982. The title is apt. The author was treated only with drugs and electroshock; no psychotherapy is mentioned. His description of the side-effects of the drugs is interesting. The book is generally upbeat and hopeful.

Flach, Frederic F. *The Secret Strength of Depression.* New York: Bantam, 1975.

**Frankl, Viktor E. *Man's Search For Meaning.* New York: Washington Square Press, 1963. Fascinating and often useful ideas rooted in a philosophical attitude toward life and depression.

**————. *The Doctor and the Soul.* second edn. New York: Bantam, 1969. More excellent ideas by Frankl.

Freud, Sigmund. Mourning and Melancholia. In Gaylin 1968, cited below.

Gaylin, Willard (ed.) *The Meaning of Despair.* New York: Science House, 1968.

Gaylin, Willard. *Feelings: Our Vital Signs.* New York: Harper and Row, 1979.

Gibson, William. *A Season in Heaven.* New York: Bantam, 1974. Interesting description of a meditation community by a first-rate dramatist.

Gilson, M. Depression as Measured by Perceptual Bias in Binocular Rivalry. Unpublished doctoral dissertation, Georgia State University. University Microfilms No. AAD83-27351, 1983. Cited by Beck, 1988.

Glatzer, Nahum (ed.) *The Dimensions of Job.* New York: Schocken, 1969.

Greenberg, Michael S., Carmelo V. Vazquez, and Lauren B. Alloy. Depression versus Anxiety: Differences in Self- and Other-Schemata. In Alloy 1988, 109–142.

*Greist, John H., and James W. Jefferson. *Depression and Its Treatment.* Washington, D.C.: American Psychiatric Press, 1984. A mainstream 'official' medical discussion of depression.

Grinspoon, Lester (ed.) *Psychiatry Update, Vol. II.* Washington, D.C.: American Psychiatric Press, 1983. A good review for professionals of the state of the art.

Gussow, Mel. Elizabeth Swados: A Runaway Talent. *New York Times Magazine,* March 5, 1978.

Heinicke, Christoph M. Parental Deprivation in Early Childhood. In Scott and Senay.

Helson, Harry. *Adaptation-Level Theory.* New York: Harper and Row, 1964.

Hildebrand, Kenneth. *Achieving Real Happiness.* New York: Harper, 1955.

Hirschfeld, Robert M. A., Gerald L. Klerman, Paula J. Clayton, and Martin B. Keller. Personality and Depression: Empirical Findings. *Archives of General Psychiatry,* September, 1983, Volume 40, 993–98.

Hoffmann, Banesh. *Albert Einstein: Creator and Rebel.* New York: Viking, 1972.

Holden, Constance. Depression Research Advances, Treatment Lags. *Science,* 15 August, 1986, 723–27

Honigfeld, Gilbert, and Alfreda Howard. *Psychiatric Drugs: A Desk Reference.* New York and London: Academic Press, 1973.

Hume, David. *Essential Works.* New York: Bantam, 1965.

***James, William. *Varieties of Religious Experience.* The all-time classic about mental illness.

————. *The Philosophy of William James.* Drawn from his own Works. Introduction by Horace M. Kallen. New York: Modern Library, 1925.

————. *Psychology.* One-volume edition: Greenwich, Ct: Fawcett, 1892/ 1963.

Janoff-Bulman, Ronnie, and Bernard Hecker. Depression, Vulnerability, and World Assumptions. In Alloy 1988, 177–192.

Johnston, Tracy. Review of *John Maher of Delancey Street* by Grover Sales. *New York Times Book Review,* August 15, 1976, 6.

Kahneman, Daniel, and Amos Twersky. Prospect Theory: An Analysis of Decision Under Risk. In *Decision, Probability, and Utility,* Peter Gardenfors and Nils-Eric Sahlin (eds.), Cambridge: Cambridge University Press, 1988.

Kaplan, Bert, *The Inner World of Mental Illness.* New York: Harper and Row, 1964. Writings by people who have suffered from mental illness.

Karasu, T. Byram. Toward a Clinical Model of Psychotherapy for Depression, I: Systematic Comparison of Three Psychotherapies. In *American Journal of Psychiatry,* 147:2, February 1990, 133–147.

Karasu, T. Byram. Toward a Clinical Model of Psychotherapy for Depression, II: An Integrative and Selective Treatment Approach. In *American Journal of Psychiatry,* 147:3, March 1990, 269–278.

Kiev, Ari. *Riding Through the Hassles, Snags, and Funks.* New York: Dutton, 1980.

Klerman, Gerald L. Evidence for Increase in Rates of Depression in North American and Western Europe in Recent Decades. In *New Results in Depression Research.* Eds. H. Hippius et al., Springer-Verlag, Berlin, 1986.

————. The Nature of Depression: Mood, Symptom, Disorder. In *The Measurement of Depression,* Guilford Publications, 1987.

————. Relationship Between Anxiety and Depression. In *Handbook of Anxiety, Vol. 1: Biological, Clinical and Cultural Perspectives.* Elsevier Science Publishers B.V., 1988, 59–82.

————. Depression and Related Disorders of Mood (Affective Disorders). In *The New Harvard Guide to Psychiatry,* Cambridge and London: Belknap Press, 1988.

Klerman, Gerald L., and Robert M. A. Hirschfeld. Personality As a Vulnerability Factor: With Special Attention To Clinical Depression. In *Handbook of Social Psychiatry,* Henderson/Burrows (eds.), Elsevier Science Publishers B.V. (Biomedical Division), 1988, 41–53.

Klerman, Gerald L., Philip W. Lavori, John Rice, Theodore Reich, Jean Endicott, Nancy C. Andreasen, Martin B. Keller, and Robert M. A. Hirschfeld. Birth-Cohort Trends in Rates of Major Depressive Disorder Among Relatives of Patients With Affective Disorder. *Archives of General Psychiatry,* July, 1985, Volume 42, 689–693.

*Kline, Nathan. *From Sad to Glad.* New York: Ballantine, 1975. By a pioneer in antidepressant medication.

*Knauth, Percy. *A Season in Hell.* New York: Harper and Row, 1975. A depression sufferer's own well-told story.

Kolata, Gina. Manic-Depression Gene Tied to Chromosome 11. *Research News,* March 6, 1987, 1139–49.

Kovacs, Maria. Psychotherapies for Depression. In Grinspoon 1983, cited above.

Kovacs, Maria, et al. Depressed Outpatients Treated With Cognitive Therapy or Pharmacotherapy. *Archives of General Psychiatry*, Vol. 38, January 1981, 33–39.

*LaHaye, Tim. *How To Win Over Depression*. Grand Rapids: Zondervan, 1974.

**Lazarus, Arnold, and Allen Fay. *I Can If I Want To*. New York: Morrow, 1975. Excellent commonsense advice for improving your life, consistent with the analysis given here.

***Lewinsohn, Peter M., Ricardo F. Munoz, Mary Ann Youngren, Antonette M. Zeiss. *Control Your Depression*. Englewood Cliffs: Prentice-Hall, 1978. One of the very best self-help books for depression, emphasizing 'social learning' and behavioral exercises.

Lowen, Alexander. *Depression and the Body*. Baltimore: Penguin, 1973.

Mahoney, Michael J., and Carl E. Thoresen. *Self-Control: Power to the Person*. Monterey, Ca: Brooks/Cole, 1974.

Maslow, Abraham. *Toward a Psychology of Being*. second edition, New York: Van Nostrand, 1968.

McKinney, William T. Jr., Stephen J. Suomi, and Harry F. Harlow. New Models of Separation and Depression in Rhesus Monkeys. In Scott and Senay.

Mendels, Joseph (ed.) *Psychobiology of Depression*. New York: Spectrum Publications, distributed by Halsted Press, 1975.

Miller, Ivan W., William H. Norman, and Gabor I. Keitner. Cognitive-Behavioral Treatment of Depressed Inpatients: Six- and Twelve-Month Follow-up. *American Journal of Psychiatry*, 146:10, October 1989, 1274–79.

Musson, Robert F., and Lauren B. Alloy. Depression and Self-Directed Attention. In Alloy 1988, 193–222.

Myers, Gloria, as told to Diane Clark. Clinical Depression: Victim Recalls 'Living Death'. *Champaign-Urbana News Gazette*, Oct. 30, 1977. 10B.

Naranjo, Claudio, and Robert E. Ornstein. *On the Psychology of Meditation*. New York: Viking, 1971.

Nelson, R. Eric, and W. Edward Craighead. Selective Recall of Positive and Negative Feedback, Self-control Behaviors, and Depression. *Journal of Abnormal Psychology*, 1977, Vol. 86, No. 4, 379–388.

*NIMH. *Helpful Facts About Depressive Disorders*. Washington, D.C.: 1987.

Oatley, Keith. *Best-Laid Schemes: The Psychology of Emotions*. Cambridge: Cambridge University Press, 1992.

Ostow, Mortimer. *The Psychology of Melancholy*. New York: Harper and Row, 1970.

**Papalos, Dimitri I., and Janice Papalos. *Overcoming Depression*. New York: Harper and Row, 1987. A practical manual for what to do when depression strikes you or a person you care about.

Peterson, Christopher, Barbara A. Bettes, and Martin E.P. Seligman. Depressive Symptoms and Unprompted Causal Attributions: Content Analysis. *Behavioral Research and Therapy*, Vol. 23, No. 4, 1985, 379–382.

Peterson, Christopher, and Martin E. P. Seligman. Causal Explanations as a Risk Factor for Depression: Theory and Evidence. *Psychological Review*, Vol. 91, No. 3, 1984, 347–374.

Plath, Sylvia. *The Bell Jar.* New York: Bantam, 1971.

Rehm, Lynn P. Self-management and Cognitive Processes in Depression. In Alloy 1988, 143–176.

Royko, Mike. How To Ease That Hangover. *Chicago Daily News,* January 1–2, 1977, 3.

Rubin, Theodore Isaac. *Compassion and Self-Hate.* New York: Ballantine, 1975.

**Russell, Bertrand. *The Conquest of Happiness.* New York: Signet, 1951.

Scott, John Paul, and Edward C. Senay (eds.) *Separation and Depression.* Washington: AAAS, 1973.

Scott, John Paul, John M. Stewart, and Victor J. DeGhett. Separation in Infant Dogs. In Scott and Senay.

Seligman, Martin E. P. *Helplessness: On Depression, Development, and Death.* San Francisco: Freeman, 1975.

————. *Learned Optimism.* New York: Knopf, 1991.

Seligman, Martin E. P., Camilo Castellon, John Cacciola, Peter Schulman, Lester Luborsky, Maxine Ollove, and Robert Downing. Explanatory Style Change During Cognitive Therapy for Unipolar Depression. *Journal of Abnormal Psychology,* Vol. 97, No. 1, 1988, 1–6.

Selmi, Paulette M. et al. Computer-Administered Cognitive-Behavioral Therapy for Depression. *American Journal of Psychiatry,* 147:1, January 1990, 51–56.

Selye, Hans. *Stress Without Distress.* New York: Signet, 1974.

Simon, Julian L., *Basic Research Methods in Social Science.* New York: Random House, 1969; second edition, 1978; third edition, [with Paul Burstein], 1985.

————. *Applied Managerial Economics.* Englewood Cliffs: Prentice-Hall, 1975.

————. *The Economics of Population Growth.* Princeton: Princeton University Press, 1977.

————. *The Ultimate Resource.* Princeton: Princeton University Press, 1981.

Simons, Anne D., et al. Cognitive Therapy and Pharmacotherapy for Depression. *Archives of General Psychiatry,* Vol. 43, January 1986, 43–48.

Sotsky, Stuart M., et al. Patient Predictors of Response to Psychotherapy and Pharmacotherapy: Findings in the NIMH Treatment of Depression Collaborative Research Program. *American Journal of Psychiatry,* 148:8, August 1991, 997–1008.

Steer, Robert A., Aaron T. Beck, John H. Riskind, and Gary Brown. Differentiation of Depressive Disorders From Generalized Anxiety by the Beck Depression Inventory. *Journal of Clinical Psychology,* Vol. 42, No. 3, May 1986, 475–78.

Styron, William. *Darkness Visible.* New York: Vintage, 1990

Suzuki, Daisetz T. *Outlines of Mahayana Buddhism.* New York: Schocken, 1907/1963.

Thase, Michael E., et al. Severity of Depression and Response to Cognitive Behavior Therapy. *American Journal of Psychiatry,* 148:6, June 1991, 784–789.

Tolstoy, Leo. *A Confession.* Translated by Aylmer Maude. London: Oxford University Press, 1920.

Tutko, Thomas. Winning Isn't Everything It's Cracked Up To Be. *New York Times,* July 4, 1976.

Vaillant, George E. The 'Normal Boy' in Later Life: How Adaptation Fosters Growth. *Harvard Magazine,* November–December 1977, 46–61.

*Watts, Alan W. *The Meaning of Happiness.* New York: Harper and Row, 1940; Perennial Library edition, 1968.

Weil, Andrew. *The Natural Mind.* Boston: Houghton Mifflin Company, 1972.

Wells, Kenneth B., et al. The Functioning and Well-being of Depressed Patients. *Journal of the American Medical Association,* August 18, 1989, 262:7, 914–19.

Wender, Paul, and Donald F. Klein. *Mind, Mood, and Medicine.* New York: Farrar, Straus, and Giroux, 1981.

Wilde, Oscar, in Burnett 1958.

Woolf, Leonard. *The Journey Not the Arrival Matters.* New York: Harcourt Brace Jovanovich, 1975.

Zigler, Edward and Marion Glick. Is Paranoid Schizophrenia Really Camouflaged Depression? *American Psychologist,* April, 1988, 284–290.

NOTES

INTRODUCTION

1. NIMH. 1987.
2. Elkin et al. 1986, abstract.
3. Wender and Klein 1981, 39.
4. Greist and Jefferson 1984, 72.
5. Seligman 1975, 73.
6. Papalos and Papalos 1987, 88.
7. Greist and Jefferson 1984, 78.
8. Miller, Norman, and Keitner 1989.
9. Papalos and Papalos 1987, 41.

1. THE NATURE OF THE TROUBLE AND THE FORMS OF HELP

1. Carnegie 1944.
2. Seligman 1975.
3. Russell 1930, 15, italics added.
4. "Cognitive techniques are most appropriate for people who have the capacity for introspection and for reflecting about their own thoughts and fantasies" (Beck 1976, 216).

2. WHAT IS DEPRESSION? HOW DOES IT FEEL TO BE DEPRESSED?

1. 1967, 5–6.
2. Lowen 1972–1973, 191.
3. Lowen, 21.
4. Lowen, 23.
5. Lowen, 99.
6. Seligman, 1–2.
7. Seligman, 2–3.
8. Russell 1930–1951, 15.
9. Quoted by Greist and Jefferson 1984, 6.
10. Alvarez 1971, 124–26.
11. Meyers 1977.
12. Custance, in Kaplan 1964, 56–58.

13. Brooks in Kaplan, 84; 1965, 439–440.
14. Tolstoy 1920, 18–22.
15. Plath 1971, 104, 105, 129, 130.

3. NEGATIVE SELF-COMPARISONS, COMBINED WITH A HELPLESS FEELING, ARE THE PROXIMATE CAUSE OF DEPRESSION

1. Nelson and Craighead 1977; for a review of some other studies on the thoughts of depressives, see Beck 1976, 125–28.
2. Beck 1976, 108.
3. Beck, 113.
4. Bowlby 1969, 1980. Technical point for the professional reader only: This view, though phrased as learning theory, is consistent with the psychoanalytic view: "At the bottom of the melancholiac's profound dread of impoverishment, there is really the dread of starvation . . . drinking at the mother's breast remains the radiant image of unremitting, forgiving love" (Rado in Gaylin 1968, 80).
5. Scott and Senay 1973.
6. Seligman 1975, 68, 69, 91, 92.
7. Please notice that this statement in no way denies that biological factors may be implicated in a depression. But biological factors, to the extent that they are operative, are underlying predisposing factors of the same order as a person's psychological history, rather than contemporary triggering causes.
8. Campbell and Stanley in their classic treatise on experimental methods, 1963, 6.
9. Helson 1964, 126.
10. Seligman 1975.
11. Zigler and Glick have suggested that "paranoid schizophrenia" is "really camouflaged depression" (1988). I agree that both the former and the latter have a "self-referential aspect," with "great salience given to the self" (285), and they agree on "the central place of self-evaluation in depression. The core experience of depression involves the perception of the self as unworthy and inadequate" (286). But I think the argument is simpler, clearer, and more persuasive that both ailments are different modes of response to neg-comps and the ensuing pain.
12. As Gaylin (1979, 6) puts it, "[P]hobias, obsessions, and delusions are attempts to control, limit, and cope with unbearable emotional states".
13. Gaylin 1979 provides rich and thought-provoking descriptions of the feelings connected with these and other states of mind. But he does not distinguish between pain and the other states he calls "feelings", which I find confusing. (For example, see page 7). Gaylin mentions in passing that he has found very little in print about feelings, which he classifies as an "aspect of emotions" (10).

14. As Beck et al. 1988 put it, based on patient responses to a study of "automatic thoughts" using a questioner, "anxiety cognitions . . . embody a greater degree of uncertainty and an orientation toward the future, whereas depressive cognitions are either oriented toward the past or reflect a more absolute negative attitude toward the future".

Freud asserted that "when the mother-figure is believed to be temporarily absent the response is one of anxiety, when she appears to be permanently absent it is one of pain and mourning." Bowlby in Gaylin 1968, 271.

15. Klerman 1988, 66.
16. Beck 1988, 13.
17. Bowlby, vol 1, 27.
18. Bowlby, 27.
19. Bowlby, 28.
20. Gallagher 1986, 8.

4. THE MECHANISMS THAT MAKE A DEPRESSIVE

1. Hume, *Essential Works,* 4.
2. Brickman, Coates, and Bulman 1977.
3. But recent studies suggest that there is no systematic relationship between personality and depression; see Hirschfeld et al. 1983, and Klerman and Hirschfeld 1988.
4. Tolstoy 1920, p. 18.
5. Kline 1974, p. 41.
6. Gilson, 1983, abstract. Also cited by Beck 1988, 17. Another study that I cannot now find again shows depressives as being more likely to look downward when walking than normals. It seems unlikely to me that there is a genetic or glandular or chemical basis for behavior such as is revealed by studies of this sort (though when one is tired one is probably more likely to look downward than when one is fresh, and fatigue has biological correlates). Rather, it would seem that depressives have some overall view of the world which accounts for their depressed behavior, and this is consistent with the idea that learning and retraining can change the thought patterns associated with depression.
7. Eaves 1981, abstract.
8. *Science,* 6 March, 1987, 1139.
9. Kline, 63.
10. Papalos and Papalos 1987, Chapter 4.
11. Papalos and Papalos, 88, (italics in original).
12. Miller, Norman, and Keitner 1989
13. Papalos and Papalos 1987.
14. Kline 1974.
15. Russell, 1930–1951, 65.
16. Papalos and Papalos, 140.

17. Papalos and Papalos, 141.
18. Papalos and Papalos, 141.

5. THE HAND OF THE PAST IN DEPRESSION

1. Several statistical studies have shown the relationship between parental death and later depression. See, for example, Beck 1967, Chapter 14.

2. Bowlby is the foremost exponent of this viewpoint:

The hypothesis to be advanced here . . . is built on the theory of instinctive behaviour . . . It postulates that the child's tie to his mother is a product of the activity of a number of behavioral systems that have proximity to mother as a predictable outcome. Since in the human child ontogeny of these systems is slow and complex, and their rate of development varies greatly from child to child, no simple statement about progress during the first year of life can be made. Once a child has entered his second year, however, and is mobile, fairly typical attachment behaviour is almost always seen. By that age in most children the integrate of behavioural systems concerned is readily activated, especially by mother's departure or by anything frightening, and the stimuli that most effectively terminate the systems are sound, sight, or touch of mother. Until about the time a child reaches his third birthday the systems continue to be very readily activated. Thenceforward in most children they become less easily activated and they also undergo other changes that make proximity to mother less urgent. During adolescent and adult life yet further changes occur, including change of the figures towards whom the behaviour is directed.

Attachment behaviour is regarded as a class of social behaviour of an importance equivalent to that of mating behaviour and parental behaviour. It is held to have a biological function specific to itself and one that has hitherto been little considered.

In this formulation, it will be noticed, there is no reference to 'needs' or 'drives'. Instead, attachment behaviour is regarded as what occurs when certain behavioural systems are activated. The behavioural systems themselves are believed to develop within the infant as a result of his interaction with his environment of evolutionary adaptedness, and especially of his interaction with the principal figure in that environment, namely his mother. Food and eating are held to play no more than a minor part in their development. (Bowlby, 179–180)

And the work of Bowlby's co-workers on children is corrobo-

rated by the research of Harlow and his co-workers on rhesus monkeys.
3. Boyd 1969, quoted in Mahoney and Thoresen 1974, 98.

6. THE CREATION AND COLLAPSE OF VALUES

1. Tolstoy 1920, 18–22.

8. WHAT ARE YOUR DIMENSIONS?

1. Collingwood 1939–1970, 46.
2. James, 174–75.
3. Vaillant 1977, 51.

9. THE REWARDS OF DEPRESSION

1. The psychoanalytic term 'secondary gain' apparently refers to these phenomena.
2. Royko 1977, 3.
3. Bonime 1966.

10. INTRODUCING SELF-COMPARISONS COGNITIVE THERAPY

1. Ellis and Harper, 4.
2. Burns, 60.
3. Beck 1976, 2.
4. Beck, 3.
5. Johnston 1976, 6.
6. Ellis and Harper 1975, 3, 5.
7. 1976, 1.
8. Lazarus and Fay 1975, 95.
9. Quoted by James, 1958 edition, 136.
10. James, 1958 edition, 155.
11. Ellis and Harper 1975, 81.
12. Ellis and Harper 1975, 81.
13. Ellis 1987.
14. Frankl 1963, 196.

11. PLANNING AND EXECUTING A STRATEGY AGAINST YOUR DEPRESSION

1. Lazarus and Fay 1975, 116.

12. IMPROVING YOUR NUMERATOR

1. Beck 1976, pp. 15–17.
2. Ellis and Harper 1975, p. xi.
3. Again I use an example of Burns's (67) for easy comparison with his treatment.
4. See Alloy and Abramson 1988 for a review of the data.
5. Royko, 1977, p. 3.

13. SWEETENING YOUR DENOMINATOR

1. James, 119.
2. Rubin 1975, 136.
3. Tutko 1976, 2.
4. Quoted by Selye 1974, Frontispiece.
5. Ellis and Harper 1975, xi.
6. Russell 1930, esp. 47, though this may be an oversimplification of Russell's views.
7. Ellis and Harper 1975, 20, their italics.
8. James 1958, 137–38.
9. Ostow 1970, 112–13.

14. CHANGING YOUR DIMENSIONS

1. *Family Weekly,* February 26, 1978, 2.
2. Ellis and Harper 1975, 34–37.

15. THE SOUND OF A NUMERATOR CLAPPING

1. This body of research is reviewed by Musson and Alloy (1988). Wicklund and Duval (1971, cited by Musson and Alloy) first directed attention to this idea.
2. Dewey 1929, 400.
3. Seligman 1975.

4. Russell 1930, 15.
5. Vaillant 1977, 8.
6. For a review, see Beck 1976, 310–13.
7. Third edition, 1976, 285–86.
8. Vaillant 1977.
9. Gussow 1978, 19; Hoffmann 1972, 231; Woolf 1969, 128.
10. Vaillant, 128.
11. Rubin 1975, 136–37.
12. Gibson 1974, 27.
13. Hildebrand 1955, 140, 142.
14. Suzuki 1907–1963, xi.
15. The central thrust of Buddhism—to take the outstanding example —is precisely to reduce suffering, especially the suffering of depression. Authorities on Buddhism say that 'the four noble truths' are the central doctrine of Buddhism. "The essence of the doctrine, accepted by all schools, has been laid down in the four Holy Truths, which the Buddha first preached at Renases after his enlightenment" (Conze 1951, 43). These 'truths' may be summarized as follows: 1. suffering is natural; 2. craving is the cause of suffering; 3. to get rid of suffering one must get rid of craving; and 4. the way to get rid of craving is to concentrate and control one's mind and behavior, especially in meditation.
Here are the four noble truths in their entirety:

> 1. Now this, monks, is the noble truth of pain: birth is painful, old age is painful, sickness is painful, death is painful, sorrow, lamentation, dejection, and despair are painful. Contact with unpleasant things is painful, not getting what one wishes is painful. In short the five groups of grasping are painful.
>
> 2. Now this, monks, is the noble truth of the cause of pain: the craving, which tends to rebirth, combined with pleasure and lust, finding pleasure here and there; namely the craving for passion, the craving for existence, the craving for non-existence.
>
> 3. Now this, monks, is the noble truth of the cessation of pain, the cessation without a remainder of craving, the abandonment, forsaking, release, non-attachment.
>
> 4. Now this, monks, is the noble truth of the way that leads to the cessation of pain: this is the noble Eight-fold Way; namely, right views, right intention, right speech, right action, right livelihood, right effort, right mindfulness, right concentration. (Burtt 1955, 30)

Please notice the key phrase in the 'noble truths' which fits perfectly with Self-Comparisons Analysis: ". . . not getting what one wishes is painful".

16. James, 1892–1963, 175.
17. E.g. Behanan 1937–1959; Naranjo and Ornstein 1971; Benson 1975.

18. Benson and Klipper, 159–163.
19. Sutra spoken by the Sixth Patriarch, in Goddard, 515.
20. Watts 1972, 387.
21. Watts 1940, xx and xxi.

16. RELIGIOUS CONVERSION CAN CURE DEPRESSION

1. James, 166–67.
2. James, 177–79.
3. Third edition, 1976, 44.
4. The 'basic text for Alcoholics Anonymous' is the 'Big Book' which is simply called *Alcoholics Anonymous,* 1976. See Chapter 4.
5. James 1902–1958, 167.
6. Schneider 1962.

17. WAYS TO STOP FEELING HELPLESS AND HOPELESS

1. Seligman 1975 has focused our attention on the sense of helplessness which is acquired by a person through prior experience and which may therefore be shed by cognitive analysis or by behavioral practice or both. But he leaves the unfortunate impression that the sense of helplessness constitutes the entire cause of depression.
2. Seligman 1975.
3. Reviewed by Seligman 1975, 68ff.

18. VALUES THERAPY: A NEW SYSTEMATIC APPROACH FOR TOUGH CASES

1. Russell 1930, 15, italics added.
2. Scheinin 1983, 13.
3. One of my best gimmicks for banishing my own sadness-producing negative comparisons is to remind myself: If you let yourself be miserable about this minor matter today, 20 years from now won't you look back and think yourself a fool for having done so? I don't want to look back 20 years from now and think myself a fool for having wasted a perfectly good day in miserable ruminations about trivia or nonsense, and this impels me to alter my thoughts and my mood.
4. Maslow 1968.
5. Selye 1974.
6. Selye 1974, 103.

7. Frankl, 157.
8. Maslow 1950, following after Fromm.
9. Frankl, 156, 175.
10. Wilde in Burnett, 1958, 156–57.
11. Wilde, 60.
12. Tolstoy, 1920 translation, 63, 70, 71.
13. Pirkei Avoth, II–1P.
14. Hertz Version, 42.
15. Frankl 1963, 178–79.
16. Frankl, 153, 174.
17. Frankl, 178–79; see also 185.
18. Russell 1930, 14.
19. Frankl 1969, second edn., 188.

19. VALUES THERAPY AND RELIGIOUS DESPAIR

1. I am told that some religious people also become depressed when they suddenly 'feel unable to reach God'. I lack understanding of this malady and its cure.
2. See Glatzer 1969 for a selection.
3. Buber 1952, 39.
4. Buber 1952, 41.
5. Eastern religion, and especially Buddhism, aims at getting rid of our wants, together with achieving Feeling X. But most Westerners—and perhaps most Easterners, too—want *more and better wants,* rather than satisfying *or* getting rid of their present wants; economist Frank Knight pointed this out long ago, and economist Tibor Scitovsky has recently developed the theme.
6. Buber 1952, 44.

EPILOGUE: MY MISERY, MY CURE, MY JOY

1. Snyder 1976, 52.

INDEX